CW00322173

V

Autosalon, Moscow 1999: old and new Russia
Credit: Camera Press / Konstantin Zavrazhin

WEBSITE NEWS UPDATED WEEKLY
WWW.INDEXONCENSORSHIP.ORG • CONTACT@INDEXONCENSORSHIP.ORG
TEL: 020 7278 2313 • FAX: 020 7278 1878

CONTENTS

Credit: © Ivan Kyncl

Credit: Chris Steele-Perkins
/ Magnum Photos

A SAD CASE OF SURVIVAL

URSULA OWEN

'We became dissidents without actually knowing how, and we found ourselves behind bars without really knowing how. We simply did certain things we had to do and that it seemed proper to do: nothing more nor less.' This was Václav Havel in *Index*, telling us that courage is a funny thing, that we don't know we have it till we've done it. A week after the piece was published in 1979 (p39), he was in jail.

It was seven years earlier that Stephen Spender had founded *Index*, responding to a plea from Soviet dissidents Pavel Litvinov and Larisa Bogoraz Daniel (pp6, 15). The idea was that there should be 'the noise of publicity outside every detention centre and a published record of every tyrannical denial of free expression'.

Over the past 30 years, *Index* has been there for the censored and oppressed in most parts of the globe and across the political spectrum. We told the stories of the 'disappeared' in Argentina, and published the work of banned poets in Cuba (p201). We published prison letters by Ken Saro-Wiwa long before the world's media reported his tragic end in Nigeria (p157), and the work of Chinese poets who escaped from the massacre in Tiananmen Square.

We carried banned literary texts by Solzhenitsyn (p195), Sinyavskii and Brodskii, and Dubravka Ugresic's seminal essay on the 'culture of lies' at the time of the war in Yugoslavia, where media battles still go on (p44). And we have documented the implacable efforts of religious fundamentalists: Islamic, Jewish and Christian. Our alphabetical record of abuses and violations, in each issue of the magazine, gives a kind of ground's-eye-view of world history seen through the prism of individual names (p100).

There were those who thought that, with the Cold War over, *Index*'s job was largely done. The world being what it is, that was unthinkable. Only the geography of censorship has changed, and sometimes not even that. What is more, as we embark on the new millennium, ideologies discredited, borders altered, new and troubling questions have surfaced, some of them challenging the primacy of free expression itself – questions around religious extremism, relative values and cultural difference, the rewriting of history, hate speech, pornography, violence on television, freedom on the Internet – and, above all, around security and fear.

In the year that *Index* began to publish, Spain, Portugal and Greece were all ruled by military dictatorships, apartheid flourished in South Africa, the Soviet

Empire dominated Russia and Eastern Europe, China was gripped by the Cultural Revolution, the United States was at war with Vietnam and totalitarian governments were in control in many parts of Latin America and some of the newly independent countries of Africa. In all these places, and many more, it was standard for censorship to be employed as an instrument of government.

Many of these particular tyrannies have gone, only to have been replaced by others. And putting this issue together, it becomes clear, again and again, that continuities with the old world persist. So we have looked backwards as well as to the future.

Geoffrey Hosking and Irena Maryniak examine the new Russia (p8), so different from the old Soviet Union, where new battles are being fought for free expression in the media and society has sunk below the level of many third world countries. The message of Wei Jingsheng in 1979 (p92) – that corruption is the scourge of China – is chillingly confirmed 12 years later in the banned extract by He Qinglian that has engendered such hot debate (p88).

Since *Index* was founded, there have been two epochal events, the first in 1989 when the Wall came down. No longer dominated by the two opposing monoliths, the USA and USSR, the world became increasingly fragmented, the divisions aggravated by the indecent rise of nationalism, religious intolerance and ethnic rivalries. The result has been enduring wars, wounded nations and silenced voices. The sane voice of Amartya Sen (p150) tells us that only recognition of the plurality of our identities will save us from intolerance and hatred. But in Nigeria, Adewale Maja-Pearce reports on religious and ethnic hatred verging on civil war (p155), while in Ireland Ronan Bennett shows how media prejudice and stereotyping became a serious impediment to the peace process (p134). From India, with its noisily fundamentalist Hindu government, we hear from women writers struggling to make their voices heard (p206).

There are a few small hopeful signs: from Israel we publish the voice of an army refusenik (p216), which has helped to swell the as yet small opposition there to the war against the Palestinians. And in Cyprus a massive peace protest in the north of the island (p162) gave some indication of the desire for reconciliation in another bitter divide.

And then, on 11 September 2001, another epoch began. The world changed utterly. We publish two opposing responses, from Michael Ignatieff and Gore Vidal (pp60, 70), to this fateful event, but many of the other articles are informed by it. As Ronald Dworkin tells us (p58), the debate in the US over extending the 'war on terrorism' is dangerously limited. Meanwhile, Dario Fo recalls his father's words, and warns of a return of fascism to Italy (p82). Sadly, we are not yet redundant. But at least in Kabul there is cautious optimism (p172) as the cinemas and bookshops reopen and Afghan music returns to the radio. ❑

1/1975: BOGORAZ & LITVINOV, USSR
APPEAL TO WORLD PUBLIC OPINION

The judicial trial of Galanskov, Ginsburg, Dobrovolskii and Lashkova which is taking place at present in the Moscow City Court is being carried out in violation of the most important principles of Soviet law. The judge and prosecutor, with the participation of a special kind of audience, have turned the trial into a wild mockery of three of the accused – Galanskov, Ginsburg and Lashkova – and of the witnesses, unthinkable in the 20th century.

The case took on the character of the well-known 'witch trials' on its second day, when Galanskov and Ginsburg – in spite of a year of preliminary incarceration, in spite of pressure from the court – refused to accept the groundless accusations made against them by Dobrovolskii and sought to prove their own innocence. Evidence by witnesses in favour of Galanskov and Ginsburg infuriated the court even more.

The judge and the prosecutor throughout the trial have been helping Dobrovolskii to introduce false evidence against Galanskov and Ginsburg. The defence lawyers are constantly forbidden to ask questions, and the witnesses are not being allowed to give evidence which unmasks the provocative role of Dobrovolskii in the case.

Judge Mironov has not once stopped the prosecutor. But he is allowing people who represent the defence to say only that which fits in with the programme already prepared by the KGB investigation. Whenever any participant in the trial departs from the rehearsed spectacle the judge cries: 'Your question is out of order.' 'This has no relation to the case.' 'I will not allow you to speak.' These exclamations have been directed at the accused (apart from Dobrovolskii), at their lawyers and the witnesses.

The witnesses leave the court after their examination, or rather they are pushed out of the court, in a depressed state, almost in hysterics.

Witness Yelena Basilova was not allowed to make a statement to the court. She wanted to record how the KGB had persecuted her mentally sick husband, whose evidence, given during the investigation when he was in a certifiable state, plays an important part in the prosecution case. Basilova was driven out of the court while the judge shouted and the audience howled, drowning her words.

P Grigorenko [the former Soviet Major-General Pyotr Grigorenko] submitted a request that he be examined as a witness because he could explain the origin of the money found on Dobrovolskii. According to Dobrovolskii,

Galanskov gave him this money. Grigorenko's request was turned down on the pretext that he is allegedly mentally ill. This is not true.

Witness Aida Topeshkina was not allowed to make a statement to the court in which she wanted to give facts showing the falsity of Dobrovolskii's evidence. Topeshkina, an expectant mother, was physically ejected from the courtroom while the audience howled at her.

The courtroom is filled with specially selected people, officials of the KGB and volunteer militia, who give the appearance of an open public trial. These people make a noise, laugh, and insult the accused and the witnesses. Judge Mironov has made no attempt to prevent these violations of order. Not one of the blatant offenders has been ejected from the hall.

In this tense atmosphere there can be no pretence that the trial is objective, that there is any justice or legality about it. The sentence was decided from the very start.

We appeal to world public opinion, and in the first place to Soviet public opinion. We appeal to everyone in whom conscience is alive and who has sufficient courage. Demand public condemnation of this shameful trial and the punishment of those guilty of perpetrating it. Demand the release of the accused from arrest. Demand a new trial with the observance of all legal norms and with the presence of international observers.

Today it is not only the fate of the three accused which is at stake – their trial is no better than the celebrated trials of the 1930s which involved us in so much shame and so much blood that we have still not recovered from them.

We pass this appeal to the western progressive press and ask for it to be published and broadcast by radio as soon as possible – we are not sending this request to Soviet newspapers because that is hopeless.

Signed: **Larisa Bogoraz Daniel**, *Moscow, V-261, Leninskii Prospect 85, Flat 3;*
Pavel Litvinov, *Moscow, K-1, Ulitsa Alexei Tolstoy 8, Flat 78.* ❏

Reprinted from The Times *Saturday 13 January 1968*

TELEGRAM TO MOSCOW

We, a group of friends representing no organisation, support your statement, admire your courage, think of you and will help in any way possible:

Signed: Cecil Day-Lewis, Yehudi Menuhin, WH Auden, Henry Moore, Stephen Spender, AJ Ayer, Bertrand Russell, Julian Hartley, Mary McCarthy, JB Priestley, Jacquetta Hawkes, Paul Scofield, Igor Stravinsky, Stuart Hampshire, Maurice Bowra, Mrs George Orwell ❏

THE NEW RUSSIA

FROM THE RUBBLE OF THE USSR, A NEW RUSSIA IS EMERGING, MARKED BY A TASTE FOR LAW AND ORDER AND A RENEWED URGE TO CONTROL THE MEDIA

Credit: Heidi Bradner

THIRTY YEARS ON
GEOFFREY HOSKING

RUSSIAN WRITERS AND JOURNALISTS
NO LONGER HAVE TO FEAR THE
NOTORIOUS GULAG BUT THE MEDIA
IS ONCE MORE UNDER PRESSURE AS
PUTIN ATTEMPTS TO RESTORE THE
'STRONG STATE' OF EARLIER TIMES

In 1972, the year *Index* first appeared, Andrei Siniavskii was released from a labour camp. A well-known scholar and literary critic, he had spent seven years there for writing and circulating short stories satirising the Soviet system under the pen-name of a Jewish underworld figure, Abram Terts. The stories were in the form of *skaz*, in which the author deliberately adopts the voice of one or more of his characters as his narrative language. The prosecution at his trial had interpreted the text with flat-footed literalness, as if each character was simply expressing Siniavskii's own opinions. His conviction seemed to threaten all writers using analogous devices, and it aroused the Soviet intelligentsia to collective oppositional action as never before. Sixty-three Moscow writers wrote to the Supreme Soviet, warning that 'learning and art cannot exist if neither paradoxical ideas can be expressed nor hyperbolic images used as an artistic device. In our complex situation today we need more, not less, freedom for intellectual and artistic experiment.'

The trial was held in camera, but Alexander Ginzburg succeeded in compiling a transcript that he circulated in *samizdat*, a recent neologism which meant 'self-publishing' – typing out copies with ever fainter carbon paper and circulating them among friends. For that humble chronicler's task, filling in what George Orwell called a 'memory hole', he too was arrested and tried.

And so a chain process was launched which led to the *Chronicle of Current Events*, a *samizdat* journal that baldly, without editorial comment, recorded instances of the Soviet authorities violating their own laws in dealing with their own citizens.

Another product of the chain process was *Index on Censorship* itself.

Soviet society was going through a strange phase in its own evolution. Mass terror had ceased at least 20 years earlier, and the Communist Party had condemned it. However, the 'socialist legality' which succeeded it was far from guaranteeing freedom of speech. Marxism-Leninism remained the single compulsory ideology, and serious dissent from it was not permitted. Similarly, criticism of more than minor details of government or party policy was banned. Writers and journalists, indeed everyone working regularly in the creative arts and the media, were organised in professional unions, which offered them a whole range of benefits, such as comfortable (though not grand) apartments, good medical care, cheap holidays and subsidised spells at 'creative retreats' designed to restore oxygen to brains benumbed by endless official campaigns about this, that and the other. In return, the unions expected their members to participate in those same campaigns and not to rock the boat with experimental or critical texts.

By the 1970s, the party had learned to leave the policing of literature almost entirely to writers themselves. The knack was to find competent but minor ones, appoint them to the command posts in the Writers' Union, give them privileges and material benefits, and leave them to quash non-conformists. Second-raters at the top could be relied on to fear and resent original young writers coming up from below, not so much for their ideological sins as for their originality, vigour and questing spirit, which elderly hacks found both threatening and baffling. And so writers would spend much of their time squabbling over minor perks and status symbols, as described in Vladimir Voinovich's stories, *The Ivankiad* and *The Fur Hat*.

Since mass terror no longer existed, however, it was possible for courageous spirits among the ordinary members of the Writers' Union to protest in semi-public against the suppression of free speech. They would do so by circulating round robins among friends and then 'publishing' them in the *Chronicle*, sending them to western journalists and having them broadcast over foreign Russian-language radio stations such as the BBC and the Voice of America – and of course disseminated in *Index*. Protest of that kind could lead to unpleasant sanctions but was no longer a suicide mission. One could say that a certain nonconformist public opinion emerged, especially among writers and scientists. After all, literature enjoyed considerable prestige among the public, since it was the most interesting form of printed matter available to the newly literate masses, while the Soviet leaders needed first-rate scientists for their economic and military programmes and simply could not afford to alienate them.

Now fast forward 30 years. Free speech is again under threat, but in a completely different way. As the Soviet Union fell apart, the nomenklatura elite, especially its middle and lower ranks, moved smartly to convert their administrative power into property and money, exploiting their fading political privileges to secure themselves a commanding position in the emerging free market. President Boris Yeltsin was prepared to let them rip and, indeed, to sell off large parts of the state economy to them at knock-down prices, in return for political support.

Thus Russia came to be dominated by 'oligarchs', very rich men who typically had a stake in industry, the banks, foreign trade and the media. They all made money by legally dubious means – in any case, the law was fluctuating and unclear – so they were all vulnerable to challenge in the courts by their enemies, as well as to the cruder threats of contract killers.

Chechnya exemplified the problems of the new Russian state in spades. Its president, Dzhokhar Dudaev, declared independence, making it a safe base for local oligarchs who traded in drugs and arms, and siphoned off some of the oil in the pipelines crossing its territory to finance criminal operations and terrorism not only in Russia but in Europe and the United States as well. When the Russian army invaded in December 1994, to restore order, it was unable to cope with its nimbler partisan opponents and had to settle for a humiliating peace that left Chechnya virtually independent.

What were writers and publishers to do in the new conditions? Literature was no longer a uniquely prestigious cultural product; it had become just one commodity like any other, subject to the dictates of the market. On bookstalls one could see, jostling side by side, Pushkin, Solzhenitsyn, cheap thrillers, pornography, astrological tables, guides to yoga and manuals on how to set up your own business. Publishers and newspapers accommodated themselves to these tastes as best they could. They were, in any case, in a declining market, far outstripped by television.

Censorship was the least of their problems. One benefit of Yeltsin's easygoing attitude to public life was that the media was relatively free. Some newspapers and television stations reported frankly the appalling blunders made by the military in the first Chechen war, as well as the corruption of commanders, some of whom vied with each other to seize the assets formerly controlled by local tycoons. Yet, though the public read about these abuses, it did not seem to care very much. Most people were too preoccupied with bare survival in a harsh world to join political movements or to protest.

Moscow 1992: 'Have your photo taken with Mr Gorbachev outside our brand new McDonald's.' Credit: Chris Steele-Perkins / Magnum Photos

Vladimir Putin came to power pledging to restore the power of the state. It is not easy at the moment to assess that attempt. It would be simple to condemn it, since it began with the launch of another violent war in Chechnya, fought in a manner that disregarded the rights of peaceful civilians and seemed calculated to turn the republic into a territory in which *only* bandits and terrorists can make a living.

On the other hand, the Russian state does need to be strengthened. Its weakness in the face of over-mighty oligarchs and criminals has been the most distressing feature of life in post-Soviet Russia. It has meant that taxes cannot be collected, and so doctors, schoolteachers and other public servants cannot be paid, or only after long delay in inflated roubles. The results can be seen in the deterioration of educational standards, in the neglected state of the hospitals and the declining life expectancy of the population. A weak state is literally lethal.

In any case, one reason why the Chechen wars have been so destructive and demoralising is that the Russian state does not have full control over its own armed forces. As Anna Politkovskaia has shown, some soldiers are drug addicts, prepared to sell anything, even their weapons, to finance their habit. Some of their officers are trading in drugs, weapons or oil siphoned from pipelines. Funds earmarked for medicine, food supplies or reconstruction work are sucked into the black market. As Politkovskaia notes in her recent book, *A Dirty War: a Russian reporter in Chechnya* (Harvill Press, London 2001), 'The moral of this story is that the State does not exist in Russia.'

So far Putin has dealt with such problems not by trying to eradicate them – or, if he has tried, he has been unsuccessful. He has reacted by trying to suppress the media reports about them – a classic case of shooting the messenger. His officials have harassed courageous journalists who try to make the truth known. He has given the go-ahead to those who would exploit the financial vulnerability of all media operations to undermine the more outspoken newspapers and television stations. Evidently, he sees a strong state as one that is not seriously criticised by the media. That is an illusion: crime, corruption and misuse of power exist in all countries, and it is often the media that first points the finger at particular abuses and crimes. To deprive oneself of its services is to grant immunity to criminals and corrupt officials, and to degrade the quality of public life. A free media is the ally of a strong state and also fulfils the vital role of curbing its excesses. That is a lesson Putin seems not yet to have learned. ❏

Geoffrey Hosking is professor of Russian history at the School of Slavonic and Eastern European Studies, London University

LIVING THE MOVIES

LARISA BOGORAZ

NOT ALL THE CHANGES FROM SOVIET
TIMES SEEM ENTIRELY SATISFACTORY
TO VETERAN DISSIDENTS

There are times when it seems as though my contemporaries and I are the actors in some highly instructive film series with the overall title *Free Speech in Twentieth-Century Russia*. By my reckoning, we have reached *Free Speech, IV*. But let's begin at the beginning.

The original film, *We Live not Feeling the Land beneath our Feet*, was followed by *Free Speech II: From Samizdat to Glasnost*. It portrayed an author who, the moment he had finished writing an article, a book, a poem not entirely loyal to the authorities, meticulously took one carbon copy from the typewriter, wrapped it in polythene and buried it in the snow. Other copies were given to friends to hide. Finally, one was circulated from person to person and, from that moment, the work began a life of its own. It might cross the state frontier of the USSR – with or without its author's knowledge – and return as a published book. We needed no reminder of the likely fate of its author should that happen.

I have a number of such scrolls on my bookshelf; they were revealed when the snows melted. The paper is blackened at the edges and, in places, the writing is indecipherable. It is the manuscript of Anatolii Marchenko's *Live Like a Normal Person*. Alongside it is the same book, published five years ago in Moscow.

In March 1980, when Marchenko was already under arrest, our friend the biologist Boris Kulaev spotted some packages in our courtyard which the thawing snow had revealed. He took them to Moscow and his wife, Naomi Botvinnik, retyped the text that had survived. Andrei Sakharov wrote a preface and I sent it abroad with someone I knew I could trust. A few years later, it was published, first in Russian, then in English.

Somewhere towards the end of *Free Speech II*, or at the beginning of *Free Speech III*, it came out in Russia, first in the literary journal *Znamya*, with the gaps and lacunae that marked its unorthodox passage to publication, and later in a collection of Marchenko's works published by Memorial.

Andrei Sakharov (1921–1989).
Credit: Susan Meiselas / Magnum Photos

I see the unfolding of this plot as a graphic illustration of how Russia has progressed from the times when its citizens had 'no correspondence rights' [a play on the Stalinist formulation when someone had been executed: relatives were informed that they had been sentenced to 'ten years without correspondence rights' – Ed] to its present state. It also gives us the answer to the question: 'Who needs glasnost anyway?' I do, for one. And so do a lot of other people.

Free Speech III: Between Glasnost and a Free Press marked the declaration of *glasnost* (openness) at the beginning of *perestroika* (restructuring) by Mikhail Gorbachev in 1985. I've no idea if he knew he'd started a process that was unstoppable and that must lead either to complete freedom of information or end up in a return to the past – like a flashback, a common enough device in sequels.

What is the difference between *glasnost* and freedom of the press? I have no ready answer so I shall cite a couple of real-life examples.

In my view, *glasnost* was when the ministry of home affairs, the federal bureau of security, the state prosecutor's office, the Duma and the armed forces in Chechnya all appointed press secretaries to keep them in touch with the people – even where these were less than effective.

Had there been publications and TV and radio stations prepared to broadcast the sort of information dug out at great risk by courageous, independent-minded journalists such as Dmitrii Kholodov (*Index* 1/01), Andrei Babitskii (*Index* 2/01) and Anna Politkovskaia (p34 and *Index* 1/02), and had the authorities, acting in accordance with their own law, not only done everything they could to obstruct the journalists and the media rather than helping them to do what was no more than their professional duty, we could have had freedom of the press. The price Kholodov, Babitskii and Politkovskaia paid for that freedom, as indeed did the independent media generally, was high.

Free Speech IV has only just gone into production and as yet has no title. With no certainty as to the outcome, *Tug-of-War* suggests itself as a working title. ❏

Larisa Bogoraz, *like her husband a dissident in Soviet times, is the widow of Yuli Daniel, one of the writers prosecuted in the show trials of 1968 that led to the creation of* Index. *Translated by Arch Tait*

CONTROL BY OTHER MEANS

IVAN ZASURSKII

THE LAST OF THE MEDIA BARONS
HAS FALLEN TO PRESIDENT PUTIN'S
NEED TO CONTROL HIS IMAGE

The nature of Russian politics in the 1990s was best described as a 'media-political system'. At a time when the state's institutions were unstable and rootless, and with Boris Yeltsin provoking one political crisis after another, the channels through which the public could be influenced were the television channels and they were crucial to the outcome of political power struggles.

When political scientists complained that Russia lacked a civilised party system and that only the communists had a mass membership party, they failed to recognise that it was the TV channels that were the real political parties. They were fundamental to the acting out of the political drama and in determining the ratings of the actors on the political stage. In the year preceding the 1996 elections they evolved into the agents, as it were, of the conventional parties and political movements. SPS (Union of Rightist Forces) and Yabloko (Apple/me-block, the liberal alliance led by Grigorii Yavlinskii) were the parties of NTV (Vladimir Guzinskii's channel); Edinstvo (Unity) belonged to ORT (main state-owned channel); Otechestvo (Fatherland) was the creature of TVTs (Moscow-based Television Centre) and the regional companies.

A prerequisite of the system was a willingness on the part of the state to tolerate the existence of powerful and at times wholly independent players in Russia's media-political structure. The reasons are simple: as a populist politician, Yeltsin remembered a time when the only people on his side had been the journalists, yet he had prevailed; and in the run-up to the presidential election – the only one that mattered – the assets of the owners of the media conglomerates became Yeltsin's political capital.

By the time of Vladimir Putin's election campaign, when the second war in Chechnya was already in the offing, it became clear that the media-political system would not survive the new election. Though the 2000 elections were managed by Yeltsin's old team, Vladimir Putin lacked his predecessor's charisma and if he was to dominate the airwaves he needed the support of the bureaucracy and direct control of the channels.

The first sign of what was to come was the auction of TVTs frequencies; the second, the removal of Boris Berezovskii from control of Channel One. The raid on Guzinskii's NTV on 11 May 2000, only four days after Putin's inauguration as president, was [at the time of writing – Ed] the final stage of a transformation that further tightened the administration's grip on the political scene. [Since then, Berezovskii's TV6 was manipulated into receivership in 2001 and is scheduled for public auction in March this year – Ed]

The Kremlin has pursued its unabashed intention of controlling the politically most influential federation-wide television stations by direct legal pressure and by use of the TV frequency licensing system. Any TV or radio company accused of infringing the law may find itself without a licence. If the authorities continue along their present course, sooner or later they will have the entire federal TV network and its power to influence the media-political system under their control.

Central control of the privately owned independent press, formed in the 1990s, is a different matter. Shut down a newspaper and it merely reappears next day under a new title and with a threefold increase in circulation; its decentralised structure makes it harder to regulate. If state control of TV becomes excessively rigorous, the press may gain a competitive edge over television and recover some of its former prestige. Journalists may also rediscover the virtues of professional solidarity when faced by official attempts to determine their news agenda.

The Web is even less manageable and may be the best guarantee that the liberalising changes in the Russian information system are irreversible. This, together with the development of satellite television may, within five years or so, see the importance of national television much reduced. Meanwhile, as the *Kursk* incident indicated, the conventional mass media is perfectly capable of mobilising public opinion when it deals with things that are of intimate concern to its audience. The public itself can be unexpectedly agile at critical moments in choosing between the information media.

On one level, the effects of the present transformation are obvious: newspapers are full of that same turgid discourse of years gone by, as unreadable today as when it was printed in *Pravda* in 1982; even the dramatic seizure and closure of NTV was reduced to little more than a footnote. Business publications may continue to provide information but most newspapers are busy dumbing down the reality of Russia today, either by touting the new 'National Idea' or by trying to exorcise its ghost. In a word, the country's press is once more profoundly provincial.

Moscow March 2000: member of the movement 'Union 2000' holds
banner declaring 'Choosing liberty! Voting against everyone!'
Credit: Camera Press / Nikishin

The changes on television, an emasculated shade of its former self and dominated by imported game shows, sports coverage and soap operas, are even more striking.

Communication is as much about withholding as transmitting. Our nostalgia-drenched media is daily less informative, more ritualised in its observance of the business of communication. To free us from the tyranny of information overload – and in the process create a sense of social stability or reality – the authorities are once again shouldering the responsibility of liberating their citizens from participation in the political process.

But all this redundant political energy must be provided with new outlets: sports, entertainment, movies, comedies, culture and science. Is it really so bad for people to cheer footballers rather than political leaders? Or watch programmes like *Morning Post, Oh, Lucky Man!* or *All About Laughter?* At least it allows us to relax in the intervals between our real interests, like visits to the cinema and a little light reading.

But there are ambiguities, too, in this transformation: the 'National Idea' or 'Great Russia' is no more than a virtual reality, one of many, directed at a particular audience. And the real opposition to this is to be found not so much within the political system as in our everyday lives – and in the medium that mediates them better than anything else: the Internet.

Opposition on the Internet today resembles the opposition to Soviet officialdom found in the *samizdat* of yesterday. But only to a point. Soviet culture was directed to the construction of Soviet reality; the *samizdat* that opposed it, whether political or pornographic, was nourished by the reality of the West. The Internet proposes no single, coherent, competing ideology. The stand-off between the media-political system and the Internet is a stand-off between different modes of social interaction: between representation and communication. On the Web, official ideology is confronted not by one, but by thousands of ideologies, all of them existing simultaneously and finding expression not in ideological arguments but in particular life projects.

There may come a time when this contradiction begins to take political shape, especially if Putin's administration succeeds in taking total control of the political arena. At that point, politics will play a much bigger part on the Web than they do today: the Internet, together with the press, will begin to structure something more like a typical alternative information system in radical opposition to what on television is currently characterised as 'the good old days'. ❏

Ivan Zasurskii is the director of the Centre for Cultures and Communication in the faculty of journalism at Moscow State University. This article first appeared in Dos'e na Tsenzuru, Index's *sister magazine in Russia, founded in collaboration with* Index *in 1997. Translated by Arch Tait*

Period	1970–85	1986–90
Political system	USSR Inc. Unified management, single authority	Upheaval. Democratic reforms, alcohol coupons, cigarette riots [shortages]
Economy	Planned, strictly structured, hierarchical. Numerous industrial lobbies. Strong black market for imported consumer goods	Changes cause disintegration. Attempt to raise efficiency of heavy industry and shortage of consumer goods. Boom in printed mass media
Wars	Foreign excursions: Asia, Africa, Afghanistan	Afghan War
Official 'national idea'	Communism	The West
Media systems	Propaganda machine	Propaganda machine supporting reforms
Methods of social control	Ideological, social rituals, propaganda, manipulation, repression	Ideology, 'soft' propaganda, persuasion, 'managed democracy'
Role of journalist	Auxiliary	Important, especially in the press
Interest in politics	Minimal	Strong
Ideology	Communist imperialism	*Glasnost*, democratisation, socialist reforms. Optimistic
Society	Highly organised, based on development of rituals and social institutions; dual Party–private morality	Transformation. First appearance of legal, small-scale enterprise. Era of optimism
Changes in mass media	As a result of its 70-year evolution under communism, the media is only a tool of propaganda	Unprecedented growth in newspaper circulation, first live coverage of political events and news. Politicisation of masses
Leading mass media	*Pravda, Izvestiia*, Radio-1 and Radio Mayak. Popular magazines: *Working Woman, Peasant Woman, Health, Behind the Wheel, Chemistry and Life, Science and Technology*. Good films and books in short supply	*Moscow News, Ogonyok, Arguments and Facts*; literary journals. Newspaper *Speed-Info*. Radio Free Europe, BBC. Boom in video and audio cassette production. Growth of mass culture market, video and audio
Opposition	*Samizdat*, political jokes, foreign radio and press in Russian. Intelligentsia subscribes to *Korea*: N Korea has Russia's problems – plus	Radical *samizdat* and conservative communists (*Soviet Russia*, etc) versus radical democrats, eg *Soviet Youth* in Riga

1991–95	1996–2000	2000–
No system. Power struggle; alternating tension–calm. Total decentralisation. Strengthening opposition	Crossroads. Strong regional leaders. Media holdings function like political parties. Elective monarchy	Centralised system based on law enforcement agencies and army. Transformation of opposition. Political system 'closed'
Triumph of commercial capital, industrial crisis. Monopolies stoke inflation. Primary accumulation of capital and privatisation: redistribution of property	State, private, joint ventures, monopolies. Mobile telecoms boom. Banking crisis, industrial recovery, formation of new economic system	Economic growth expected. Raw materials monopolies but intense competition in telecommunications and IT sectors
Two putsches in Moscow; first Chechnya campaign	Information wars; second Chechnya campaign	War against terrorism and drug trafficking (new scapegoats)
Creation of democracy	Law and order	Great Russia
'Fourth Estate': independent corporation of journalists	Media-political system, viewer society	Mixed: enhanced role of state-controlled media and Internet
Eclectic ideology, persuasion, Special Forces units and army	Manipulation via political spectacle in TV and advertising	Ideology, propaganda and manipulation against horizontal communication (Internet)
Extremely important (in alliance with authorities)	In practice, auxiliary	Auxiliary on TV, slightly more significant in press and Internet
Significant	Sporadic	Minimal
Market fundamentalism, democratic reforms, anti-communism	No coherent value system. Public relations, dramatic conflicts	National (strong state and capitalism); poly-cultural post-industrial society
Free: chaotic and unintegrated with islands of growth. Power struggle between new property-owners exceeds legal limits. Social differentiation begins	Fragmented, changing but stable. Time of money. New social stratification on basis of consumption. Role of new business grows	Structured using hierarchy of signs. Growing role of Orthodox Church. Dual morality: divorce between private and public, socially accepted and real
Media become fully independent of original state sponsors. Circulation falls because of high price of paper and delivery	Sophisticated PR techniques. Mass media discredited by information wars. Satellite TV and Internet. Segmentation of spheres of consumption	State becomes dominant power centre, totally controlling symbolic reality. Partly compensated for by rapid growth of Internet and growth of power of mass media
Arguments and Facts, Izvestiia, Moscow Young Communist, Independent Newspaper, Trader (Kommersant), Russian Radio and TV, NTV. Regional TV. Commercial channels take Hollywood to the masses	Russian Public TV (ORT), NTV, FM-radio, quality press (*ID Kommersant*); specialised, including women's journals (*Liza, Cosmopolitan,* etc). Internet media grows (Gazeta.ru; lenta.ru; polit.ru). Film production develops	Russian Public TV, entertainment channels, FM-radio station, mass publications (*Young Communist Pravda, Izvestiia,* etc; commercial magazines, film industry, Internet publications, consumer segments of quality and mass culture
Communist newspapers (*Pravda, Soviet Russia*), nationalist publications (*Day*); publications of anarchist, ecologist subcultures, etc	Communist, nationalist and alternative publications (*Herbs and The Will, Radek, Eco-Defence, Anti-militarist*); publications of human rights organisations, etc	NTV and other mass media owned by Gusinskii. Alternative press and counter-culture on Internet; former 'mainstream' liberal polit.ru. Tendency to abandon politics

DEATH IN RUSSIA

IRENA MARYNIAK

> MEDICINE IS A SCIENCE DEALING WITH THE
> TREATMENT ONLY OF THE RICH AND FREE.
> IN RELATION TO EVERYONE ELSE, IT IS
> MERELY A THEORETICAL SCIENCE DEALING
> WITH HOW THEY WOULD BE CURED IF THEY
> WERE RICH AND FREE – *NOTES OF A*
> *PHYSICAN* (NINETEENTH CENTURY)

What is the most beautiful thing in life? The struggle for freedom. And what is even more beautiful? This. Take it down.

Zhigulev beer	100 grams
Shampoo (*Sadko the Rich Merchant*)	30 grams
Anti-dandruff shampoo	70 grams
Insect repellent	20 grams

Infuse some shag into the mixture and serve.

Venedikt Erofeev, *Moskva-Petushki*

Moskva-Petushki (*Moscow Circles*), Venedikt Erofeev's 1970s novella about being out of it on the streets and suburban railways of Moscow, is as much a cult book today as it was when it circulated in the Soviet Union in *samizdat*.

The story is a tumbling challenge to rationality, an ultimately tragic declaration of non-participation and, more gleefully, an exploration of those other spheres of consciousness and experience touched with the help of a little drink: 'From the sufferings at Kursk Station, through the purgatory at Kuchino to the reveries at Kupavna, to the light and Petushki. *Durch leiden – licht.*' Because, as all Russians know, nothing oversteps those apparently impenetrable barriers of status and style as effectively, companionably and affably as half a litre of vodka. Particularly so if you're on an *elektrichka* – one of those clattering suburban trains that take you out of the Styx into the city where, on public holidays at least, the sun always shines. That may be because squads of military planes have sprayed any approaching cloud formation with silver iodide to ensure that the provinces get the downpour but the burnished domes of the capital are sure to look their best. For this is it, the heart of the Russian dream where you pays your money and you takes your chance, and where 15 to 20 people, mostly drunk and homeless, died daily from exposure this winter.

Thirty years ago, Erofeev's hero Venichka might have warmed up in an *elektrichka*, but these days most radiators have been ripped out and he'd probably have trouble finding a seat. The number of trains to and from the city centre has been cut threefold. Daily commuting has been described in the Russian press as a 'cataclysm'. Two hours' crush in battered carriages with broken windows and puddles slopping about the floor makes for a different kind of companionship. A former prisoner with multi-drug-resistant TB may find himself breathing into the jowls of a paediatrician or a teacher. Paediatricians and teachers may be in a position to bribe doctors to treat them if they pick up the infection but their patients and pupils may be less lucky.

The ex-prison inmate is most likely to go the way of Venichka and the other 20 million Russians who have migrated into spirits and home-brewed variations of vodka.

Alcohol poisoning kills about 35,000 people a year in Russia, most of them men of working age. Life expectancy was highest during the legendary and hugely unpopular anti-alcohol campaign instigated by Mikhail Gorbachev in 1985. The initiative faltered within two years, and a Russian now consumes an average of 4.4 gallons of alcohol a year. Men can expect to live to 60, women can hope to reach 72; since 1990, the death rate has risen by one-third while births are down by almost 40%. Alcohol, drugs, TB, Aids, syphilis and hepatitis C are blamed most. As Russia moved towards the free market, an excess of 2 million deaths above the norm was recorded. One Russian paper called it 'genocide'. In the West, academics acknowledge that it's a figure unprecedented in peacetime.

At present, Russia's population of 145 million is shrinking by 750,000 a year. By 2050, it could be down to 100 million, estimates US demographer Murray Feshback. The US population, currently at 289 million, is expected to rise to 396 million over the same period. Russian predictions are even more pessimistic, warning of a possible drop to 70 million. Deaths exceed births by almost two to one; infectious disease is up; two-thirds of pregnancies are aborted; the suicide rate is one of the highest in the world. Putin's economic adviser, Andrey Iliaronov, has pointed to 2003 as 'the year of reckoning' when the demographic crisis, a crumbling infrastructure and foreign debt may combine to cripple Russia's remaining productive capacity and its ability to help itself.

The temptation for many may be to harp back to the days of Empire, the 1960s for instance, when life expectancy in communist Europe was equal to, or higher than, that in the West. Under the Soviet regime, the state assumed an absolute responsibility for health that was certainly restrictive for individuals but provided a safety net that protected people from the worst consequences of real poverty. Housing, education and employment were guaranteed; bread, vodka and cigarettes were cheap. But the health security the state notionally gave the state also took away. Essentials and palliatives were readily available but fresh food wasn't. Ham-fisted environmental policies left air, land, water and people poisoned. The Soviet Union was the first industrialised country to record a rise in infant mortality and a decline in life expectancy. In 1979, unfavourable figures were deleted from the published census and locked away in a safe whose combination was known only to a select few. They were released only in 1988, under *glasnost*.

Yet the Soviet Union did put 3 to 4% of its GDP into health care while post-communist spending on it dropped to 1 to 2%. Scarce resources have led to a lack of even basic sanitation in many Russian hospitals today while the best doctors serve elite groups privately. Bribery is the norm. A remark from the 19th-century *Notes of a Physician* carries a troubling resonance: 'Medicine is a science dealing with the treatment only of the rich and free. In relation to everyone else, it is merely a theoretical science dealing with how they would be cured if they were rich and free.'

This is nothing short of a disastrous state of affairs in a country where an estimated 7% of civilians and 40% of prison inmates have TB. The penitentiary system is heavily overloaded, with over 1 million detainees, and the disease continues to spread, aided by overcrowding, errors and delays in diagnosis, poor therapy and a hopelessly inadequate diet. An article by Anatoly Yershov in *Izvestiya* describes conditions in the prisons of the Nizhny Novgorod region: 'Two hundred and forty inmates out of 1,500 prisoners in the Kaisk colony have nowhere to sleep . . . that is why there are often two patients to one bed and inmates take turns in inhaling fresh air through the barred window. Because of overcrowding in the colony's hospital, 300 prisoners with tuberculosis have to stay outside the hospital, spreading infection throughout the colony.'

Control of the disease is hampered by budget cuts and poor co-ordination between prison and health officials. The Harvard Report on TB in Russia has called the prison system an 'epidemiological pump, releasing into the society hundreds of thousands of infected persons annually'. In 1999,

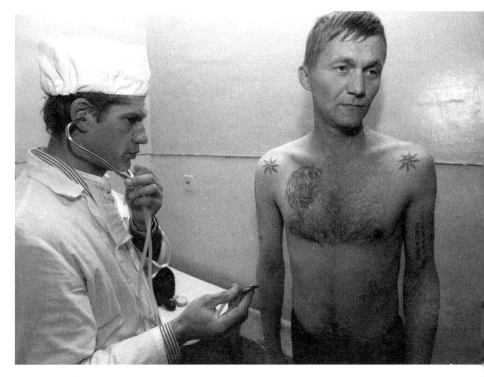

Russia 2001: testing time in the TB gulag
Credit: Heidi Bradner

Nezavisima gazeta wrote that of the 300,000 prisoners discharged each year, probably 80% were infected; 10% had active TB and many would not receive treatment. There are concerns, too, that the emerging parallel epidemic of HIV in Russia, said to be assuming proportions approaching those in Africa, will amplify the number of active TB cases among the carrier population.

Aids has an ill-documented history in Russia. The first case was recorded in 1986 and widely publicised in the USSR as a disease associated with corrupt lifestyles. Sex education was absent from Soviet schools and attempts to introduce it since have fallen victim to resistance from religious and conservative groups. The late 1980s and early 1990s, which witnessed a belated 'sexual revolution' in Russia, also saw an increase in IV drug-taking and a surge in prostitution. No attempt was made to provide information about HIV to the public until the mid-1990s. Then, in 1998, a law was introduced classifying drug addicts as criminals: anyone with Aids or syphilis who had contracted the disease through drug abuse could be imprisoned. This ensured that few addicts would seek Aids testing or treatment for fear of arrest. Vadim Pokrovskii of the Federal Centre for Aids Prevention, Russia's leading HIV/Aids epidemiologist, estimates that 5 to 10 million will die of Aids after 2015, most aged between 15 and 29. The Russian Central Bureau of Epidemiology has predicted that there will be 2 million cases of HIV in Russia by the end of 2002.

Testing has been widespread but mostly compulsory and sometimes carried out without the knowledge or consent of patients. Anyone who tests positive may be refused treatment if he can't pay the black market, or get experimental medication without knowing what it is he's getting or, indeed, without having been told that information about his condition may be made public. The *SPID-Infosvyaz* website reports that in Moscow an Aids doctor employed an HIV-positive patient to befriend other positives and get the names of their sexual partners. Each name provided to the government was paid for. In the mid-1990s, in Rostov, a number of people lost their jobs after reports that they were on a list of men suspected of having gay sex with an Aids victim who had died.

Recent reports in the Russian media have tended to suggest, oddly, that the number of Aids cases is falling. The disease has become 'confined to the circle of drug addicts', the argument goes, where the 'level of recidivist crime is high'. In December 2001, *Nezavisima gazeta* rebuked the government for inadequate policing, lenient sentencing of addicts and a shortage of treatment centres while laying the blame for an increasingly thriving drugs trade squarely with minorities: Azerbaijanis, Chechens and Tajiks.

The overwhelming influence of government on the Russia media is telling and making for reporting that is bland, eager to find evidence of increased stability and to suggest that those responsible for jeopardising the state's security and future are identifiable and should be punished. In lieu of information, people are being plied with the promise of a lifestyle already enjoyed by those with elite status, once party members and now moneyed capitalists, who consume what most Russians can't afford and have choices, chances and an autonomy that the majority don't. Perhaps 30% of the population have made some kind of progress economically, but many are left clutching at national or religious identity to bolster their fragile perception of themselves and the lives they must lead.

Sociologist Yuri Levade says in *Argumenty i fakty* that the public mood is improving: 73% of Russians now declare they trust Vladimir Putin. Even people who haven't been paid for months are willing to say that they believe the government is doing a lot to improve matters. Putin's democratic credentials are not a priority because, Levade says, 'the notion of democracy has become diffuse. The word has been juggled with too much.' A saviour at the helm is more important. Comparisons are being drawn between Putin and Peter the Great. The image of a strong, internationally respected leader combined with the time-honoured myth of the good in conflict with a nefarious elite of boyars – one-time media magnates and oligarchs Boris Berezovskii and Vladimir Gusinskii – have taken root in the public imagination.

The media fiddle as Russia burns and the government plays on the faint hope that a consolidation of public spirit will, somehow, turn the country around. Because that may be the only hope left. ❑

Irena Maryniak

OLD BOOKS FOR NEW – AND OLDER

JUDITH VIDAL-HALL

IN WHAT LOOKS SUSPICIOUSLY LIKE A
NEW FORM OF CENSORSHIP, RUSSIAN
VIGILANTES ARE CLEANING UP THE
LITERARY SCENE IN MOSCOW

First it was TV6; then that sturdy veteran Karl Marx, no longer considered suitable for the new Russia; now it's the bad boy of contemporary Russian literature who's in their sights.

In a manner more reminiscent of China's Red Guard or Hitler's over-zealous storm troopers than of the old Glavlit, Vladimir Putin's moral brigades are on the march, determined to cleanse Mother Russia from literature that might sully her image at home and abroad.

'We feel certain authors can damage the Russian spirit,' says Vasilii Yake-menko, leader of Walking Together, a youth organisation with close links to Putin's Unity Party. On the other hand, he adds, there are those that are 'useful' and should be promoted by the state. His organisation is proposing a 'book exchange' in Moscow through which they propose to substitute for more suitable literature the works of Marx and Victor Pelevin, a best-selling author who is equally scathing about old Soviet or Putin-new Russia, and whose flouting of sexual taboos, still strong among an older generation brought up on Soviet puritanism, has made him something of an icon to Russian youth.

For 'suitable' read 'patriotic'; and the man in the uncomfortable position of being thus promoted by Walking Together, is, says Yakemenko, Boris Vasiliev, one-time Soviet writer of the old style who has 'perpetuated the tradition of Russian literature in which it is the soul that feels pain and not the head that is aching after a drinking bout'.

No one is happy, least of all Vasiliev, who appears to be more embarrassed than anything else by being held up as an unwitting paragon of Russian letters. But what do Marx and Pelevin have in common? 'In the old days, everyone was supposed to live the life according to Marx,' says Yakemenko. 'Today, our younger generation are being encouraged to live life according to Pelevin.' He plans to organise book drops throughout Moscow where people can exchange their Marx and Pelevin for a volume of short stories by Vasiliev.

What Pelevin, who has a considerable reputation abroad for such surreal and often scurrilous collections of short stories as *A Werewolf Problem in Central Russia* and *The Life of Insects* or for novels such as *Omon Ra* and *Buddha's Little Finger*, thinks is not on record, but the media and intellectuals have led a string of protests. *Izvestia* dismissed the whole thing as 'silly' and the culture minister called the campaign 'youthful waywardness'. Putin's office has remained silent and, undeterred, Walking Together are determined to take their campaign further. 'This is only a beginning,' says Yakemenko. 'We ugently need to set up a special commission that will decide which writers should be published and who is suitable to represent Russia abroad.'

Which might not sound quite so alarming if it weren't for the fate of Boris Berezovskii's TV6. In November last year, Walking Together launched a public attack on the channel in an 'open letter to the government' denouncing the 'moral depravity' of certain programmes put out by the opposition channel. Berezovskii has since fled abroad, and the channel, which has been put into receivership, is due to be auctioned off at the end of March and is likely to end in hands sympathetic to the present government.

With Vladimir Guzinskii's NTV already in hands sympathetic to Putin, the loss of TV6 marks the end of nationwide independent television and could have repercussions way beyond Moscow. Since the end of communism in 1991, a vigorous network of some 600 regional TV stations has sprung up across Russia. They have mainly been spared interference from the centre and have built up a reputation as an alternative news source to the official line. TV6's network included 156 regional stations covering all major cities and reaching an audience of over 80 million. In addition to local programming, they broadcast shows form TV6. If the fate of NTV's regional network after the break-up of the parent company is anything to go by, the network could be in serious trouble.

Since the April 2001 takeover of Guzinskii's Media-MOST corporation by the state gas company Gazprom, TNT, its regional TV network of over 100 stations in 582 cities with an audience of 75m, has been subjected to increased interference from the parent company. Efforts at the end of last year by local bosses to buy out their stations have met with no response. Meanwhile, intervention from the Kremlin is sending the message to local political bosses that they, too, can pile on the pressure if coverage by their local TV station is not entirely to their liking. The temptation to self-censorship, now that the last independent TV outlets are at risk, is considerable. ❑

JVH

MIDDLE GAME

VICTOR PELEVIN

Lucy was lying on her back looking at the ceiling. Nellie was pensively examining her profile with its delicate down of face powder.

'Listen, girl,' she whispered. 'Promise me one thing. Promise me you won't just get up and walk out, no matter what I tell you. All right?'

'I promise, Nellie. Of course I do.'

'You haven't noticed anything odd about me?'

'Of course not.'

'Well, all right . . . No, I can't go on. Kiss me . . . That's good. Do you know who I used to be?'

'Heavens, Nellie, what difference does it make?'

'No, I don't mean like that. Have you heard about transsexuals? The sex-change operation?'

Lucy felt a sudden wave of fear breaking over her and her breasts began to ache painfully. She drew away from Nellie slightly.

'Yes, Nellie. What about it?'

'Well, then,' Nellie gulped. 'Only hear me out. I used to be a man. My name was Vasily, Vasily Tsyruk. I was the secretary of a regional committee of the Young Communist League. I used to walk around in, well, a suit, and a collar and tie, wearing a waistcoat and chairing endless meetings . . . carrying dossiers on people around in my briefcase . . . agendas, minutes . . . Well, anyway, I would be going home in the evening, and on the way I had to pass this hard-currency restaurant, limos, women like you, everybody laughing, and me walking past in this prissy waistcoat, with my YCL lapel badge and my prissy moustache, carrying my prissy briefcase to cap it all, and they would all hoot with laughter and pile into all these cars! "Well," I thought, "so what. I'll soon be a party member, and before you know it I'll be an instructor in the city committee." I had it all going for me. "I'll live it up in restaurants that'll put this one in the shade. Never mind the town, I'll paint the whole world red . . ." But then, one evening, I went to a Solidarity-with-the-Palestinians party and this drunk Arab called Avada Ali went and threw a glass of tea in my face, and people in the regional committee of the party started asking questions and wondering why Comrade Tsyruk got tea thrown in his face when it never happened to other comrades. Anyway, I got an official reprimand and it went down in my file. And me already a candidate for party membership! I practically went out of my mind! And then I read in the *Literary Gazette* about this Professor Vishnevskii who did this operation for, well, queers, only don't think I was gay . . . I was just reading about how they inject these hormones and change your whole personality and way of thinking, and my old personality and way of thinking had really let me down. Anyway, to cut a long story short, I sold my old Moskvich and went for six operations one after the other. They injected me with endless hormones, and a year ago I came out of the clinic with my hair long and feeling a different, er, woman. Everything seemed different. I walked down the street and even the snowdrifts didn't seem real. They were like the cotton wool round a Christmas tree. Then I suppose I got used to everything, only recently I have had this feeling everybody is looking at me and that they know all about me. And then I met you and I thought, right, I'll test whether I really am a woman or . . . Lucy, what's wrong?'

Lucy had moved away and was sitting by the wall pressing her knees to her breasts with both arms. There was a silence.

'Do I disgust you?' Nellie whispered. 'Am I disgusting?'

'So you did have a moustache,' Lucy said, and tossed back a lock of hair from her face. 'And perhaps you remember you had a deputy called Andreii Pavlov? Only you called him Creep.'

'I do remember,' Nellie said in amazement.

'You even sent him out for beer. And then you saddled him with a personal dossier over that poster propaganda cock-up, when someone drew Lenin on the propaganda board wearing gloves, and Felix Dzerzhinskii without a shadow!'

'How do you know all . . . ? Creep? Is it really you?' ❏

Victor Pelevin is one of the most controversial of Russia's younger generation of writers. 'Middle Game', the story from which this excerpt was taken, was first published in Love and Fear, Glas New Russian Writing, No 4 1993. See also Index 3/1996. Translated by Arch Tait

CLEANING UP

ANNA POLITKOVSKAIA

UNDER THE BANNER OF WAR ON
TERRORISM, THE RUSSIANS HAVE
TAKEN ADVANTAGE OF THE LICENCE
TO KILL

Do you still think you should be supporting the war in Chechnya because of some aim that's being pursued? To stop things getting worse?

We have reached a stage in Russia now where every schoolchild knows that Chechnya is being 'sanitised', and adults no longer bother with the inverted commas. 'Sanitisation' in this sense entails thoroughly sorting out someone or something and, on the whole, we prefer not to enquire too closely into who or what. For this meaning of a virtuous 19th-century verb we have the war in Chechnya to thank, and more particularly the high-ranking military brass who routinely update us on television with the latest news from Russia's Chechen ghetto, popularly known as the 'Zone of Anti-Terrorist Operations'.

Grozny 1995: one of the unidentified Chechen dead
Credit: Heidi Bradner

It is March 2002 and the 30th month of the Second Chechen War. 'Sanitisation', if we are to believe the military, is precisely the aim of the current Special Measures. From last November until now, lunatic waves of Special Measures have been sweeping over Chechnya: Shali, Kurchaloy, Tsotsan-Yurt, Bachi-Yurt, Urus-Martan, Grozny; again Shali, again Kurchaloy; Argun again and again; Chiri-Yurt. Towns and villages are besieged for days; women wail; families try desperately to evacuate their adolescent sons – where to doesn't matter providing it's a long way from Chechnya; village elders stage protest demonstrations. Finally, we are regaled with general Moltenskoy himself, our supposed commander-in-chief of the 'Front Against Terrorism', festooned with medals and ribbons, there on the television screen, pumping adrenalin, larger than life, and invariably against a background of corpses and 'sanitised' villages. The general reports some recently achieved 'significant success'.

But they still haven't captured Emir Hattab and Djokar Basaev, and you know full well that something isn't right, because you went to school when you were little and can do enough mental arithmetic to add up the numbers of enemy fighters he claims to have caught over the past winter. It amounts to a whole regiment of them. Just the same as in last year's warfare season.

So how many fighters do these people have? What exactly does 'sanitisation' involve? What is the truth, and who is telling it? What have these Special Measures actually turned into? What is their aim? Last, and most important, what are their results?

'I was relieved when they took us out to be shot.'

'Relieved? What about your parents? Didn't you think about them then, and how sad they would be?'

Mahomed Idigov, recently taken out to be shot, is 16. He is a pupil in the tenth grade of School No 2 in the town of Starye Atagi, Grozny Province. He has a favourite pair of jeans, a much-loved Walkman, and a stack of pop music cassettes which he enjoys listening to. He's a typical 16-year-old. The only disturbing thing about him is his eyes, which have the level steadiness of an adult's. They don't go with his teenager's skin problems and adolescent gawkiness. There something wrong, too, in the measured way Mahomed relates the story of what was done to him. In the course of 'sanitisation', he was subjected to the same electric torture as the grown men. Having themselves been tortured, these men pleaded with Russian officers not to torture the boy but to torture them again in his place. 'No way,' was the reply. 'We get good counter-terrorist information out of schoolboys.'

When I ask about his parents, Mahomed pauses for a time. His eyebrows finally arch childishly as he tries not to cry. He manages, and replies clearly and directly, as you can when something's over,

'Other people get killed too.'

Indeed. Why should Mohamed have it easier than other people? Everybody is in the same situation.

The 'sanitisation' of Starye Atagi from 28 January to 5 February was the second time the town had been 'sanitised' in 2002, and the 20th time since the beginning of the Second Chechen War. It is subjected to Special Measures nearly every month. The official explanation is plausible: with a population of around 15,000, Starye Atagi is one of the largest towns in Chechnya. It is 20km from Grozny and ten from the so-called 'Wolves' Gate', as Russian soldiers call the entrance to the Argun Ravine. It is considered a trouble-spot full of terrorist wahhabites and their sympathisers.

But what has this to do with Mahomed? On the morning of 1 February, when the 20th 'sanitisation' was at its most ferocious, masked men seized the boy from his home in Nagornaia Street, threw him like a log into a military truck and took him to the 'filtration point', where he was tortured.

'It was very cold that day. First we were "put against the wall" for several hours, which means you stand with your hands up and your legs apart, facing the wall. If you try to lower your arms you get beaten immediately. Any soldier who walks past is likely to hit you. They unbuttoned my jacket, pulled up my sweater and cut it into strips with a knife, like a clown's jacket.'

'Why?'

'Just to make me feel the cold more. They saw I was shivering.'

I can't bear it. Mahomed is too dispassionate. I can't bear the calm, thoughtful look on his face as he relates his appalling story. I wish this child would at least cry and give me something to do. I could comfort him then.

'Did they hit you a lot?'

'All the time. On the kidneys. Then they put me on the ground and dragged me through the mud by the neck.'

'What for? Did you know why they were doing it?'

'Just because. For fun.'

'But were they trying to get something out of you?'

'For a whole day there was nothing. They just hurt me. They took me to interrogation in the evening. They interrogated three of us. They showed me a list and said, "Which of these people are fighters? Where are they treated for injuries? Who is the doctor? Whose house do they sleep at? Which of your neighbours is feeding them?" I answered, "I don't know."'

'And what did they say?'

'They said, "Do you need some help?" And they tortured me with electric current. That's what they mean by helping. They connected the wires and turned a handle, like on a telephone. The more they turned it the stronger the current that passed through me. They asked me where my older brother, "the Wahhabite", was as well.'

'And is he a Wahhabite?'

'No, of course not.'

'What did you say?'

'I didn't say anything.'

'And what did they do?'

'They passed the current through me again.'

'Did it hurt?'

Mahomed's head on his thin neck slumps down below his shoulders, into his angular knees. He does not want to answer, but it is an answer I need.

'It hurt a lot then?'

'Yes.'

'Is that why you were relieved when they took you out to be shot?'

Mahomed is shaking as if he has a high fever. Behind him is an array of bottles with solutions for medicine droppers, syringes, cotton wool, tubes.

'Whose is this stuff?'

'It's for me. They damaged my kidneys and lungs.'

There are a lot of people in the room, but it's as silent as if we were in an uninhabited, soundproof bunker. The men are completely motionless. Somewhere outside the Idigovs' house the nightly artillery barrage is starting, but nobody so much as stirs at its uneven booming which sounds like the drums at a funeral.

I realise that this war, which from force of habit we still call an 'anti-terrorist operation', has been lost. It can't be continued solely for the momentary gratification of a group of people who long ago took leave of their senses. The silence is broken by Mahomed's father, Isa, a haggard man whose face is deeply etched with suffering.

'I was wounded serving in the Soviet army. I served on Sakhalin. I know the way things are. But! During the last "sanitisation" they took my oldest son. They beat him up and let him go, and I decided to send him as far away as I could, to people I know, where he'd be safe. Was I wrong to do that?

During this "sanitisation" they've crippled my middle son, Mahomed. What am I to do? My youngest is already 11. How long will it be before they start on him? Not one of my sons is a gunman. They don't smoke or drink. How are we supposed to live?'

I do not know. I only know that this is unacceptable. I know too how it has come about: our entire country has joined hands to follow the lead of our great statesmen (and not only Russia, but Europe and America too), and at the beginning of the 21st century we are acquiescing without a murmur in the torture of children in a present-day European ghetto mendaciously called a 'zone of anti-terrorist operations'. The children of this ghetto will never forget what we have done.

Do you still think you ought to be supporting this war because of some aim that's being pursued and to stop things getting worse? Things cannot get worse. We have lost all sense of the morality and restraint we were taught in less tumultuous times, and something more vile and loathsome than we could ever imagine has erupted from the murkiest depths of our souls. ❏

Anna Politkovskaia is special correspondent in Chechnya of Novaia gazeta.
Translated by Arch Tait

MARCHING IN STEP

VÁCLAV HAVEL

DEMOCRACY CANNOT PROSPER WITHOUT
A FREE MEDIA AND THE RIGHT TO SPEAK
ONE'S MIND, SAYS CZECH DISSIDENT
AND PLAYWRIGHT TURNED PRESIDENT

President Havel, you have stood up for freedom of expression and have paid the price: almost five years in prison. What is the secret of the courage to resist?

Based on personal experience, I would say this courage does not come as the result of a single moment in a person's life in which he or she decides to become a brave man or women or to stay a coward for ever. It is, rather, a development in which a person takes the first step he or she thinks is the right one, and then the next . . . and the next . . . until it becomes a step-by-step process. Naturally, this is based partly on the decisions the person is making but also on the circumstances: a person's character plays a role but quite often the decisive influence comes from outside. Many brave people have surprised themselves by the discovery of their courage.

Not so long ago, here in Prague Castle, I decorated two Czech journalists, Petra Prochazkova and Jaromir Stetina, who have been working in Chechnya and Afghanistan. When I think about them, I believe it was probably not so much a matter of them deciding at the beginning of their careers to become heroes but rather a particular situation that engaged their professional curiosity and integrity as journalists and drew them ever further in until they found themselves in serious danger. They had to prove their readiness to deal with whatever confronted them: to take risks, to make sacrifices, to resist pressure. At a certain point, I think they became attracted to reporting from dangerous regions; now, back in the peace and quiet of Prague, I know they get restless and want to go somewhere else.

How do you assess developments in free expression in this region in the ten years since the demise of the Soviet Union?

Basically, I believe you can observe an irreversible process towards democracy and freedom of expression throughout Central and Eastern Europe, including the Balkans. However, in the 12 years since the collapse of communism, we have experienced countless things that were entirely new and unexpected. In some countries, development has been faster than anyone could possibly have predicted; in others, this process has proceeded along a circuitous route with many surprising diversions and detours along the way.

Furthermore, the change of generations has played a part. Most of the journalists working today were only ten or 15 years old when the democratisation process started. They have grown up and studied in an environment that is much closer to true democratic values than earlier generations. There is also another important factor in the development of freedom of expression in this part of the world: globalisation. The access to information from virtually all over the world makes it increasingly difficult to keep societies closed and to exercise strong control of the media.

What challenges do you see ahead?

There is, of course, still a long way to go in some countries in the region; I hope the international community will pay attention to this and help to push the process forward. But there is something else I want to draw attention to. It's my impression that there is a threat to free expression in some countries that has nothing to do with direct political oppression or censorship, but that could, in 50 years or so, become the biggest threat to free expression. I'm talking about complex issues – economic interests in particular – that could affect freedom of speech. Italy could provide us with the first example.

In situations like this, voluntary, non-governmental human rights and civic groups have an important part to play because these communities, by definition, are the ones that can stand up against manipulation and censorship, as much in its economic guise as in its more conventional forms.

Another issue is directly related to the challenges to democracy that terrorist organisations represent [*Index* 2/2002, 'Squeeze on democracy'] – and to the response of the democratic world.

This is a difficult issue. I can see this potential conflict between freedom and security from both sides: I used to be an independent critic of politicians, looking in from the outside; then I became a politician myself. So, to some extent, I can understand politicians getting upset because the press gets to know everything; sometimes it leaks information that is still a matter of debate among politicians. And it is sometimes true that it is better that politicians announce things first before any revelations are made in the press.

Nevertheless, I believe freedom should always be given priority. At the same time, the media's treatment of security issues must be guided by responsibility and by their professional standards, both of which we have a right to demand from them.

Governments in Central and Eastern Europe, as in the Czech Republic, have been criticised in past months for interfering with the media, trying to control them. What is your view on these cases?

I have always appreciated it when my own country has been legitimately criticised. I said the same under communism; why should I feel any differently or be offended by it now?

However, the historical context is important. In post-communist countries, the media situation is complicated, largely as a result of the vast changes these countries have already undergone and are, indeed, still going through. The West has not gone through the same dramatic transformation of ownership and privatisation.

In this transformation process, a thousand and one temptations have been generated, including the attempt to link political and economic power. This process needs constant monitoring by the media and civil society, and well-researched, substantive criticism is not just welcome, it is imperative for the continued development of democracy.

Let me quote a US judge who once said that the horrors with which we are flooded from the tabloid press are just a very small price that we pay for the gift of freedom.

President Havel, in about a year you will step down as president of the Czech Republic. What do you plan for your retirement?

If God gives me the health and strength, I want to put together a book of reflections analysing as frankly as possible my experience during my almost 13 years in office. The press often asks me what I consider to have been my biggest mistakes. But as is evident to me from what they write about me and my mistakes, they have not noticed the biggest ones – and I am not inclined to make their life easier by telling them myself. ❏

Václav Havel, President of the Czech Republic, was interviewed by Mette Terkelsen, deputy editor-in-chief of Kristeligt Dagblad, Denmark; Eberhard Ebner, publisher of Südwest Presse, Germany; Kees van Zweeden, Central European senior correspondent for the Dutch media group GPD; Michal Klima, CEO of Economia OnLine, Czech Republic, and Mogens Schmidt, assistant director-general of World Association of Newspapers, Paris

5/1979: VÁCLAV HAVEL, CZECHOSLOVAKIA

How are ordinary, decent people to react to the imposition of a repressive regime, how much should they risk in showing their opposition to it? These questions were raised by Ludvik Vaculik in a feuilleton *he wrote in December 1978, which brought an indignant reply from Václav Havel, excerpted below, as well as a dozen other dissidents. Havel was arrested and imprisoned soon after this appeared in* Index.

Without exaggeration: none of us can know in advance how much we can bear, nor what we may be made to bear. That can only be known by your calculating model of a sensible, decent man within the limits of the law. None of us decided in advance that we wanted to go to jail, indeed none of us made a conscious decision that he or she wanted to become a dissident.

We became dissidents without actually knowing how, and we found ourselves behind bars without really knowing how. We simply did certain things we had to do and that it seemed proper to do: nothing more, nor less. Happy are those who are decent and haven't landed in jail. But why should those who had that misfortune be set apart from the others? Is it not usually quite arbitrary who lands in it and who doesn't? Those whom you call heroes, suggesting that they are overdoing things, didn't get locked up for their ambition to become martyrs – they were locked up because of the indecency of those who put people in jail for writing novels or for playing tapes with the music of unofficial musicians.

No one wants to go to jail. If people were to take your advice and calculate the risks involved in the fashion of a thief deciding whether to burgle a supermarket, there would, for long time now, have been in our country not a single expression of solidarity with an unjustly persecuted person, not a single truthful novel or free song, not even a single *feuilleton*. For how can we be sure that tomorrow they won't start putting people away for writing *feuilletons*?

Maybe all you meant to say was that the quiet and inconspicuous humiliation of thousands of anonymous people was worse than the occasional arrest of a well-known dissident. Undoubtedly. But the question surely is, why did they arrest the dissident? Mainly, if you think about it, just because he had tried to tell the truth about that quiet and inconspicuous humiliation of thousands of anonymous people. ❑

2/1983: GYORGY KONRAD, HUNGARY

Hungary's best-known writer, Gyorgy Konrad, is in the paradoxical position of having some of his best work published abroad but not in Budapest. This article was written by him specially for Index on Censorship.

The censors these days are not obsessive characters, only lazy, gloomy and averse to anything extreme. Thirty years ago they were strong, and society under their feet was weak; now as society grows in strength, the censors suffer from world-weariness. However, the dialogue of censorship and anti-censorship can never be silenced on the stage of our innermost soul. This dialogue may at present resemble that of Samuel Beckett but it may develop into that of Chekhov and – who knows? – maybe into that of Shakespeare. There comes a mysterious moment when, all at once, a majority tires of its grumbling hopelessness. That is when a new historical period begins.

To live in an atmosphere of censorship – as I have ever since I can remember – isn't much fun. It is like a slowly enveloping fatigue; it is to see nothing but faces made boring by fear and conformity. Their eyes say: you must not, it is not sensible, or opportune . . . Not a day passes without my hearing something about censorship; it clings to my mind like thistledown. Always I feel censorship's heavy atmospheric pressure; its fustiness is all-pervading. Whatever I write, I don't bother offering it for publication. I'm not in the mood to defend or to bewail my condemned sentences (judge inadmissible). Of course, this is only a mental game anyway, as I am a black-listed author.

Greetings to you, little listening device, behind the ceiling of my country retreat. It's good to know that there is an ear above, noting my every sigh. To rattle on my typewriter, to speak into my tape recorder, all gives me a feeling of cheerful defiance.

. . .

Although I live in defiance of it, censorship still fills my life to the brim.

Censorship is the Great Lie, constantly recreating itself; an imposed trusteeship from the cradle to the grave, a lingering fog of fear, inside which the primordial rule of the system becomes invisible. This rule is that nothing must escape censorship; without it, state socialism would be impossible. Censorship is not a distant authority: it is you, your own self. ❏

2/1972: CENSORSHIP OF WRITERS, YUGOSLAVIA
LETTER FROM YUGOSLAVIA

The political and police action taken by the Yugoslav authorities against intellectuals has continued on a somewhat diminished scale. At the time of writing, early in July, the measures taken against writers, journalists and university faculty members in Croatia have probably passed their peak, although a number of trials are still in progress and the largest trial of all – that of a dozen leaders of the cultural organisation Matica Hrvatska – is due to be held in the autumn. At the same time, although in a considerably milder form at the moment, a similar action has been started against Serbian nationalism. This has led to the banning of a number of newspapers and other publications and even to trials of journalists, publicists and faculty members in Belgrade and Novi Sad. It is true to say that the majority of cases concern people who are known for their Croatian nationalist or Serbian nationalist tendencies but there has also been a gradual increase of cases in which intellectuals whose beliefs have nothing at all to do with nationalism have been subject to banning orders or trials. This leads one to the conclusion that it is no longer only nationalistically minded people who are suffering but a much wider circle of Yugoslav intellectuals who are now experiencing less freedom of expression than they enjoyed up till September last year.

At the end of May, the Central Committee of the League of Communists of Croatia published in Zagreb a document under the title 'Report on the Position of the League of Communists of Croatia Regarding the Infiltration of Nationalism into its Ranks'. Leafing through the 310 pages of this report one finds the names of about 200 Croatian writers, journalists, school-teachers and university faculty members who have either had difficulties with the authorities in the course of the last few months, or can expect them in the near future. The accusations made against them in the report are extremely varied, but the material forming the basis of these accusations is almost always the same: quotations from writings or public speeches made before the time of the recent emergency. Thus it is fair to say that the guilt of all the accused Croatian intellectuals comes down to one and the same thing, namely that they freely and publicly aired opinions and ideas which until December 1971 were considered legitimate and legal in Yugoslavia but are now politically unpalatable and in some cases are being interpreted as a matter of criminal prosecution ...

Serbia until now has not come under the same kind of pressure as Croatia but there are signs that the situation there, too, is growing difficult for writers, intellectuals and scholars. The evidence for this is contained in a Serbian Party document very similar to the Croatian report. The Serbian document, published by the Central Committee of the League of Communists of Serbia is entitled 'Documentation of the Roots, Ideology, Phenomena and Actions of Nationalism in Serbia' and has been summarised in the 2 July number of the Belgrade weekly *NIN*. In general, the Serbian document appears milder than the Croatian report. There are relatively few direct attacks on personalities, although a number of intellectuals are referred to as possessing pronounced nationalist tendencies ... Somewhat sharper are the accusations levelled against certain institutions and publishers labelled as 'hotbeds of nationalism'.

In general, it may be said that the rest of the country has been much less affected by the present trend than Serbia and especially Croatia. In Bosnia and Herzegovina, the intellectual climate has always been less liberal than in many of the other republics, so that it is not uncommon for change to be imposed on publishing houses and newspapers. In Macedonia and Montenegro the republican party organisations have so far limited themselves to criticism. And it is only in Slovenia, the northernmost and most developed of the Yugoslav republics, that there have been echoes of the events in Croatia ...

All these measures place a question mark over previous expectations of a steady move in the direction of greater freedom of expression in Yugoslavia and hopes that its unique variant of communism would prove amenable to this freedom. Since the measures taken may still be characterised as mild, there is a possibility that they may be stopped within a short period of time. Otherwise, if they gather momentum, one fears that a far larger number of Yugoslav writers and intellectuals will be affected before very long. ❑

'GH'

1994: MEDIA, YUGOSLAVIA
THE CULTURE OF LIES

Is it possible for the media to provoke war? I permit myself the theory that the war on the territory of Yugoslavia began several years ago with the posterior of a completely innocent Serbian peasant. I still remember his surname: Martinovica. For months the poor man, who was allegedly found in a field with a bottle in his backside, became a topic in many Yugoslav newspapers and of TV stations, particularly in Serbia. Some maintained that Martinovica had been raped with a beer bottle by Albanians, others that he was a pervert who had been masturbating with the bottle. Others again affirmed that he had been raped by Serbs so that they could blame the Albanians. Yet others, the most fundamental, calculated on the basis of the nature of the injury that Martinovica had himself jumped on to the bottle from a nearby tree. His sorrowing and numerous offspring gave statements in their father's favour, teams of doctors disagreed in public about the various possibilities of injury and self-injury. Martinovica spent the whole time in his hospital bed smiling feebly at the anxious TV viewers. The media made a political spectacle of Martinovica's backside, quite in keeping with the Balkan spirit.

So the case of Martinovica simply confirmed the belief of the Serbian people that the Serbian leader Slobodan Milosevic's decision – to change the constitution violently and revoke the autonomy of Kosovo and Vojvodina – was more than justified! So the masses became accustomed to participating passionately and collectively in that miserable and tasteless media story. And so they confirmed, once again, their receptivity to any kind of media manipulation.

After Martinovica there was an abundance of 'evidence', which the Serbian media 'milked' to the full, of 'genocide' carried out against the Serbian minority by Albanians (!); and numerous Serbian woman sprang up from somewhere, having been raped by (who else but) Albanians. Justifying themselves by their injured national pride and the national myths served up by the media, Serbian nationalists collectively supported the Serbian repression of the Albanians in Kosovo, or took an active part in it themselves.

And since in these cursed Balkan lands every little lie becomes a truth in the end, every spoken word becomes reality, so just a few years later, a male and, from a psychoanalytical point of view, deeply homosexual war came about, and the war strategy of rape became cruel everyday reality. The women

who were to be raped were, of course, completely innocent, their bodies simply serving as a medium for the transmission of male messages.

The media only discovered anew what they knew already: that promiscuity with leaders, with their political pretensions and aims, functions perfectly; they also discovered what they may not have known before – the scale of their power! They quivered with satisfaction at the confirmation that a lie very easily becomes legitimate truth; they were astonished at the realisation that in the absence of other information people believe what is available to them; that even despite other information, people believe what they want to believe, their media: in a word, their custom-built myths.

And the infernal media campaign was able to continue. In Serbian newspapers there began to appear articles about the *ustasha* camps during World War II (and no one could deny their truthfulness, because they existed and in them perished Serbs, Gypsies, Jews and also Croats!). There began to be more and more pictures of the camps on Serbian television. Croats began increasingly to be called criminals, '*utashas*'. Serbian newspapers were full of horrifying stories of 'necklaces of Serbian children's fingers', worn by the Croat '*utashas*'; of the 'genocide' that the Croats were again preparing to carry out against the innocent Serbs.

The Serbian media propaganda (orchestrated by the Serbian authorities and the Serbian leader) finally achieved what it had sought: a reaction in the Croatian media. And when the Croatian media also filled with tales with 'necklaces of Croatian children's fingers' worn round their necks by Serbian 'cut-throats', the preparations were laid for war.

Today, in what is still wartime, no Serbian newspapers can be found in Croatia (and if there were no one would buy them), nor are there Croatian papers in Serbia (and if there were no one would believe them); television programmes waging a war to the death can only be received with satellite aerials. Which is hardly necessary in any case as the programmes are identical. The Serbs put together information in their interest, the Croats in theirs. Telephone links between Croatia and Serbia have not been functioning for a long time.

Growing out of the worn-out Yugoslav system, following the same old habits, the media have succeeded in legalising lies. From being a political and journalistic way of behaving, lies have developed into a war strategy, and as such have rapidly become established as morally acceptable. ❏

Dubravka Ugresic

IS THIS THEN THE END?

DRAGUTIN HEDL

HUGE FINES COULD FINALLY SPELL
THE END OF CROATIA'S BEST-KNOWN
SATIRICAL WEEKLY

Croatia's *Feral Tribune*, a weekly paper famed for its ferocious attacks on the country's rulers over the past decade, may have to close as a result of crushing fines imposed for offending a lawyer and upsetting in similar manner the daughter of a famous sculptor. The court actions are seen as a way of circumventing the need for direct government intervention to protect those in power from the sharp tongue of *Feral* and others.

Based in Split, *Feral Tribune* was a tireless critic of the late hardline nationalist president, Franjo Tudjman, and was constantly in trouble (*Index* 4/1996). After his death, the paper turned its guns on the reputedly more moderate prime minister, Ivica Racan.

Two recent court rulings found that *Feral* had 'inflicted mental anguish' on the subjects of its comment. The paper was ordered to pay fines totalling some 200,000 kunas (cUS$27,000), a sum well beyond its means. The court also blocked the paper's bank accounts, leaving its future in jeopardy. Despite temporarily staving off closure, the future looks bleak: the paper is facing about 70 more judgements on similar charges and its management are convinced the outcome will be the same

Legislation imposing huge fines for 'mental anguish' was a favourite weapon against a refractory press in Tudjman's time, devised as a way of crippling awkward media financially without having recourse to police action to close them down. When Racan came to power in January 2000, his government refused to change the legislation. Its indifference towards media freedom reflects its own vulnerability to criticism. At least 1,200 charges similar to those brought against *Feral*, most of them filed by politicians and public figures, are waiting their turn in the Croatian courts and could determine the fate of other media outlets. Media analysts are convinced that the fate of *Feral* is crucial in determining whether other papers will continue to criticise the authorities – or back down in the event of an adverse judgement.

One commentator, Jurica Pavicic of the Zagreb daily *Jutranji list*, said the *Feral* case was a revival of a policy – to which *Feral* was no stranger – used by Tudjman's Croatian Democratic Union (HDZ) against media that poked their noses where they were not wanted: financial blackmail.

Feral editor-in-chief Heni Erceg said: 'The present judiciary is headed by the same people who persecuted us for nine years during Tudjman's regime. I do not believe anyone issued directives to the judges, as was the case in Tudjman's time, but the result is the same. Racan and his coalition have done nothing to reform the judiciary. It is a cancer in Croatian society.'

The head of the Association of Croatian Judges, Vladimir Gredelj, dismissed the complaints and accused *Feral* management of whipping up 'mass hysteria' against judges. '*Feral* and its arrogant, irresponsible reports are to blame for this, not the judiciary,' he said.

The Croatian journalists' association, the country's Helsinki human rights committee and its PEN Centre have spoken up in *Feral*'s defence. Even President Stipe Mesic has shown solidarity with *Feral*.

Unlike Mesic, Prime Minister Racan has made no public comment on the case. When asked why he had refused to be interviewed by the paper, Racan replied, 'There's already too much of me in *Feral* as it is.'

To many Croatians, it seems absurd that *Feral* could be shut down now, under a new regime that Europe regards as 'democratic', when it managed for a decade to survive all that the dictatorial Tudjman regime threw at it. ❑

Dragutin Hedl *is Croatian project editor for International War and Peace Reporting*

ARTICLE 19, Global Campaign for Free Expression, would like to congratulate Index on Censorship for its commitment to freedom of expression over the last 30 years. Our work as organisations has largely been complementary; we look forward to working together more closely on this important issue of common concern.

PRIVATE LIVES IN QUM

OMID SALEHI

The private lives of the mullahs of Qum, Iran's theological centre, are seldom exposed to the outside world, and never before now to the photographer's gaze.

With the help of friends in the religious schools in Qum, Omid Salehi, a young Iranian photographer, was able to enter their world and bring the everyday life of the clergy to a wider audience. His photographs show the simple human face of a group that has all too often been presented only as stereotypes that appeal to western prejudice. Here, rather than in the forefront of the political affray, are Iran's mullahs at home with their children, teaching, enjoying a gentle massage, making a cup of tea, trying – not undisturbed – to pray . . . In short: a normal humdrum day.

'I had the opportunity to live with Haj Amjad, a teacher of younger clergy, and began to understand much that had been closed to me,' says Salehi. 'At first they were suspicious of me: what's this guy doing, without a beard, with a camera in his hand and always looking at us through the end of a lens? But after a while, they began to talk and we could begin to form a relationship.' *JVH*

Omid Salehi is a co-founder of 135 Photos, a new photo agency in Iran specialising in documentary and media photography

Among the minarets of Qum: the call to prayer
Credit: all photographs by Omid Salehi

STRANGE NEW WORLDS

'RESTRICTIONS ON PERSONAL LIBERTY,
ON THE RIGHT OF FREE EXPRESSION,
INCLUDING FREEDOM OF THE PRESS, ARE
ALSO PERMISSIBLE BEYOND THE LEGAL
LIMITS OTHERWISE PRESCRIBED' –
ADOLF HITLER, 1933

Cuba, Playa Giron, 1961: Castro surveys wreckage of
US plane brought down in the 'Bay of Pigs' invasion
Credit: © Bob Henriques / Magnum Photos

WAR WAS EVER THUS: THE SENTIMENTS ARE THE SAME, AS ARE THE THREATS TO LIBERTY SINCE THE DECLARATION OF AMERICA'S LATEST WAR — ON TERRORISM

USES AND ABUSES

RONALD DWORKIN

THE RIGHT TO FREE EXPRESSION,
ALREADY THREATENED BY THE
EXIGENCIES OF THE WAR ON TERRORISM,
SHOULD NOT BE FURTHER ABUSED BY
WRONG-HEADED APPEALS IN ITS NAME

Freedom of speech is constantly under threat, not just in dictatorships but in democracies as well, and we must struggle to defend it at almost any cost. But that freedom is also sometimes mistakenly invoked to try to block important democratic reforms. Both these dangers are illustrated, as this 30th anniversary issue of *Index* appears, by fresh events in the United States.

War is always a bad time for free speech, because political and social pressures chill any genuine criticism of, or even debate about, government's security and military measures. Following the catastrophe in New York last September, the Bush administration adopted new legislation and policies defining the crime of terrorism in breathtakingly broad terms, permitting preventive detention of suspected terrorists, allowing conversations between them and their lawyers to be monitored, and substantially broadening surveillance powers. (I described these measures in the *New York Review of Books* in February.) But few of the organisations or politicians who have traditionally defended civil liberties spoke out in protest, and those who did were told by the attorney-general that they were aiding terrorists themselves.

In recent weeks, following the military successes in Afghanistan, President George W Bush has floated a proposal to carry the war against terrorism to other nations as well, including Iraq, North Korea and Iran, countries he declared form an 'axis of evil'. The public debate over the wisdom and feasibility of this frightening and portentous plan should be full and free. But when the Democratic Senate majority leader, Tom Daschle, questioned the plan in a tentative way, the Republican minority leader, Senator Trent Lott, rounded on him. 'How dare Senator Daschle criticise President Bush while we are fighting our war on terrorism?' he declared. That is politics, of course, but it is dangerous politics. It threatens to weaken democracy just when it needs to be strong.

In March, the United States Congress adopted, after many years of debate, a law sharply limiting the contributions that rich individuals and corporations may make to political parties to use in election campaigns. The prior law had limited direct contributions to political candidates to make political campaigns more equally financed, and to reduce the power of rich contributors to extract preferential treatment from politicians in return for large contributions. But the law permitted unlimited contributions (called 'soft money') to political parties rather than to candidates, and parties were permitted to use those funds in ways that supported their candidates. That exception destroyed the scheme: in the 2000 presidential election, a total of just under US$500 million of soft money was put at the disposal of the two candidates, Bush and Al Gore. The prior law also prohibited private individuals and organisations from paying for TV commercials that explicitly advocated a vote in favour of one candidate. But it permitted them to pay for commercials supposedly about political issues that were thinly disguised endorsements of one candidate. Once again, the exception destroyed the policy: such 'issue' ads became a prominent part of every election campaign.

The new law eliminates the soft money exception, and prohibits, within 60 days of an election, such thinly disguised private television commercials. A group of lawyers ranging from very conservative (including Kenneth Starr, who prosecuted President Clinton in the Monica Lewinsky scandal) to very liberal (including Floyd Abrams, a famous free-speech lawyer who has represented the *New York Times* in many important free-speech cases) has announced that it will sue to have the new law declared an unconstitutional violation of the First Amendment's right to free speech.

That claim confuses a citizen's right to present his opinions and convictions to the public at large, which is of course at the centre of free speech, with the very different idea that he is entitled to spend as much as he wishes in doing so even when the result is to distort democracy by making politicians depend on rich organisations with legislative agendas, rather than on wider public appeal. Contribution and publication restrictions would be illegitimate if they permitted so little expenditure that unknown politicians or unfamiliar groups or interests could not carry their message to the people. But the contribution and expenditure limits under the new law are generous and have no such effect: they are designed simply to reduce the distortion of the public debate that money has wrought in US politics for years. It seems a travesty to appeal to free speech to try to preserve that distortion. ❏

Ronald Dworkin *is Quain professor of Jurisprudence at the University of London. His most recent book is* Sovereign Virtue *(Harvard University Press)*

THE GOLDEN SECTION: TERROR, RIGHTS AND REASON

MICHAEL IGNATIEFF

INDEX WAS CREATED IN THE DAYS OF THE COLD WAR TO EXPOSE THE TERRORS OF THE SOVIET SYSTEM. TODAY THE CHALLENGE IS DIFFERENT BUT THE SAME MORAL AND RATIONAL CLEAR-SIGHTEDNESS IS ESSENTIAL IN THE CONFRONTATION WITH TERROR

It's interesting to commemorate the 30th anniversary of a Cold War institution – this magazine – at the precise moment that a new cold war has begun. Just as a president proclaims a war against evil, it's instructive to remember the intellectual atmosphere that prevailed when another president proclaimed a war against an evil empire.

When people make this comparison, of course, they usually do so in order to denounce the intellectual atmosphere of a war on terror. What those who oppose US military action dislike about the atmosphere since 11 September is the oppressive moralism, the coercive appeals to patriotism, the rights violations of detainees, the renewed xenophobia and the general chill on free speech.

Viewed from another angle, however, the atmosphere post-11 September is simply what life is like when societies, by a large majority, make up their mind that they need to stand together against attack. In such times, societies tighten up. The same liberal democracies that appear anomic and amoral in times of peace can seen moralistic and menacing in times of war. Indeed, war offers the only society-wide experience of community that liberal democracies ever offer.

Community – especially moral community – is not easy on free thought. The risks of censorship, as usual, are probably less serious than those of self-censorship. But these in turn may be less of a danger, especially in Europe, than the tyranny of a miasmic compound of reflexive anti-Americanism, guilt and confusion, all dressed up as *Guardian*-reading common sense.

Thinking straight about the dangers ahead is not easy, but it is worth recalling one lesson from the Cold War. Those who hated Soviet tyranny, despised communist lies and prayed for the early demise of the whole wretched system turned out to be right. Simple moral conviction often sees history straight.

Consider the case of *Index* itself. When Stephen Spender and other British liberals set it up in 1972, *Index* was a fiercely moralistic project. Spender loathed Soviet tyranny at a time when many European intellectuals still made excuses for communism, or when they were edging towards the indulgence of tyranny that went by the name of détente. Spender's moralism was at some remove from Ronald Reagan's but it helped Spender to see clearly, and *Index* wouldn't exist without the heritage of that clear sight.

The challenge for liberals in the old Cold War was to balance the conviction that communism was an evil mistake with the equal conviction that there were some exceedingly stupid and illiberal ways to fight it: such as an endless arms race; such as supporting authoritarian regimes simply because they happened to have anti-communist credentials; such as subverting democratically elected governments because they proclaimed socialist or communist sympathies and so on; such as locking up communists at home. Balancing simple conviction with complex intuitions about how to keep faith with that conviction was what it meant to think seriously about a war against the evil empire.

Now, as the new cold war against terror begins, the same balancing act will be required. We shall have to balance moral conviction with sustained thinking about what policies, what actions, will or will not work. But we shouldn't be afraid to start from simple moral intuitions.

There is such a thing as terrorism, and it is an evil. Why? Because it seeks to frighten human beings rather than persuade them; because it replaces the ballot box with the bullet; because it provokes terror in return; because, fundamentally, violence is the enemy of rational politics and rational politics is the only hope we have to create justice and peace. The fundamental sin of terrorism is not just that it kills and maims innocent human beings: it corrupts faith in the possibility of rational, ie, peaceful, political change.

What counts as terrorism is supposed to be an interesting and complex question but it is not fundamentally interesting at all. Jeremy Greenstock, UK ambassador to the UN, was right when he said, 'You know it when you see it.' Any threat or use of violence to terrorise or intimidate civilians for political ends counts as terrorism. Any use of violence by state parties directed at civilians to keep them in subjugation counts as terrorism.

There is no iron law that requires peoples struggling against subjugation and oppression to resort to terror in pursuit of their aims. Armed struggles for national self-determination that confine their use of force to strictly military targets are bona fide liberation movements, if those movements first exhaust all peaceful political means. Those that attack civilians deliberately are terrorists.

Those who say the difference between civilians and government or military targets is a meaningless legalism have given up on the struggle to control the often necessary use of violence in human life. Those who say that non-combatant civilians who support acts of oppression are as guilty as those who carry them out help to create the moral atmosphere in which terror becomes permissible. Non-combatant immunity is the principle that distinguishes warfare from barbarism. Terror is an offence against rational politics. But it is also an offence against warfare. And war, Clausewitz said, is 'the continuation of politics by other means', a legitimate continuation where a people's survival is threatened.

Those who say that one man's terrorist is another man's freedom fighter dishonour genuine freedom fighters. Martin Luther King achieved a revolution in American civil rights – against the dogs and the police of the American South – without resorting to terror. Mahatma Gandhi freed the Indian subcontinent without resorting to terror. Andrei Sakharov helped free an empire from tyranny without resorting to terror. The civil rights movement in Northern Ireland in the 1960s did more for the rights of the Catholic minority than 75 years of nationalist terrorism.

Those who say you cannot stop terror with military force don't know what language terror speaks. It understands and respects only force. Those who say that collateral damage and terror are the same thing don't know the difference between a mistake and a crime. Those who say that America's many crimes and mistakes disqualify it from the right to defend itself are allowing political conviction to make fools of them. States that don't defend themselves do not survive. European peoples who have spent more than 50 years sheltering behind US security guarantees are engaging in bad faith if they pretend that they would prefer not to be defended by US bombers in Afghanistan. Societies that long since gave up the capacity to defend themselves militarily have no business objecting to being defended by those who can. Nobody supposes the USA is perfect. But its sins of commission and omission are irrelevant in this case. Good causes are often defended justly by persons with less than clean hands, just as good causes are sometimes lost by persons who prefer moral perfection to effective, if morally dubious, action.

The claim that America or Americans 'had it coming' is either nonsensical or an apologia for terror. What is nonsensical – as well as offensive – is the claim that 3,000 individual human beings – dishwashers, bond traders, cops, firemen, secretaries – deserved anything, let alone violent and terrible death. It is a justification of terror, and not merely an explanation, to claim that terror can be interpreted as an act that represents, embodies, speaks for the cause of the poor and excluded. The central impersonation of terror is the claim that violence represents anyone. It defames the Palestinians and colludes in a hijacking of Islam to suppose that Osama bin Laden represents the people or his faith. The reverse is – or ought to be – true. Anyone who uses terror automatically disqualifies himself or herself from any claim to represent anyone.

The world is a violent and unjust place. The sufferings of the Palestinians demand remedy. But it is wrong in principle, and fatal in practice, to treat terror as the representative of respectable political demand and to respond with political concessions.

The only responsible response to acts of terror is honest police work and judicial prosecution in courts of law, linked to determinate, focused and unrelenting use of military power against those who cannot or will not be brought to justice.

Operation Enduring Freedom logo. A US naval draftsman created it while deployed as part of the operation
Credit: © Rex Features

I take these truths to be self-evident. Many Europeans do not, and many people in the Arab world would take all of this as apologetics for US imperialism. I don't much care. We do live in the shadow and under the shelter of US power. We might wish it were otherwise but it is not. If I can't defend myself against terror, if the government whose passport I carry cannot, I would rather have the US do it for me than any other power that comes to mind.

If there is a cold war atmosphere surrounding the war on terror, it is not because there is oppressive unity on these issues but, in fact, because there is deep and enduring moral division. When fundamentals are at stake, people feel bullied by each other's certainties. But that merely means they feel the pressure of making up their own minds. And that pressure is a good thing. In this war, it really is the case that you are either on one side or on the other. It's a time to make up our minds.

Making up your mind about the fundamentals also means making up your mind about the details. The problem here is that having simple convictions about the rights and wrongs of terrorism is not necessarily a compass for finding the right path on such policy questions as: should Iraq be next? Should Guantanamo prisoners have Geneva Convention rights? Should asylum and refugee law be tightened up?

How far the war on terror should go – whether it should extend to Iraq, Iran, North Korea, Somalia, the Philippines, Yemen, Sudan and so on – is not a question that can be answered in advance. It all depends on the evidence. The world is full of nasty regimes. They have to constitute a credible threat of terror in order to justify military action. That credible evidence is not yet forthcoming. What seems nonsensical – or ideological – is the idea that the USA is making up the threat. The reality of Iraqi experimentation with chemical and biological agents, and the seriousness of Saddam Hussein's attempts to create weapons of mass destruction, is beyond serious doubt. North Korea has let one million of its own people starve while attempting to create and export ballistic missile technology. Iran has supported terrorist groups in the Middle East for 20 years. This is the world we actually live in, and it seems childish to blame the US messenger who persists in waking us up to realities we would rather not attend to.

What to do about these threats is not obvious. Containment is better than bombing, but containment has its limits. We may have to take some difficult risks. One of the lessons of the last decade, ironically, is that our anticipations of risk, in using military force, are usually alarmist. It turns out to be easier to do hard things than we thought. This is the testimony of Desert Storm, Bosnia 1995 and Kosovo 1999. In each case, those who advocated military action were told that the risks might be prohibitive. In each case, they were proved wrong. This in itself tells us nothing about the risks of taking military action against Iraq or North Korea some time in the future. But it should tell us something about the penchant we all have to frighten ourselves into complacent helplessness.

There is no reason to suppose that a war on terror has to be lawless or barbaric. There have been moments when it has seemed to be but, as usual, we are asking the wrong questions. European liberals, shocked by pictures of the conditions of confinement at Guantanamo, tended to forget that the detainees, if left in detention in Afghanistan, would probably be dead, killed by Afghan captors. Guantanamo is a side issue: the Red Cross has access, the USA understands it has to observe the spirit, if not the letter, of the Geneva Convention, and many of the captives will consider themselves lucky to be in Cuba rather than in the hands of the Northern Alliance.

A more real issue is how to maintain some element of public scrutiny – by NGOs, media and elected officials – of a war waged by Special Forces and undercover agencies.

Afghanistan was a special operations war, and special operations are a Conradian world in which the rules are significantly different from those in regular battle: you kill prisoners because you do not have the means to repatriate them; and you kill civilians who risk disclosing your location to an enemy. Controlling military power is democracy's enduring challenge; secret military and intelligence power is the most difficult to control. The press has begun to uncover special operations mistakes in Afghanistan and it must do more, or we will have no control whatever over the war waged in our name.

Human rights organisations, especially Human Rights Watch, are doing an excellent job maintaining scrutiny of US air operations, investigating collateral damage incidents, publicising the use of cluster munitions, and arguing with air targeteers and lawyers about what the Geneva Convention allows in terms of proportionality, military necessity and other restraining principles on the use of military force. These organisations are our canaries in the mine, our best hope to make sure that the military force used in our name does not end up disgracing us.

On the domestic front, especially in the USA, the unexpected strength of the civil liberties lobby has forced the administration to use federal criminal courts to try terrorist suspects, instead of the military tribunals announced in

November. This battle – over how to bring justice to those suspected of terrorist offences – is not over, but it is a mistake to assume that the US administration has everything its own way. The point here is that there is so much for citizens to do, to pressure, lobby, argue, in order to make sure that security does not trump liberty and order does not prevail at the expense of justice.

The worst aspect of the intellectual atmosphere of the war on terror, as in the Cold War, is a sense of fatalistic passivity and helplessness about the vast geostrategic battle going on over our heads. In reality, as the examples above are intended to show, there is plenty for citizens to do. Keeping the war just, keeping it on target, keeping it in the light and not in the dark: all these are essential duties of citizenship, and we cannot assume that anybody but us will do it.

Only citizens – people with a strong sense of belonging to a civic community – can insist that their fellow citizens of Muslim or Middle Eastern origin continue to be treated with dignity and respect. This is an obligation, not just of common decency but also of basic citizenship and the equality of rights.

But the obligations are reciprocal. It can't be right to be a citizen and fund terror abroad. It can't be right to abuse the freedoms of a free society in order to plot the murder of others. 11 September was a terrible reckoning with the limits of multicultural integration in Europe. Most white liberal Europeans didn't have the slightest knowledge of the Muslim communities in our midst. Most were stunned to discover that an Egyptian architecture student in a college in Hamburg could harbour such cold-eyed designs on a world that had accepted him for study. Most could not believe that a Pakistani former student at the LSE could delight in the kidnap, torture and murder of a US journalist, for no other reason than that he was Jewish and American. Most could scarcely believe that a British subject, born of Muslim and non-Muslim parents, could be so seriously disaffected by life in Britain that he would be willing to turn himself into a bomb on board a commercial airliner. It would be as foolish to pretend that these cases are typical of the state of mind of most of the Muslims who have come to live in our midst as it would be to pretend that these are isolated fanatics with nothing to tell us about the multicultural experience in Europe in the 1990s. It's no good pretending a multicultural society can be held together by a pact of mutual indifference between ethnic communities living separately from each other in a set of intellectual and spiritual bell jars. We need to talk, and the talk will be hard and uncompromising. There are rules of civility, and we need to reinforce them instead of pretending that we can get by ignoring each other with rituals of feigned tolerance.

In our search for bases, allies and intelligence abroad, the war on terror will lead us to make various pacts with the devil; and here we need to learn from our mistakes in the war against the evil empire. What we learned then, or should have learned, is that in moral and political terms we have a principal agent problem whenever we use proxies. Proxies were used to subvert the Sandinista regime in Nicaragua; proxies were used to fight the Soviets in Afghanistan. Eventually, proxies end up disgracing or embarrassing the principal agent – the USA – who arms and supplies them. Proxies are a problem. We should either do the business ourselves or not do it at all. And if we have to use proxies, as in our use of the Northern Alliance, then we have to keep them under control.

A broader lesson from the Cold War is that the maxim 'the enemy of my enemy is my friend' is the common sense of fools. We allied ourselves with some dubious company in the Cold War simply because they proclaimed themselves enemies of communism. One by one, the Shah of Iran, Pinochet of Chile, Suharto of Indonesia turned out to be incapable of developing and maintaining the stability of their regimes. Eventually, they lost power and the USA and its allies lost influence and leverage with them. We are rushing to make the same mistake now. It is a fool's game to cosy up to the Sudanese, the Chinese, the Uzbeks and the Russians if, in the process, we forget that these are all steady, inveterate human rights violators. We should care about human rights not just because they are good in themselves but because rights observance is critical to regime stability, and if we want friends that last, we had better choose ones that are both stable and rights observant.

An anniversary like this one reminds us, as we head into an age of iron, that we have been at war before and we have won before. We won before because we kept our nerve, because we held to certain simple moral intuitions, and because we really had no other choice. We have no other choice now. It is a time to be as tough as we can be, and as intelligent too. ❏

Michael Ignatieff is the director of the Center for the Politics of Human Rights at the Kennedy School of Government, Harvard University

1/1997 & 1/1999: MUMIA ABU-JAMAL, USA
CAPITOL PUNISHMENT & THE WAR ON THE POOR

The journalist and Black Panther activist Mumia Abu-Jamal was sentenced to death in 1982 for his alleged killing of a policeman in 1981. His prosecution was riddled with inconsistencies and Abu-Jamal has always protested his innocence, maintaining the original case was politically – and racially – charged.

His execution was ultimately set for August 1995 by the then governor of Pennsylvania, Tom Ridge, who signed the death warrant four days before Abu-Jamal's appeal was to be filed. One month later, Abu-Jamal was denied a retrial by Judge Albert Sabo, who had been the sentencing judge in 1982. Abu-Jamal and his lawyers continue to fight the sentence; meanwhile, he remains on death row.

The death penalty is a creation of the state, and politicians justify it by using it as a stepping stone to higher political office. It's very popular to use isolated cases – always the most gruesome ones – to make generalisations about inmates on death row and justify their sentences. Yet it is deceitful; it is untrue, unreal. Politicians talk about people on death row as if they are the worst of the worst, monsters, etc. But they will not talk about the thousands of men and women in our country serving lesser sentences for similar and even identical crimes. Or others who, by virtue of their wealth and ability to retain a good private lawyer, are not convicted at all. The criminal court system calls itself a justice system, but it measures privilege, wealth, power, social status and – last but not least – race, to determine who goes to death row.

Why do Pennsylvania's African-Americans, who make up only 9 per cent of the population, comprise close to two-thirds of its death row population? Because its largest city, Philadelphia, like Houston and Miami and other cities, is a place where politicians have built their careers on sending people to death row. They are not making their constituents any safer. They are not administering justice by their example. They are simply revealing the partiality of justice.

Never forget that the overwhelming majority of people on death row are poor. Most of them cannot afford the resources for an adequate defence to compete with the forces of the state, let alone money for a decent suit to wear in court. The OJ Simpson case illustrated (again) the kind of defence you get is the kind of defence you can afford. In Pennsylvania, New Jersey

and New York, in Florida, Texas, Illinois, California – most people on death row are there because they could not afford what OJ could, namely the best defence.

One widespread argument favouring the death penalty is that it deters crime. Study after study has shown that it does not. If capital punishment deters anything at all, it is rational thinking. How else would it be conceivable in a supposedly enlightened, democratic society? Until we recognise the evil irrationality of capital punishment, we will only add, brick by brick, execution by execution, to the dark temple of Fear. How many more lives will be sacrificed on its altar?

In every phase and facet of national life, there is a war being waged on America's poor. Poor mothers are targeted for criminal sanctions for acts, which, if committed by mothers of higher economic class, would merit treatment at the Betty Ford Centre. In youth policy, governments hasten to close schools while building prisons as their graduate schools. Xenophobic politicians hoist campaigns to the dark star of imprisonment for street beggars, further fattening the fortress economy. The only apparent solution for homelessness is to build more prisons.

In America's 90s, to be poor is not so much a socio-economic status as it is a serious character flaw. Statistics tell a tale of loss and want so dreadful, that Dickens, of *A Tale of Two Cities* fame, would cringe. Consider: 7m people homeless with less than $200 in monthly income. Thirty-seven million people – 14.5% of the nation's population – living below poverty levels. Of those, 29% are African-Americans, meaning over 10.6m blacks living in poverty. Both wings of the ruling 'Republicrat' Party try to outdo themselves with ever more draconian measures to restrict, repress, restrain and eliminate the poor.

Outgunned industrially by Japan and Germany, the US has embarked on a low-technology, low-skilled, high-employment scheme that exploits the poor, the stupid and the slow via a boom in prison construction. More and more Americans are guarding more and more prisoners for more and more years, amid the lowest crime rate in decades.

The time is ripe for a new, brighter, life-affirming vision that liberates, not represses, the poor who, after all, are the vast majority of this earth's people. Neither serpentine politics, nor sterile economic theory which treats them – people – as mere economic units, offer much hope. For the very politicians they vote for spit in their faces while economists write them off as 'non-persons'. ❑

THE END OF LIBERTY

GORE VIDAL

THIS PIECE ORIGINATED IN A COMMISSION BY THE
DAILY MAIL, WHICH THEN DROPPED IT. *VANITY FAIR*
COMMISSIONED VIDAL TO UPDATE AND ELABORATE.
AFTER A THREE-MONTH DELAY THAT MAGAZINE ALSO
DROPPED IT. IT WAS THEN OFFERED TO SEVERAL UK
NEWSPAPERS, WHO TURNED IT DOWN. IT APPEARED
LAST YEAR IN ITALY IN A COLLECTION OF VIDAL'S
ESSAYS ENTITLED *LA FINE DELLA LIBERTÀ: VERSO
UN NUOVO TOTALITARISMO?* THIS IS ITS FIRST
PUBLICATION IN ENGLISH

According to the Quran, it was on a Tuesday that Allah created darkness. Last
11 September, when suicide-pilots were crashing commercial airliners into
crowded American buildings, I did not have to look to the calendar to see
what day it was: Dark Tuesday was casting its long shadow across Manhattan
and along the Potomac River. I was also not surprised that despite the seven
or so trillion dollars we have spent since 1950 on what is euphemistically
called 'Defence', there would have been no advance warning from the FBI
or CIA or Defense Intelligence Agency.

While the Bushites have been eagerly preparing for the last war but two
– missiles from North Korea, clearly marked with flags, would rain down on
Portland, Oregon, only to be intercepted by our missile-shield balloons –
the foxy Osama bin Laden knew that all he needed for his holy war on the
infidel were flyers willing to kill themselves along with those random
passengers who happened to be aboard hijacked airliners. Also, like so many
of those born to wealth, Osama is not one to throw money about. Apparently, the airline tickets of the 19 known dead hijackers were paid through
a credit card. I suspect that United and American Airlines will never be
reimbursed by American Express whose New York offices Osama – inadvertently? – hit.

On the plane that crashed in Pennsylvania, a passenger telephoned out to
say that he and a dozen or so other men – several of them athletes – were
going to attack the hijackers. 'Let's roll!' he shouted. A scuffle. A scream.
Silence. But the plane, allegedly aimed at the White House, ended up in a

Gore
Vidal

La fine della libertà
Verso un nuovo totalitarismo?

Fazi Editore

Cover of Italian edition of The End of Liberty
Credit: Fazi Editore

field near Pittsburgh. We have always had wise and brave civilians. It is the military and the politicians and the media that one frets about. After all, we have not encountered suicide bombers since the kamikazes, as we called them in the Pacific where I was idly a soldier in World War II. Japan was the enemy then. Now, bin Laden . . . The Muslims . . . The Pakistanis . . . Step in line. The telephone rings. A distraught voice from the United States. 'Berry Berenson's dead. She was on Flight . . .' The world was getting surreal. Arabs. Plastic knives. The beautiful Berry. What on earth did any of these elements have in common other than an unexpected appointment in Samarra with that restless traveller Death?

The telephone keeps ringing. In summer I live south of Naples, Italy. Italian newspapers, TV, radio, want comment. So do I. I have written lately about Pearl Harbor. Now I get the same question over and over: isn't this exactly like Sunday morning 7 December 1941? No, it's not, I say. As far as we *now* know, we had no warning of last Tuesday's attack. Of course, our government has many, many secrets which our enemies always seem to know about in advance but our people are not told of until years later, if at all. President Roosevelt provoked the Japanese to attack us at Pearl Harbor. I describe the various steps he took in a book, *The Golden Age*. We now know what was on his mind: coming to England's aid against Japan's ally, Hitler, a virtuous plot that ended triumphantly for the human race. But what was – is – on bin Laden's mind?

For several decades there has been an unrelenting demonisation of the Muslim world in the American media. Since I am a loyal American, I am not supposed to tell you *why* this has taken place but then it is not usual for us to

examine why *aNYThing* happens other than to accuse others of motiveless
malignity. 'We are good,' announced a deep-thinker on American television,
'They are evil,' which wraps that one up in a neat package. But it was Bush
himself who put, as it were, the bow on the package in an address to a joint-
session of Congress where he shared with them – as well as all of us somewhere over the Beltway – his profound knowledge of Islam's wiles and ways:
'They hate what they see right here in this Chamber.' A million Americans
nodded in front of their TV sets. 'Their leaders are self-appointed. They hate
our freedoms, our freedom of religion, our freedom of speech, our freedom
to vote and assemble and disagree with each other.' At this plangent moment
what Americans' gorge did not rise like a Florida chad to the bait?

Should the 44-year-old Saudi Arabian bin Laden be the prime mover, we
know surprisingly little about him. We can assume that he favours the Palestinians in their uprising against the European- and American-born Israelis,
intent, many of them, on establishing a theocratic state in what was to have
been a common holy land for Jews, Muslims and Christians. But if Osama
ever wept tears for Arafat, they have left little trace. So why do he and
millions of other Muslims hate us?

Let us deal first with the six-foot seven-inch Osama who enters history
in 1979 as a guerrilla warrior working alongside the CIA to defend Afghanistan against the invading Soviets. Was he anti-communist? Irrelevant question. He is anti-infidel in the land of the Prophet. Described as fabulously
wealthy, Osama is worth 'only' a few million dollars, according to a relative. It
was his father who created a fabulous fortune with a construction company
that specialised in building palaces for the Saudi royal family. That company is
now worth several billion dollars, presumably shared by Osama's 54 brothers
and sisters. Although he speaks perfect English, he was entirely educated in
the Saudi capital, Jeddah; he has never travelled outside the Arabian penin-
sula. Several siblings live in the Boston area and give large sums to Harvard.
We are told that much of his family appears to have disowned him while
many of his assets in the Saudi kingdom have been frozen.

Where does Osama's money now come from? He is a superb fund-raiser
for Allah but only within the Arab world; contrary to legend, he has taken no
CIA money. He is also a superb organiser within Afghanistan. In 1998, he
warned the Saudi king that Saddam Hussein was going to invade Kuwait.
Osama assumed that after his own victories as a guerrilla against the
Russians, he and his organisation would be used by the Saudis to stop the
Iraqis. To Osama's horror, King Fahd sent for the Americans: thus were infi-

dels established on the sacred sands of Mohammed. 'This was', he said, 'the most shocking moment of my life.' 'Infidel', in his sense, does not mean a*NYT*hing of great moral consequence, like cheating sexually on your partner; rather, it means lack of faith in Allah, the one God, and in his Prophet.

Osama persuaded 4,000 Saudis to go to Afghanistan for military training by his group. In 1991, Osama moved on to Sudan. In 1994, when the Saudis withdrew his citizenship, Osama was already a legendary figure in the Islamic world and so, like Shakespeare's Coriolanus, he could tell the royal Saudis, 'I banish you. There is a world elsewhere.' Unfortunately, that world is us.

In a 12-page 'declaration of war', Osama presented himself as a potential liberator of the Muslim world from the great Satan of modern corruption, the United States.

When Clinton lobbed a missile at a Sudanese aspirin factory, Osama blew up two of our embassies in Africa, put a hole in the side of an American warship off Yemen, and so on to the events of Tuesday, 11 September. Now President George W Bush, in retaliation, has promised us not only a 'new war' but a secret war. That is, not secret to Osama but only to us who pay for and fight it. 'This administration will not talk about any plans we may or may not have,' said Bush. 'We're going to find these evil-doers . . . and we're going to hold them accountable' along with the other devils who have given Osama shelter in order to teach them the one lesson that we ourselves have never been able to learn: in history, as in physics, there is no action without reaction. Or, as Edward S Herman puts it, 'One of the most durable features of the US culture is the inability or refusal to recognise US crimes.' When Osama was four years old, I arrived in Cairo for a conversation with Nasser to appear in *Look* magazine. I was received by Mohammed Heikal, Nasser's chief adviser. Nasser himself was not to be seen. He was at the Barricade, his retreat on the Nile. Later, I found out that a plot to murder him had just failed and he was in well-guarded seclusion. Heikal spoke perfect English; he was sardonic, cynical. 'We are studying the Quran for hints on birth control.' He sighed.

'Not helpful?'

'Not very. But we keep looking for a text.' We talked off and on for a week. Nasser wanted to modernise Egypt. But there was a reactionary, religious element . . . Another sigh. Then a surprise. 'We've found something very odd, the young village boys – the bright ones that we are educating to be engineers, chemists and so on – are turning religious on us.'

'Right-wing?'

'Very.' Heikal was a spiritual son of our eighteenth-century Enlighten-
ment. I thought of Heikal on Dark Tuesday when one of his modernised
Arab generation had, in the name of Islam, struck at what had been, 40 years
earlier, Nasser's model for a modern state. Yet Osama seemed, from all
accounts, no more than a practising, as opposed to zealous, Muslim. Ironically, he was trained as an engineer. Understandably, he dislikes the United
States as symbol and as fact. But when our clients, the Saudi royal family,
allowed American troops to occupy the Prophet's holy land, Osama named
the fundamental enemy 'the Crusader-Zionist Alliance'. Thus, in a phrase, he
defined himself and reminded his critics that he is a Wahhabi Muslim, a
Puritan activist not unlike our Falwell-Robertson zanies, only serious. He
would go to war against the United States, 'the head of the serpent'. Even
more ambitiously, he would rid all the Muslim states of their western-
supported regimes, starting with that of his native land. The word 'Crusader'
was the giveaway. In the eyes of many Muslims, the Christian West, currently
in alliance with Zionism, has for 1,000 years tried to dominate the lands of
the Umma, the true believers. That is why Osama is seen by so many simple
folk as the true heir to Saladin, the great warrior king who defeated Richard
of England and the western crusaders.

Who was Saladin? Dates 1138–1193. He was an Iraqi Kurd [born in
Takrit, Saddam Hussein's home village, in what is now Iraq]. In the century
before his birth, western Christians had established a kingdom at Jerusalem,
to the horror of the Islamic Faithful. Much as the United States used the
Gulf War as pretext for our current occupation of Saudi Arabia, Saladin
raised armies to drive out the Crusaders. He conquered Egypt, annexed
Syria and finally smashed the Kingdom of Jerusalem in a religious war that
pitted Mohammedan against Christian. He united and 'purified' the Muslim
world, and though Richard Lionheart was the better general, in the end he
gave up and went home. As one historian put it, Saladin 'typified the
Mohammedan utter self-surrender to a sacred cause.' But he left no government behind him, no political system because, as he himself said: 'My troops
will do nothing save when I ride at their head . . .' Now his spirit has
returned with a vengeance.

The Bush administration, though eerily inept in all but its principal task,
which is to exempt the rich from taxes, has casually torn up most of the
treaties to which civilised nations subscribe – like the Kyoto Accords or the

nuclear missile agreement with Russia. As the Bushites go about their relent-
less plundering of the Treasury and now, thanks to Osama, Social Security (a
supposedly untouchable trust fund) which like Lucky Strike green has gone
to war, they have also allowed the FBI and CIA either to run amok or not
budge at all – leaving us, the very first 'indispensable' and at popular request
last global empire, rather like the Wizard of Oz doing his odd pretend-magic
tricks while hoping not to be found out. Latest Bushism to the world: 'Either
you are with us or you are with the Terrorists.' That's known as asking for it.

To be fair, one cannot entirely blame the current Oval One for our
incoherence. Though his predecessors have generally had rather higher IQs
than his, they, too, assiduously served the 1% that owns the country while
allowing everyone else to drift. Particularly culpable was Bill Clinton.
Although the most able chief executive since FDR, Clinton, in his frantic
pursuit of election victories, set in place the trigger for a police state which
his successor is now happily squeezing.

Police state? What's that all about? In April 1996, one year after the
Oklahoma City bombing, President Clinton signed into law the Anti-
Terrorist and Effective Death Penalty Act, a so-called 'conference bill' in
which many grubby hands played a part including the bill's co-sponsor,
Senate majority leader Bob Dole. Although Clinton, in order to win elections, did many unwise and opportunistic things, like Charles II he seldom
ever said an unwise one. But faced with opposition to anti-terrorism legislation – which not only gives the attorney-general the power to use the
armed services against the civilian population, neatly nullifying the Posse
Comitatus Act of 1878, but also, selectively, suspends habeas corpus, the heart
of Anglo-American liberty – Clinton attacked his critics as 'unpatriotic'.
Then, wrapped in the flag, he spoke from the throne: 'There is nothing
patriotic about our pretending that you can love your country but despise
your government.' This is breathtaking since it includes, at one time or
another, most of us. Put another way, was a German in 1939 who said that
he detested the Nazi dictatorship unpatriotic?

There have been ominous signs that our fragile liberties have been
dramatically at risk since the 1970s when the white-shirt-and-tie FBI re-
invented itself from a corps of 'generalists' trained in law and accounting into
a confrontational 'Special Weapons and Tactics' (aka SWAT) Green Beret-
style army of warriors who like to dress up in camouflage or black ninja
clothing and, depending on the caper, the odd ski mask. In the early 80s, an
FBI super-SWAT team, the Hostage 270 Rescue Team, was formed. As so

often happens in United States-speak, this group specialised not in freeing hostages or saving lives but in murderous attacks on groups that offended them, like the Branch Davidians – evangelical Christians who were living peaceably in their own compound at Waco, Texas, until an FBI SWAT team, illegally using army tanks, killed 82 of them, including 25 children. This was 1993.

Post-Tuesday, SWAT teams can now be used to go after suspect Arab-Americans or, indeed, anyone who might be guilty of terrorism, a word without legal definition (how can you fight terrorism by suspending habeas corpus since those who want their corpuses released from prison are already locked up?). But in the post-Oklahoma City trauma, Clinton said that those who did not support his draconian legislation were terrorist co-conspirators who wanted to turn 'America into a safe house for terrorists'. If the cool Clinton could so froth, what are we to expect from the overheated Bush post-Tuesday?

Incidentally, those who were shocked by Bush the Younger's shout that we are now 'at war' with Osama and those parts of the Muslim world that support him should have quickly put on their collective thinking caps. Since a nation can only be at war with another nation state, why did our smouldering if not yet burning bush come up with such a phrase? Think hard. This will count against your final grade. Give up? Well, most insurance companies have a rider that they need not pay for damage done by 'an act of war'. Although the men and women around Bush know nothing of war and less of our Constitution, they understand fund-raising. For this wartime exclusion, Hartford Life would soon be breaking open its piggy bank to finance Republicans for years to come. But it was the mean-spirited *Washington Post* that pointed out that, under US case law, *only* a sovereign nation, not a bunch of radicals, can commit an 'act of war'. Good try, W. This now means that we the people, with our tax money, will be allowed to bail out the insurance companies, a rare privilege not afforded to just any old generation.

Although the American people have no direct means of influencing their government, their 'opinions' are occasionally sampled through polls. According to a November 1995 CNN-Time poll, 55% of the people believe: 'The federal government has become so powerful that it poses a threat to the rights of ordinary citizens.' Three days after Dark Tuesday, 74% said they thought: 'It would be necessary for Americans to give up some of their personal freedoms.' 86% favoured guards and metal detectors at public buildings and events. Thus, as the police state settles comfortably in place, one can imagine Dick Cheney and Donald Rumsfeld studying these figures, trans-fixed with joy.

'It's what they always wanted, Dick.'

'And to think we never knew, Don.'

'Thanks to those liberals, Dick.'

'We'll get those bastards now, Don.'

It seems forgotten by our amnesiac media that we once energetically supported Saddam Hussein in Iraq's war against Iran, and so he thought, not unnaturally, that we wouldn't mind his taking over Kuwait's filling stations. Overnight, our employee became Satan – and so remains, as we torment his people in the hope that they will rise up and overthrow him – as the Cubans were supposed, in their US-imposed poverty, to dismiss Castro a half-century ago, whose only crime was refusal to allow the Kennedy brothers to murder him in their so-called Operation Mongoose. Our imperial disdain for the lesser breeds did not go unnoticed by the latest educated generation of Saudi Arabians, and by their evolving leader, Osama bin Laden, whose moment came in 2001 when a weak American president took office in questionable circumstances.

The *New York Times* is the principal dispenser of opinion received from corporate America. It generally stands tall, or tries to. Even so, as of 13 September, the *NYT*'s editorial columns were all slightly off-key.

Under the heading 'Demands of Leadership' the *NYT* was upbeat, sort of. It's going to be OK if you work hard and keep your eye on the ball, Mr President. Apparently Bush is 'facing multiple challenges, but his most important job is a simple matter of leadership.' Thank God. Not only is that *all* it takes, but it's simple, too! For a moment . . . The *NYT* then slips into the way things look as opposed to the way they ought to look. 'The Administration spent much of yesterday trying to overcome the impression that Mr Bush showed weakness when he did not return to Washington after the terrorists struck.' But from what I could tell no one cared, while some of us felt marginally safer that the national silly-billy was trapped in his Nebraska bunker. Patiently, the *NYT* spells it out for Bush and for us, too: 'In the days ahead, Mr Bush may be asking the nation to support military actions that many citizens, particularly those with relations in the service, will find alarming. He must show that he knows what he is doing.' Well, that's a bull's-eye. If only FDR had got letters like that from Arthur Krock at the old *NYT*.

Finally, Anthony Lewis thinks it wise to eschew Bushite unilateralism in favour of cooperation with other nations in order to contain Tuesday's darkness *by understanding its origin* while ceasing our provocations of cultures opposed to us and our arrangements. Lewis, unusually for a *New York Times* writer, favours peace now. So do I. But then we are old and have been to the wars and value our fast-diminishing freedoms unlike those jingoes now beating their tom-toms in Times Square in favour of an all-out war for other Americans to fight.

As usual, the political columnist who has made the most sense of all this is William Pfaff in the *International Herald Tribune* (17 September 2001). Unlike the provincial war-lovers at the *New York Times*, he is appalled by the spectacle of an American president who declined to serve his country in Vietnam howling for war against not a nation nor even a religion but one man and his accomplices, a category that will ever widen. Pfaff:

'The riposte of a civilised nation, one that believes in good, in human society and opposes evil, has to be narrowly focused and, above all, intelligent.

'Missiles are blunt weapons. Those terrorists are smart enough to make others bear the price for what they have done, and to exploit the results.

'A maddened US response that hurts still others is what they want: it will fuel the hatred that already fires the self-righteousness about their criminal acts against the innocent.

'What the United States needs is cold reconsideration of how it has arrived at this pass. It needs, even more, to foresee disasters that might lie in the future.'

War is the no-win, all-lose option. The time has come to put the good Kofi Annan to use. As glorious as total revenge will be for our war-lovers, a truce between Saladin and the Crusader Zionists is in the interest of the entire human race. Long before the dread monotheists got their hands on history's neck, we had been taught how to handle feuds by none other than the god Apollo as dramatised by Aeschylus in *The Eumenides* (a polite Greek term for the Furies who keep us daily company on CNN). Orestes, for the sin of matricide, cannot rid himself of the Furies who hound him wherever he goes. He appeals to the god Apollo who tells him to go to the UN – also known as the citizens' assembly at Athens – which he does and is acquitted on the grounds that blood feuds must be ended or they will smoulder for ever, generation after generation, and great towers shall turn to flame and incinerate us all until 'The thirsty dust shall never more suck up the darkly steaming blood . . . and vengeance crying death for death! But man with man and state with state shall vow the pledge of common hate and common friendship, that for man has oft made blessing out of ban, be ours until all time.'

Let Annan mediate between East and West before there is nothing left of either of us to salvage.

The awesome physical damage Osama and company did us on Dark Tuesday is as nothing compared to the knockout blow to our vanishing liberties – the Anti-Terrorism Act of 1991 combined with the recent request to Congress for additional special powers to wire-tap without judicial order; to deport lawful permanent residents, visitors and undocumented immigrants without due process, and so on. Even that loyal company town paper the *Washington Post* is alarmed:

'Justice Department is making extraordinary use of its powers to arrest and detain individuals, taking the unusual step of jailing hundreds of people on minor . . . violations. The lawyers and legal scholars . . . said they could not recall a time when so many people had been arrested and held without bond on charges – particularly minor charges – related to the case at hand.'

This is pre-Osama:

Restrictions on personal liberty, on the right of free expression of opinion, including freedom of the press; on the rights of assembly and associations; and violations of the privacy of postal, telegraphic and telephonic communications and warrants for house searches, orders for confiscations as well as restrictions on property, are also permissible beyond the legal limits otherwise prescribed.

The tone is familiar. It is from Hitler's 1933 speech calling for 'an Enabling Act' for 'the protection of the People and the State' after the catastrophic Reichstag fire that the Nazis had secretly lit.

Only one congresswoman, Barbara Lee of California, voted against the additional powers granted the president. Meanwhile, a *NYT*-CBS poll notes that only 6% now oppose military action while a substantial majority favour war 'even if many thousands of innocent civilians are killed'. Most of this majority are far too young to recall World War II, Korea, even Vietnam. Simultaneously, Bush's approval rating has soared from around 50% to 91%. Traditionally, in war, the president is totemic like the flag. When Kennedy got his highest rating after the debacle of the Bay of Pigs, he observed, characteristically: 'It would seem that the worse you fuck up in this job the more popular you get.' Bush, father and son, may yet make it to Mount Rushmore though it might be cheaper to redo the handsome Barbara Bush's lookalike, George Washington, by adding two strings of Teclas to his limestone neck, in memoriam, as it were.

'Urgent Fury' 1983: US marines storm Grenada
Credit: © Phillip Jones Griffiths / Magnum Photos

Finally, the physical damage Osama and friends can do us – terrible as it has been thus far – is as nothing to what he is doing to our liberties. Once alienated, an 'inalienable right' is apt to be for ever lost, in which case we are no longer even remotely the last best hope of earth but merely a seedy imperial state whose citizens are kept in line by SWAT teams and whose way of death, not life, is universally imitated.

Since VJ Day 1945 ('Victory over Japan' and the end of World War II), we have been engaged in what the great historian Charles A Beard called 'perpetual war for perpetual peace'. I have occasionally referred to our 'enemy of the month club': each month a new horrendous enemy at whom we must strike before he destroys us. I have been accused of exaggeration, so here's the scoreboard from Kosovo (1999) to Berlin Airlift (1948–49). You will note that the compilers, Federation of American Scientists, record a number of our wars as 'ongoing', even though many of us have forgotten about them. We are given under 'Name' many fanciful Defense Department titles like 'Urgent Fury', which was Reagan's attack on the island of Grenada, a month-long caper that General Haig disloyally said could have been handled more briefly by the Provincetown police department. In these several hundred wars against communism, terrorism, drugs or sometimes nothing much, between Pearl Harbor and Tuesday 11 September 2001, we always struck the first blow. ❑

Gore Vidal's latest book, in which this essay will appear, is The Last Empire (Time Warner Books, 2002)

WWW For Gore Vidal's 'scoreboard' ⇨ www.indexonline.org

IS THIS THE NEW FASCISM?

DARIO FO

THE APATHY AND INCOHERENCE OF
THE LEFT ARE LETTING THE ITALIAN
RIGHT HAVE IT ALL THEIR OWN WAY

The new face of Italy is the face of apathy: no energy, no interest, no passion. What we are witnessing is a stream of acts of sheer folly and hypocrisy on the part of the various political groupings as they adjust to the overall climate of fascism, almost to the point where they are adopting its language and its behaviour. They trot out the same old litany of slogans: liberty, struggle, fatherland, Italy, defending the race, our civilisation's culture, roots of our civilisation.

Added to this is what is being called 'the conflict of interests'. Not even Mussolini ever actually adopted a policy of sharing out favours, neither for himself nor for those who accepted the logic of his regime (always excepting his choice of Fiat as the flagship of the nation's industry). But nowadays we have Agnelli [the Agnelli Foundation established in 1966 by FIAT to celebrate the centenary of the birth of its founder, Senator Giovanni Agnelli – Ed], who spotted the way the wind was blowing and changed tack all of a sudden, as did the banks, the major finance houses and so on. And all that stands in their way is an absurd, timid nothingness, an opposition that scarcely seems to exist. Our role is simply to be dissidents attempting to make up for the absence of any political opposition. I saw what happened at the Social Democrats' congress: it was as if they were paralysed. 'We must change or we will die,' they cried. And, having said that, they stood frozen like pillars of salt. When you see someone like Pierferdinando Casini, the president of the Chamber of Deputies, coming out with a statement that belongs directly to left-wing politics, such as: 'Before we change anything in the RAI [state-owned TV channel] we have to resolve the conflict of interests,' then you know the world's gone mad.

Here is a right-wing politician co-opting the voice of a non-existent left. We are put in the absurd position of hearing Casini saying to his followers: 'Steady on now, you've gone far enough.' Even if it's all sorted out afterwards with some sort of hypocritical gesture or in the end with nothing at all, it's they, the right wing, that have managed to speak, not the opposition.

But there are signs of something new, especially among students and young workers, though also among older people: the beginnings of movements that bear witness to a wonderful process of renewal.

But instead of greeting them with open arms, instead of offering them support or applauding their actions, the left runs away from them as if it found them repugnant. On the day of the great peace march against the war in Afghanistan, the left decided it preferred to go off on a barbecue, or wave little flags to cheer on the fleet as it left for the Far East. And let's be clear: these are the same people who are responsible for the first moves to sell off state schools, despite the protests of teachers and others who rejected the transformation of schools into private businesses. Before we create a new kind of school, a private school, we should to do more to restore order to those we already have, the state schools. But to return to the Paris meeting on the decline in democracy – a very evident phenomenon in my own country – at which I spoke. I would not want the fact that I have to go to Paris to make a speech calling for at least a minimum of reflection to be compared with what happened when that other absolutist government came into being, the one my father told me about. He became a political refugee in France while still very young. Even so, it is disturbing to hear those who lived through those times saying they feel as if they are reliving the 1920s, the years in which fascism was born.

All you have to do is read the newspapers to see how Silvio Berlusconi's [President of the Council/prime minister] own lawyer dares to storm out of the courtroom, yelling: 'There's no justice any more!' Not to mention the advocates who support Berlusconi's own lawyers in calling for the intervention of the justice minister and the Northern League, the Berlusconi government's own watchdog.

What we're faced with is the craziest of paradoxes, worthy of a surreal farce such as *Ubu Roi*: laws are being framed to suit the king, ministers are being appointed from among his courtiers and their sole function is to protect his interests. And what does the public do? It applauds. At best, someone does an indignant little burp to show that they're finding it a bit hard to digest. All of which suggests that Il Cavaliere and his employees have a clear conscience when it comes to holding the reins of power with the knowledge they can act with complete impunity. They feel they've nothing to fear: 'They'll never pin anything on us.' And all this is straight from the horse's mouth. I heard a member of the government say when they were organising a meeting with the centre-left: 'We'll have an olive branch in one hand and a gun in the other.' Those were his exact words.

Rome, 29 April 2001: supporters of SS Lazio display racist banners in Rome's Olympic Stadium – a not uncommon sight at Italian soccer matches
Credit: AFP Photo / EPA / ANSA / Alessandro Bianchi

It's true. The new-style fascism is already with us. It's in their language, it's in the way they express themselves – the way, first of all, that they talk about Italy plc, about the party as a limited company, so that everybody is a company employee with the big manager in the middle. 'Vae victis!' has always been a fascist slogan. Nowadays it's all perfectly obvious from the body language, the words, the attitudes, the arrogance of these members of the ruling class who are given to thumping the table or to bellowing, 'You're getting on my nerves!' or, 'You're sacked' (as in the case of the minister for communications) or, 'Arabs out!' or, 'They can go and build their sodding mosques somewhere else!' or, 'They can just stay in their ghettos!' Well, there's a new idea. Anybody who's different, anybody who doesn't conform – into the ghetto!

There are times when this state of affairs really gets to me, with a dull melancholy. It's true that I go on working in the theatre, and it's true that in our line of work we get the chance to take this kind of discourse to pieces.

It's true that audiences react; but these audiences are self-selecting. The most wonderful thing, despite it all, is this magnificent surge, this rising sun that illuminates the vision of the young people that we have to help, that we have to inform and to whom we must tell the truth.

But nowadays, in our country, we don't have a Jean-Paul Sartre to go and say what he has to say in the universities as he did in 1968 when he gave a lecture about the theatre of situation, political theatre, the people's theatre, and concluded by quoting the words of Alberto Savinio: 'Oh Men, recount your story!'

Today, the problem is not that of chronicling the present or recording the spirit of the age. Not only are most theatre producers and directors, thanks to a series of agile U-turns, more or less recent converts to the right, but the majority of intellectuals seem to be asleep, or pretending to be somewhere else, pretending to have other things to think about. ❏

Dario Fo, *Italian dramatist and actor, was awarded the Nobel Prize for Literature in 1997. Translated from French by Mike Routledge*

1/1972: GEORGE MANGAKIS, GREECE

Below is an excerpt from George Mangakis's 'Letter to Europeans', written from his cell in one of the Greek junta's prisons. Then 48 and a leading criminal law academic, Mangakis was dismissed from his university post in February 1969 after having been unanimously elected to the chair of Penal Law in the University of Athens. He was accused of a lack of spiritual conformity with the regime and five months later was arrested, interrogated and tortured on a charge of having participated in terrorist activities. In 1970, he was sentenced to 18 years' imprisonment.

It has become quite clear to me. It had to be this way. From the moment my country was humiliated, debased, it was inevitable that I should go underground. It was an inexorable spiritual imperative. My whole life had been leading me to that imperative. Since childhood, I was taught to gaze upon open horizons, to love the human face, to respect human problems, to honour free attitudes. At the time of World War II, I was an adolescent; I lived through the Resistance; it left its moral mark on me. It has now become clear that it was to be the most vital inspiration force in my life. At last I can explain many things that happened to me between then and now. And so when the dictatorship came, I was already committed to the Resistance without knowing it. I was carrying my own fate within me. Nothing happened by chance, by coincidence. Only the details were accidental. Diabolically accidental. But the general direction, the orientation, was rooted securely within me. Therefore it is not by mistake that I now find myself in prison. It is quite right that I should be here. What is horribly wrong is that this prison should exist at all. . . .

I would like to write about a friendship I formed the autumn before last. I think it has some significance. It shows the solidarity that can be forged between unhappy creatures. I had been kept in solitary confinement for four months. I hadn't seen a soul throughout that period. Only uniforms, inquisitors and jailers. One day, I noticed three mosquitoes in my cell. They were struggling hard to resist the cold that was just beginning. In the daytime they slept on the wall. At night they would come buzzing over me. In the beginning, they exasperated me. But fortunately I understood. I, too, was struggling hard to live through the cold spell. What were they asking from me? Something unimportant. A drop of blood – it would save them. I couldn't

refuse. At nightfall I would bare my arm and wait for them. After some days they got used to me and they were no longer afraid. They would come to me quite naturally, openly. This trust is something I owe them. Thanks to them, the world was no longer merely an inquisition chamber. Then one day I was transferred to another prison. I never saw my mosquitoes again. This is how you are deprived of the presence of your friends in the arbitrary world of prisons. But you go on thinking of them, often.

During the months when I was being interrogated, alone before those men with the multiple eyes of a spider – and the instincts of a spider – one night a policeman on guard smiled at me. At that moment, the policeman was all men to me. Four months later, when the representative of the International Red Cross walked into my cell, once again I saw all men in his friendly face. When one day they finally put me in a cell with another prisoner and he began to talk to me about the thing he loved most in life – sailing and fishing boats – this man, too, was all men to me. It is true then that there are situations in which each one of us represents all mankind. And it is the same with these papers: I have entrusted them to a poor Italian prisoner who has just been released and who was willing to try to smuggle them out for me. Through him I hope they will eventually reach you. That man again is all men to me. But I think it is time I finished. I have raised my hand, made a sign. And so we exist. We over here in prison, and you out there who agree with us. So: *freedom, my love.* ❏

CHINA'S LISTING SOCIAL STRUCTURE
HE QINGLIAN

As a result of the corrupt accumulation of wealth by the top few, China's society has regressed to a worse state than anything Mao fought against; the allure of the World Trade Organisation is a golden fantasy that will exacerbate the divisive trends of the drive to free markets; crimes committed by peasants and workers on the scrap heap of socialism have gone from random acts of opportunism to organised attacks on wealth; many of those in power have the cash and the will to leave this sinking ship and should do so before they're locked in the hold.

So says the author of the most controversial book to be published in China in recent years. The essay from which this excerpt is taken appeared in the March 2000 issue of the journal Shuwu (House of Books). *It sold out within ten days, only to be denounced by the propaganda department of the Central Committee of the* CCP *as a 'liberal' document guilty of 'inciting antagonism between the different strata of Chinese society'. He Qinglian was demoted from her editorial position at the* Shenzhen Legal Daily *and placed under domestic surveillance. She is believed to have left the country since. Her article continues to provoke intense unofficial discussion and has been compared to Mao's 1920s* Analysis of Classes in Chinese Society *as a gripping class analysis of contemporary China.*

The class structure of Chinese society has undergone a profound transformation since the beginnings of the reform-policy period in 1978. The elite, previously selected on a political basis, is now also being recruited on the basis of 'wealth' and 'merit', profoundly affecting the underlying social structure. They are forming their own interest groups, social organisations and lobbying channels beyond the existing political ones. The working class, hitherto the constitutionally decreed 'leading class', and the peasantry, the 'semi-leading class', have both been marginalised; intermediate social organisations are developing apace.

Reforms have reallocated the possession of social resources, principally the process of privatisation of judically public assets by the power-holding stratum. Its most striking feature has therefore been a glaring inequality in the distribution of national resources – the starting point of the restructuring of class relations in China in the past 20 years.

Though the total size of the elite that now controls a stock of 'all-encompassing capital' is not large, it enjoys commanding power over political, economic and cultural life. Most of its members made their fortunes not through technological innovation or industrial enterprise but by reproducing and exploiting monolithic positions of power to accumulate personal wealth.

By 1995, corruption had developed from the individual to an organisational stage, with leaders of social organisations utilising the public authority entrusted to their institution or state apparatus for 'power–money exchanges'. Lower-level social organisations mobilised the public resources under their control to bribe upper-level organisations for more financial support, better administrative deals or business opportunities. In the Zhanjiang city corruption scandal, the party secretary, the mayor and leading government departments figures were involved – and caught. Similar exposures bedevil the army.

Corruption developed to a systemic stage and has permeated the bulk of the party and state apparatus, becoming an established arrangement within institutions, as official posts are traded as counters in the redistribution of political, economic and cultural power. Official campaigns against corruption are no longer real threats to it but are instruments of political leverage and blackmail for personal gain. The power and wealth of the few keep them on top but the crudity of their route to enrichment means that society has no moral respect for them.

Chinese society today can now be broadly categorised into a small elite layer, a much larger middle layer and a burgeoning layer of marginalised groups beneath (although these layers' composition and relations remain fluid). Within the elite are three distinct groupings: political, economic and intellectual.

Together, China's political and economic elite today comprises about 7 million people, or 1% of the employed population. The political elite consists of top state officials, high- and middle-ranking local officials, and functionaries of large state-owned, non-industrial institutions. Many members rose up from the planned-economy system, using their previous administrative roles to ensure a smooth access to market opportunities – and thus to reconstitute themselves and their families as members of the 'second pillar', the economic elite. Many could claim a literal blood-kin relationship with the ruling political elite due to insignificant changes in personnel since before the reform era. Elite cadres began to 'love the market' in the mid-1980s and soon understood how to turn the power they wielded into the personal accumulation of wealth, beginning the process of reconstituting themselves into a property-holding class.

The lifestyles of the two major elite circles – political/governmental and economic – share some basic features: high-speed living, limited spare time, abundant consumption and similar tendencies in their leisure pursuits and sexual proclivities. This is because the 'cultural consumption' of the political elite – whether sexual consumption or general entertainment – mostly takes place in the purlieus of the economic elite. Urban spatial structures are changing, too. In the larger, more developed cities, concentrated elite neighbourhoods and mini-urban communities are forming, reflecting the demands of the ruling groups' transformed lifestyles.

The roots of China's problems today lie, among other factors, in the backward and anachronistic, irrational cadre selection. There is no examination or open democratic system. Mystification surrounds the whole process in which leaders 'discover' a talent, ministries 'take care' of gifted people or a party boss picks out a 'successor'. Such patterns readily generate corruption: appointments are based on personal connections, incompetents cannot be removed and positions are literally sold. Many corruption cases never reach the public eye. Judged by their behaviour, these are power-holders of very low quality. In general, a political elite should not only display competence in social administration but be capable of considering the interests of classes other than its own, if only to protect its own position in the long run, by allowing them some share in the distribution of common resources. Unfortunately, the current power elite in China cannot do either. Its mentality is expressed rather in the adage 'Power must be utilised before its expiry date.' Posts freely referred to as having 'gold content' are inseparable from fraud and corruption.

More and more economic policies are based not on considerations of any overall national interest but on a nexus of benefits to a specific social group. Critical issues for the national economy such as the restructuring of lopsided industrial sectors or cleaning up banks' bad debts remain unresolved because tackling them would affect some private vested interests. Production of family cars continues to 'develop' under various special favours. Property construction is out of control, paralysing the banks with bad loans. Cheaper flats for people would hurt vested interests so aren't built. Measures that would allay social discontent, like forbidding the use of public vehicles for

Shanghai, China:
US automobile; 'exclusive'
health club. How the 1% live
Credit: Panos / Chris Stowers

private purposes, or cutting down on official banquets, exist only on paper. By contrast, policies that exploit public authority to further elite interests, like those designed to facilitate lay-offs and cut welfare benefits, are rushed through with rare determination.

In early 1999, official policies and pronouncements boosted the stock exchange without restraint, helping certain interest groups to lift a bear market with the stimulus of public funds and bank loans. Once the market was artificially inflated, these groups sold off quickly, leaving small players to absorb the losses. This serves only to make quick fortunes for the new rich. Such suicidal policies are testimony to the myopia of a political and intellectual elite that has lost confidence in the future of the country in its hands. The government of the PRC has made its choice between the elite and the majority of the people. The reason lies not only in the tilting social basis of the ruling party but in a more general slide towards a 'rent-seeking society'. The ship named China is sinking under the devoted efforts of a power elite that has long prepared a retreat for its family members. When it is no longer possible to be a CCP cadre, it will be time for a comfortable retirement abroad. ❏

He Qinglian was born in Hunan in 1956. After numerous teaching jobs she worked for the Shenzhen municipal party committee and on the Shenzhen Legal Daily. *In August 1996, she completed a book on the social and economic ills of China after two decades of reform. Nine publishers refused it, fearing its explosive nature, and it eventually appeared in Hong Kong under the title* China's Pitfall. *An expurgated version was published in Beijing in January 1998, prefaced by Liu Ji, then an adviser to Jiang Zemin. The book sold 200,000 legal copies and vastly more pirated ones*

5/1979, 1/1980, 2/1981, 5/1986:
WEI JINGSHENG, CHINA

Wei Jingsheng was born into a militant communist family of veteran cadres from China's 1949 revolution and received a 'revolutionary education' throughout his childhood. Barely 16 at the start of the Cultural Revolution in 1966, he became a Red Guard but was imprisoned for four months as the revolution turned in on itself and its masters. The process of disillusionment had begun.

When the democratic movement was launched in 1978, he founded the journal Explorations *in which he published his essay 'The Fifth Modernisation' from which the following excerpt is taken. The essay appeared in three parts on Peking's Democracy Wall. It criticised China's leaders, accusing them of making empty promises to the people. Wei renewed this criticism in* Explorations *in 1979, attacking Deng for his change of attitude to the democratic movement.*

He was arrested in spring 1979 and sentenced to 15 years' imprisonment and three years' deprivation of human rights, for 'counter-revolutionary activities'. He now lives outside China.

The bourgeois democracy of the West allows its citizens to express their will by means of elections, and even if the popular will is misguided, the people can right their mistake. So no 'bourgeois politician' dares ignore the opinion of the electorate or risks being thrown out. But the 'proletarian politicians' can resort to the big stick to force the 'proletarian masses' into submission. The people can then do little but contemplate the politicians' successful rise to power and wonder at their life of pleasure and debauchery.

Western workers can go on strike and demonstrate, thus influencing the organisation of their work, as well as their living conditions. The Chinese workers and peasants must content themselves with the salary that Marx defined as the 'bare essentials for the keep and reproduction of the labour force'.

The westerners, who have already got so many rights, find that these are not enough. Among the Chinese, who know nothing but discipline, there are those who want to reinforce it still further. In the West, the protection of citizens' rights is one of the duties of government. In a 'socialist country', the citizen's only right is to obey a ruling minority.

Now the organs of the proletarian dictatorship interrupt us: 'At least, in our society, we have solved the problem of hunger.'

Really? Perhaps it would be better to let 'the dark face of socialism' – those people who beg on street corners – answer this question. Perhaps the millions of peasants and workers who, if they aren't careful, might end up as beggars too, should answer.

What of those 20 million compatriots who died of hunger during the three years of 'natural catastrophe'? Liu Shaoq did well to say: '30% natural catastrophe. 70% human disaster.' What does he mean by human disaster? He means that which was brought about by those tyrannical leaders, the Marxist-Leninist fascists. And which disaster? That of totalitarianism, a minority toying with 900 million lives.

'Stop!' the arse-lickers who have benefited from the regime say. 'In capitalist countries there is no equality between the sexes.' Do they imagine that men and women are equal because they submit to the same oppression, because they lead the same life, more wretched than that of pigs and dogs, and work like galley slaves in order to benefit their lordships – gracefully termed socialist accumulation?

'Please!' the professional slaves can't take any more. 'In capitalist countries there are prostitutes.' This time they should turn to their own whore, the police, and ask how many clandestine prostitutes there are in China and the USSR? And how many young girls are ready to serve the top leaders at any time?

And how many young girls are dispatched to work in the depths of the countryside because they refused to serve their leaders? Lacking any statistics, one might just enquire of the foreign visitors or of those Chinese who acquired foreign currency.

Is this the ideal society for which so many heroes have shed their blood and sacrificed their lives? Is this the society for which millions of workers strive with all their hearts? Is this the inexorable law of the development of history? ❑

INSIDE THE AXIS
ANDREW LAM

A GROUP OF IRANIAN WRITERS AND
INTELLECTUALS GIVE THE LIE TO
GEORGE W BUSH'S 'AXIS OF EVIL'

President Bush may list Iran as part of an 'axis of evil' but writers and intellectuals on this dry and weedy coral island 25 miles south of the mainland say democracy may yet thrive in their country.

In a project designed by President Mohammad Khatami, the reformist leader re-elected in 2001 in Iran, some 30 writers gathered to meet foreign authors and thinkers recently in a programme titled 'Dialogue Among Civilizations'. Though censorship remains strong in Iran, especially in matters of politics and religion, most Iranians here agreed that recent years have delivered a strong and steady push towards social liberalisation.

In fact, these days Iranians are quick to compare life 'before the election' and 'after the election'. The elections were seen as a mandate for Khatami's reformist policies. The ban on satellite dishes was lifted, for instance, and use of the Internet, albeit small, is growing quickly. Western music is coming back; bookstores are full of titles that had previously been censored. Books by Sama Behrangi, a pre-revolutionary leftist writer of children's stories, and works by the leftist poet Khorsro Golsorkhi are prominently displayed. Translations of western authors such as Isabel Allende, Danielle Steel and Michael Crichton sell briskly.

'We still can't write: "The man and the woman lie down on the bed and make love,"' says Asadollah Amaraee, a 47-year-old translator of western novels. 'We have to write: "The man and the woman lie on the bed and take turns counting the number of light bulbs above their bed." But everyone understands what we mean.'

Iranian writers, he says, are pushing at the boundaries all the time. But that isn't without risks. When a Swedish scholar voiced surprise to a 30-something Iranian writer that the government regarded fiction seriously enough to hold a seminar on the topic, the author answered, 'Yes, seriously enough to have a few [authors] disappeared and a few assassinated as well.'

Ayatollah Khomenei's death in 1989 and the subsequent battle between conservatives and reformists put Iran into gridlock. The economy suffered with 30% inflation and unemployment still hovers at 17%. But in the 2001 elections, the reformists triumphed, overturning the conservative domination of the country's parliament, though the conservatives still hold important levers of power like the presidency and the judiciary. The parliament had previously blocked reform efforts by Khatami, who had become Iran's fifth president in 1997.

Now, says Mohammed Sharifi, the author of 16 novels, things are slowly changing for the better. Tiny aspects of social life, nuances that many foreigners wouldn't notice, are, in fact, indicators of important changes: 'Before the election, you couldn't applaud after someone read their work on stage. Now, people applaud like mad.'

At a recent celebration of the opening of the Grand Darius – a five-star resort by the sea with 20-metre-tall columns – the hotel owner, an Iranian tycoon who owns a dozen hotels in Europe, flew in 160 dancers and musicians from Tehran. A woman wept quietly as a quartet played on stage. 'I haven't heard Mozart since before the revolution,' she says. 'You don't know how good this feels.'

As for the Iranian tycoon, many said he is betting tens of million of dollars that the trend in Iran is towards more liberalisation. After all, he is not expecting many foreign tourists to come any time soon, even if Kish is meant to be a visitor-friendly resort. Alcohol is still banned everywhere in Iran and Kish is no exception. The swimming pools are empty, for men and women cannot legally swim together. Beaches, too, remain gender-segregated. Men and women cannot touch in public, and women still must be covered with headscarves and tunics.

Dr Shiva Kambari, an Iranian novelist who lives in Germany, says freedom must be appreciated in small steps. 'It has to be incremental. No one really wants another revolution. But definitely everybody wants an evolution toward more social freedom.'

'It's a step up from before the election,' agreed the woman who was moved by Mozart. 'Before the election, women sat on one side of the amphitheatre and men on the other. Now we can sit together.' Iran has a long way to go, she adds, fidgeting with the scarf on her head to keep it from being blown away by the wind. 'We still have the US embargo and we are very afraid of Mr Bush.' Then she pauses and smiles. 'But we've come a long way, too.' ❏

Andrew Lam is associate editor of the Pacific News Service

TURNING BACK THE CLOCK
TOM FAWTHROP

THAILAND'S REPUTATION AS A HAVEN
OF PRESS FREEDOM IN THE REGION
HAS BEEN ENDANGERED BY THE
GOVERNMENT'S AGGRESSIVE ATTEMPTS TO
INTIMIDATE LOCAL AND FOREIGN CRITICS

After a series of critical reports on the Thai government by the Hong Kong-based *Far Eastern Economic Review* (FEER), Thailand Inc hit back. The 10 January issue of the magazine was deemed a 'threat to national security' by Thai Special Branch police and the magazine banned inside the kingdom.

After another critical report on the Thai government's handling of the economy on 7 February, the PM's office ordered the Special Branch to blacklist FEER's two Bangkok-based reporters and threaten them with deportation. State security agencies had not been used in this way by a Thai government since the dark days of military rule.

Thaksin Shinawatra, the telecommunications tycoon who became prime minister last year, believes the nation should be run in the same way as he runs his Shinawatra Corporation boardroom: the boss gives the orders, his minions obey. In his vision of the new Thailand Inc there is little room for dissent and opposition.

In March came further evidence that Thaksin's drive to tame the media was turning the clock back to an earlier era of dictatorship: the government forced the 24-hour cable news channel UBC8 to drop the independent news service provided by the Nation media group. He denied that the action taken against the Nation news service was political but once again warned the media to be 'constructive' in its reports.

Since Thaksin, leader of Thai Rak Thai (Thai Love Thai) took over as PM, most media have either been intimidated or won over with government largesse. Thaksin's conflict of interests and control over the media – his corporation owns ITV channel – is comparable to Berlusconi's role in Italy.

Special Branch censors were soon at it again with a threat to seize all copies of the 2 March issue of *The Economist* with its special survey on Thailand if it was distributed. In a manner that reeked of Singapore-style media control and internet censorship, Thai police spokesman Major General Pongsapat Pongcharoen went further and insisted that the Thai authorities

What possibly upsets him?

Abac pollsters have been in hot water following their latest survey on government performance. Following are findings that must have angered powers-that-be the most

Please list the problems that you think have affected the government's image? (Respondents may list more than one):

1 Conflicts of interest involving government members
2 Telecommunications contract conversion
3 PTT shares sell-off
4 Economic woes and lack of clear-cut goals
5 Proposal to open casinos in Thailand
6 Providing tax benefits to car businesses close to politicians in power
7 Explosions at an arms depot in Nakhon Ratchasima

Thaksin Shinawatra: offending front page of Bangkok's Nation
Credit: Tom Fawthrop

would demand that the London-based weekly remove its 'Survey on Thailand' from the Web. *The Economist* has not complied.

According to an opinion poll released in February, it appears that Thaksin's popularity is on the wane. Shortly after releasing their poll, Assumption University's Abac Poll team were surprised to receive a series of visits from high-ranking military officers and Special Branch police.

Anger over the media campaign was fuelled days later by the revelation that AMLO – the Anti Money Laundering Organisation – had secretly ordered commercial banks to release confidential details of the assets and transactions of certain Thai journalists and NGO leaders who had one thing in common: they are known as vocal critics of the Thaksin government. AMLO's mandate is supposed to be a non-partisan investigation into unusual wealth derived from such sources as drug-trafficking, prostitution, illegal gambling and fraud.

Many Thai journalists and NGOs don't have to cast their minds back very far to remember the dark days of Thai military dictatorships, bloody coups d'état and the silencing of the media. After the 1992 massacre of pro-democracy demonstrators in Bangkok, Prime Minister General Suchinda Krapayoon was forced to resign, democracy was restored and a new constitution was approved in 1997 which for the first time fully recognised citizens' rights and enshrined press freedom.

FEER, owned by Dow Jones Group, eventually made an ambiguous apology for 'any misunderstandings' over their report that 'the Thai king was highly critical of the prime minister's performance'. The government was able to save face, and *FEER*'s two Bangkok-based correspondents were able stay in the country. ❏

Tom Fawthrop *is a freelance journalist and film-maker based in SE Asia*

TESTING TIMES AHEAD

With the implementation of a draconian new media law in the wake of an election the opposition disputes as fraudulent and the government claims is a ringing endorsement of President Robert Mugabe, Zimbabwe's journalists are gearing up for what could become a confrontation with the authorities.

'There will definitely be a lot more pressure now. The international community has condemned the elections and their media has agreed with them,' says Lewis Machipisa, correspondent of the IPS news agency in Harare. 'The first casualty will be the independent press because the government will accuse them first. It will be watching the papers a lot more carefully now.'

Zimbabwe's media has been sharply divided into pro-government, represented by the Zimbabwean Broadcasting Corporation and newspapers such as the *Sunday Mail*, and the independent sector led by the *Daily News*, the *Financial Gazette* and the *Zimbabwe Independent*.

The state media has broadcast the news of President Mugabe's re-election without reference to statements by opposition leader Morgan Tsvangirai and election observers that the voting was flawed. Machipisa says that he, along with other accredited journalists, were able to visit polling stations during the voting but added there were many reasons to doubt the election results. 'If you're talking about whether elections are free and fair, you have to start with the pre-election period,' he says. 'The opposition parties were intimidated from going into rural areas and denied any access to public airwaves.'

The only time the state media mentioned the fact that there was an opposition was when Tsvangirai was charged with plotting to kill Mugabe. Then a raft of laws was introduced whittling down the potential opposition vote – by banning postal votes, for example,. Election officials were all appointed by the government and there were administrative delays in issuing cards to first-time voters in districts where the opposition was known to be strong.

The government has also been playing a cat-and-mouse game with foreign journalists. It banned correspondents from Britain's BBC and introduced a rule denying accreditation to any non-Zimbabwean journalists. This was later reduced to any non-resident of Zimbabwe but information minister Jonathan Moyo insisted that journalists who entered the country undercover and worked without accreditation would be 'tracked down and punished'.

Although Zimbabwe's state and independent media produce sharply diverging views, Machipisa says journalists from the two camps rely on each other to get access to the sharply polarised sides of the country's political life. 'As a journalist in the independent sector, there are times at pro-government demonstrations when you feel very uncomfortable. Particularly in my case when people learn that I'm working for the BBC. Sometimes you really have to be buddy-buddy with the guys from the state media so they can protect you,' he says. 'But it works both ways. Because there is such a deep dislike of public press and television among supporters of the opposition, then it is the journalists from the independent sector who say: "No, we are all here as one body," and keep the crowd away from state sector journalists.'

Journalists have been actively intimidated by Mugabe's 'veterans', supporters who claim to have fought in the war of independence against the white supremacist government of Ian Smith in the 1970s. The *Daily News* had its bureau in Bulawayo bombed and, last month, Basildon Peta, a leading independent journalist who works for the *Financial Gazette*, fled to South Africa to join his family after repeated threats on his life.

Peta had been the first journalist to be arrested under a new law passed in January curbing press freedoms. It contains such broad provisions as outlawing 'unethical journalism' and any article that promotes 'alarm, fear and despondency'.

Machipisa says the country's journalists will have to keep their heads down in the coming days and weeks. '[Iindependent journalists] should detach themselves from the politics of the day; they have to be mindful of the fact that no story is worth your life. People should know when the situation is tense it is better to live to fight another day than to become a dead hero.' At the same time, he says, journalists from the private sector have agreed not to write anonymously except when it would be absolutely life-threatening to do otherwise. 'Sometimes the government says if you are not ashamed, why be anonymous or use pseudonyms. So we have taken a decision not to use pseudonyms,' he adds.

Machipisa feels the independent media has a vital role to play in the coming days. 'I think we shall feel obliged to get down to the bottom of the election, find out what happened and how and to publish it in a way that will force the authorities and the courts to do something about it.' ❑

Lewis Machipisa was interviewed by John West

A censorship chronicle incorporating information from Agence France-Press (AFP), Alliance of Independent Journalists (AJI), Amnesty International (AI), Article 19 (A19), Association of Independent Electronic Media (ANEM), the BBC Monitoring Service Summary of World Broadcasts (SWB), Centre for Human Rights and Democratic Studies (CEHURDES), Centre for Journalism in Extreme Situations (CJES), the Committee to Protect Journalists (CPJ), Canadian Journalists for Free Expression (CJFE), Democratic Journalists' League (JuHI), Glasnost Defence Foundation (GDF), Human Rights Watch (HRW), Information Centre of Human Rights & Democracy Movements in China (ICHR DMC), Instituto de Prensa y Sociedad (IPYS), the United Nations Integrated Regional Information Network (IRIN), the Inter-American Press Association (IAPA), the International Federation of Journalists (IFJ/ FIP), the Media Institute of Southern Africa (MISA), Network for the Defence of Independent Media in Africa (NDIMA), International PEN (PEN), Open Media Research Institute (OMRI), Pacific Islands News Association (PINA), Radio Free Europe/Radio Liberty (RFE/ RL), Reporters Sans Frontières (RSF), Transitions Online (TOL), the World Association of Community Broadcasters (AMARC), World Association of Newspapers (WAN), World Organisation Against Torture (OMCT), Writers in Prison Committee (WiPC) and other sources including members of the International Freedom of Expression eXchange (IFEX)

AFGHANISTAN

The Afghan independent newspaper *Kabul Weekly* returned to the streets on 24 January after more than five years' absence. The weekly, with seven pages in Pashto and Dari and three pages in French and English, costs 2,000 afghanis, about the price of a loaf of bread. Issue one ran items on free speech, the situation of women and the rebirth of Afghan theatre. Several groups, including Reporters Sans Frontières and Unesco, backed the paper's launch. (RSF)

The US-based Committee to Protect Journalists (CPJ) continued to quiz Washington officialdom for the truth behind the 13 November air strike on the Kabul office of **al-Jazeera** satellite TV. But in a terse letter to al-Jazeera on 6 December US assistant secretary of defence Victoria Clarke said the 'the building we struck was a known al-Qaeda facility in central Kabul'. The building had been in use by the station for two years. The CPJ is concerned that the US forces either did not properly check the target or deliberately bombed it to stop it transmitting. A deliberate attack on a civilian facility is prohibited under international humanitarian law. (CPJ)

US soldiers aimed their weapons at a *Washington Post* **correspondent** in Afghanistan on 10 February and threatened to shoot him if he tried to check an area where a US missile had recently hit. The US military denied the reporter's account. The *Post* tersely asked on what basis does the military in Afghan-istan 'prevent American reporters from reporting on aspects of military operations in Afghanistan?'. (*Washington Post*)

ALGERIA

Renewing their interest in the independent press, Algerian security forces ordered civilian police to haul in their staff in late January. First to be quizzed were *Liberté*'s cartoonist **Ali Dilem** and journalist **Salima Tlemçani** of the daily *El Watan*, then Mohamed Benchicou, editorial director of the daily *Le Matin* on 30 January. (*Liberté*)

On 18 February 2002, the Algiers Appeals Court prosecutor called for a one-year prison sentence without parole for **Omar Belhouchet**, *El Watan*'s editor, charged with 'attacking official bodies' in comments made to French TV in September 1995. Belhouchet had said he did not exclude the possibility that state forces as well as Islamist underground groups were involved in the killing of journalists. (RSF)

A commission set up to investigate the Berber uprising of spring 2001 reported in January that since the start of the state of emergency in 1992, power had drifted from political to military circles. The state of emergency had become a 'state of siege', it said. (www.allafrica.com /*El País*)

ANGOLA

On 27 January, journalist **Rafael Marques** was ordered by a court to pay 30,000 kwanza (approx US$950) compensation to President Eduardo dos Santos for defamation and injury. The charge relates to a 1999 article by Marques published in *Agora* newspaper, in which he referred to dos Santos as a dictator 'responsible for the destruction of the country and the promotion of corruption'. (MISA)

ARGENTINA

On 25 February, *Clarín* and *El Liberal* journalist **Julio Rodríguez** and his family received a death threat from an anonymous caller. Rodríguez believes the incident is a response to his investigation into corruption in the political and financial sectors of the province of Santiago del Estero, where he is a correspondent. The threat is the latest in a series of more than 100 threats against and violence towards journalists in Santiago del Estero (*Index* 4/2001) over the past few years. (*Clarín*)

ARMENIA

Speaking in Yerevan on 20 February, President Robert Kocharian said a much criticised draft law on the media would not be enacted without the blessing of the Council of Europe. The bill plans a new system of media licensing. It will require journalists to seek permission in writing before interviewing government personnel and pay staff the costs they incur in answering media questions. Kocharian said 'we all need free media', but it should be 'responsible'. (RFE/RL)

AUSTRALIA

Canberra's contribution to the war on terrorism includes a new bill that redefines terrorism to include dissenting political activities. Anyone who 'discloses information about national security with the intention to prejudice that security' could face a 25-year prison sentence. This includes information relating to the intelligence activities of Australia's security partners, primarily the US and UK. People may be jailed for two years for leaking 'official records of information' even if they are not tagged 'secret' − if they are, the sentence may be seven years. The bill shifts the burden of proof. The prosecution doesn't have to prove that the journalists knew or even ought to have known that the document was unauthorised. It will be the duty of the journalist to check any 'suspect' documents with the relevant authority. Charges under the new bill can be heard in secret and tribunals can ban any publication from attending. (www.wsws.org).

AZERBAIJAN

Some 100 police officers armed with rubber batons forcibly dispersed a group of about 80 members of the **Azerbaijan Democratic Party** as they demonstrated against the Azerbaijani leadership on 16 February. The protest did not have official permission. Between 20 and 40 protesters were detained. (RFE/RL)

BAHAMAS

Opposition Coalition and Labour supporters stormed the Broadcasting Corporation of the Bahamas (BCB) on 25 February, led by party leader **Dr Bernard Nottage**, calling for an end to what they claim is the ruling Free National Movement (FNM) Party's monopoly of the airwaves. The group of about 50 supporters entered the grounds of the BCB shortly after 1pm, requesting an audience with management or any reporter who was willing to hear the story. 'We are not here to harm anybody,' Nottage insisted at a press conference held just minutes before. 'We just want our 15 minutes like the others. We want to be heard also.' Nottage was met by BCB general manager Edwin Lightbourne for an impromptu meeting that lasted two hours. Trade Union Congress Leader Ubie Ferguson, the Coalition's candidate for Bain Town, also attended. (*Nassau Guardian*)

BANGLADESH

On 16 January, the Dhaka power company DASA literally pulled the plug on the independent daily *Janakantha*, allegedly on orders from government officials, cutting off the paper's print works. The paper, which has been criticising government policies under the leadership of Begum Khaleda Zia, published as normal on portable generators. (Media Watch)

On 5 February, several homemade bombs rocked the Chittagong Press Club, where journalist **Shahriar Kabir** was attending a reception to celebrate his release on bail. One bystander was killed and several others were injured.

Kabir was not harmed. Kabir, a documentary film-maker and contributor to the daily *Janakantha,* was arrested on 22 November for 'anti-state activities on the basis of intelligence reports and at the instruction of higher authorities,' according to a police report. He was released on bail on 20 January. Irene Zubaida Khan, the Secretary General of Amnesty International and Prime Minister Khaleda Zia raised Kabir's case in a face-to-face meeting in December. (AFP/IFEX/Media Watch)

In January pro-Islamist government elements complained about surveillance of mosques, madrassahs (religious schools) and Islamic centres over the border in the Indian state of West Bengal. The press in India regularly accuses Bangladesh of allowing Pakistan to launch covert attacks against India from its territory. (Tehelka.com)

The 11 February issue of *Newsweek* magazine's Asian edition was banned in Bangladesh and several other states because it reportedly carried a portrait of the Prophet Mohammed, whose depiction is considered blasphemous by Muslims. (Gulf News Online, BBC Online)

Recent publication: 'Bangladesh: Attacks on members of the Hindu minority' (AI, December 2001, 7pp)

BELARUS

A court in Hrodna fined **Mikola Markevich**, editor-in-chief of the local independent newspaper *Pahonya*, US\$320. The court found Markevich guilty of organ-

ising an unauthorised rally in defence of his newspaper on 19 November. The paper had reported links between a state-sponsored deaths squad and the disappearances of opposition figures in Belarus. It is now closed. Markevich did not admit the charge but will not appeal against the verdict. He noted: 'Present-day courts in Belarus serve only one person, not society as a whole'. (RFE/RL)

The opposition Youth Front began a three-month campaign against President Aleksandr Lukashenka's regime on 14 February by delivering valentine cards to a dozen embassies in Minsk. The inscription read: 'In times of darkness, lies, aggression, repression and dictatorship, we should remember that only love will help us overcome [them] and revive a European Belarus.' The Russian Embassy did not get a card. Later, some 30 Youth Front activists were arrested at a protest. Five days later Youth Front leader **Pavel Sevyarynets** was fined US\$1,300 for his role in the unauthorised protest. He said he was surprised he was not given a prison sentence. (RFE/RL)

The mother of **Yury Korban**, head of the Vitsebsk-based opposition youth centre Kontur, has appealed to Belarusan and international human rights organisations for help in finding her missing son. Yury left the the family house on 19 January and has not seen him since. He phoned subsequently, the last time on 23 January when he asked her to bring \$20,000 to a location in Minsk. She arrived with some money but no one turned up.

In his last conversation Yury told his mother that she would never see him again. (RFE/RL)

Prosecutor Fyodar Shvedau on 13 February demanded death sentences for the four suspected kidnappers of journalist **Dzmitry Zavadski**, missing since July 2000. The four, ex-Interior Ministry officers **Valery Ihnatovich** and **Maksim Malik**, and **Alyaksey Huz** and **Syarhey Saushkin**, have been found guilty on various counts, including murder, abduction, and robbery. However, **Syarhey Tsurko**, the lawyer representing Zavadski's wife, said the four's part in kidnapping Zavadski had not been proven. Two former staff of the Belarusan Prosecutor-General's Office said last year that Zavadski was kidnapped and murdered by a government-sponsored death squad on orders from Belarus Security Council Secretary Viktar Sheyman, who is now the country's prosecutor-general. (RFE/RL)

Belarusan officials are confiscating any material that might throw a negative light on President Aleksandr Lukashenka and his regime. CDs, videotapes and disks are being seized on the grounds that the officials do not know what is stored on them. Persons wishing to take a laptop out of Belarus now have to surrender it to the customs for checking 24 hours before departure. One victim of the new rules is likely to be the state airline, Belavia. Lukashenka's treaty of Union with Russia lifted customs controls at the Belarusan–Russian frontier. Businessmen and other travellers who find a laptop essential can simply take the night train to Moscow and fly from there. (Index on Censorship)

BOLIVIA

A new Bolivian law authorises the National Electoral Court (CNE) to control which publications may or may not publish election news in the run-up to the polls – and ban media that break the rules. The law was approved on 3 December and under Article 119 of the new law, media will have to register with the CNE. The CNE will then publish a list of approved media outlets. Media not on the list will be effectively barred from reporting the pre-election political debate. Political parties that address news to media off the list could also face sanction under Article 119. (IFEX)

BRITAIN

Ryton Police Training College in Coventry refused to display issues of the magazine for homosexuals, *Gay Times*. The college head, Chief Superintendent Stan Horlock, said the publication was not suitable for its community resource centre because the material could be 'offensive'. The Lesbian and Gay Police Association disagreed and said it was a form of 'censorship'. A number of police forces have used the *Gay Times* to advertise for new officers. (BBC Online)

London police are planning a computer register of children who look likely to become criminals in later life. Youngsters who tag buildings with graffiti, skip school, or even talk back to adults run the risk of being entered into a data-base that will monitor their behaviour as they grow up. In October, Ian Blair, London's deputy police commissioner, told the Youth Justice Board, which supervises the British juvenile justice system, that the system would collect data from teachers, social workers, doctors, police and other authorities. Special squads of police and community workers will supervise the actions of children on the registry. The director of Privacy International, Simon Davies, called it 'police profiling gone mad' and said it would only lead to 'greater criminalisation of children and heightened discrimination against certain racial groups'. (*Wired*)

The British Official Secrets Act preventing any member of the security and intelligence services from disclosing anything about their work is incompatible with the European human rights convention, counsel for **David Shayler**, the former MI5 officer, told the Law Lords on 4 February. 'There is a class whose lips are buttoned of about 10,000 people who are stopped from disclosing to outsiders any information,' said Geoffrey Robertson QC. Shayler is appealing against court rulings, which, if upheld, would prevent him from having any defence at his criminal trial. Robertson said Shayler should be able to argue in court that he disclosed the information in the public interest and out of necessity. The *Guardian* newspaper and other media organisations also argue that blanket ban means that journalists may face charges if they investigate allegations about the security services. (*Guardian*)

BULGARIA

Vesselin Stoikov, one of nine members of the Electronic Media Council that supervises radio and television, was sacked on 11 February after ongoing investigations into communist-era secret service files revealed him as a former agent. The law on radio and television stipulates that communist secret service collaborators may not serve on the Electronic Media Council. Stoikov denied the accusation and claimed it was politically motivated dismissal. (RFE/RL)

In February, the leaders of five Bulgarian evangelical churches warned of a wave of anti-Semitism spreading in the country, citing anti-semitic and Holocaust-denying literature in circulation. They singled out a book by **Volen Siderov**, deputy editor-in-chief of *Monitor*, one of Bulgaria's largest dailies, which they said was not only just a collection of classic anti-semitic stereotypes, but also targeted Roma and other minorities. (RFE/RL)

BURMA

Journalist and former editor of the magazine *Pe-Phu-Hlwanwas* **Myo Myint Nyein** was among a small group of political prisoners released on 13 February, coincidentally as a CPJ special report on Burmese journalists was released and United Nations envoy Paulo Sergio Pinheiro visited Burma to investigate human rights abuses there. 'The censorship board has told us we must not write about Aids, corruption, education, or the situation of students', said an editor of a monthly magazine cited in the CPJ report. 'We also cannot write about any bad news and we must be careful about everything political. That does not leave very much for us to publish'. Myo Myint Nyein had served more than 11 years of a 14-year prison term.

New publication: *Under Pressure: How Burmese journalism survives in one of the world's most repressive regimes*, by A Lin Neumann, CPJ Asia consultant

BURUNDI

Burundian communications minister Albert Mbonerane lifted a ban on the private news agency **Net Press** to publish news on its website, agency editor-in-chief Claude Sibomana said on 25 February. The agency had been accused of failing to respect the country's 1997 media law, requiring the media to 'avoid publishing information that is subversive, defamatory, abusive, false or even lies that are published with the sole aim of disturbing the prevailing situation in the country'. (IRIN)

CAMEROON

Questions still linger over the case of Cameroonian journalist **Georges Baongla**, publication director of the weekly *Le Démenti*, now serving five years in jail for fraud and extortion. Baongla says he was not told about the opening of his case in October 2001 and only heard about his sentence second-hand. Baongla is accused of extorting 10 million CFA francs (approx. US$13,400)

from an official at Cameroon's Ministry of the Economy and Finances. *Le Démenti* has repeatedly accused the minister of embezzling public monies during the installation of a sewer system in the country. (RSF)

CANADA

After six years of legal struggle the Canadian Human Rights Commission has ordered Holocaust denier **Ernst Zundel** to kill off his website of anti-semitic propaganda. The commission's ruling on 18 January found that the social benefits of eliminating hate speech outweighed the issues of protection of free speech, reported the *Toronto Globe & Mail*, though it accepted that ordering Zundel to 'cease and desist' from using his website was fairly futile as the material was now widely posted elsewhere on the Web. 'We now know that the Internet is not a "lawless zone", and cannot be used to promote hate,' claimed the CHRC's Chief Commissioner, Michelle Falardeau-Ramsay. 'This is all the more important in light of the tensions that have emerged since last September.' (*Toronto Globe & Mail*)

CanWest Global Communications Corporation, which owns 14 major newspapers around Canada, has drawn fire from Canadian and international free-expression groups by insisting that all newspapers print the same editorial in their pages from December. Critics argue that the policy sidelines regional voices – particularly hitting the editorial independence of its newspaper in Montreal, the English-language *Montreal*

Gazette – in favour of 'a single voice for the company's national corporate agenda'. (IFJ)

CHILE

Chilean Judge Marcos Felzenstein dropped charges against **Paula Afani Saud** of *La Tercera* newspaper, who had refused to reveal her sources for a story on a major anti-drug trafficking and money laundering operation. A new press law guaranteed her right to keep her sources secret but the force behind the operation, the State Defence Council (CDE), appealed on 18 January, demanding Afani be jailed for five years and a day. A order banning publication of the story was only sought in June 1998, after Afani's articles had been printed. 'Everything I reported on was true. No one denied this, not the police, not the court, not even the CDE,' Afani said. While the case is in progress Afani is subject to an order that restricts her movements at home and abroad. (IPYS)

On 11 December, a Santiago appeals court ruled in favour of a writ demanding that Chile's National Forestry Corporation (CONAF) allow environmental NGO**Fundación Terram** access to ecological studies that it tried to keep secret. The tribunal said CONAF's failure to provide Fundación Terram with the information interfered with 'the public's legitimate right to oversee state employees, as the matter in question is of public interest'. CONAF has now handed over the requested information. (IPYS)

The trial of **Eduardo Yanez** began on 18 February. The host of the television programme 'El termometro' is accused of defamation for comments he made about the Supreme Court in November 2001, including calling the members of the Supreme Court cowards and branding the judicial process 'corrupt' and 'immoral'. The case is the latest in a series presided over by Judge Jordan, who banned **Alejandra Matus**'s *Black Book of Chilean Justice* (*Index* 4/1999, 6/1999, 2/2001, 4/2001) in 1999. If guilty, the broadcaster could face up to five years in prison. The trial continues. (HRW, RSF, *El Mundo*, *Pagina 12*)

CHINA

A play by China's exiled Nobel Literature Prize-winner, **Gao Xingjian**, whose work is banned on the mainland, was aired on government-run Radio TV Hong Kong. *Weekend Quartet*, an hour-long radio drama adapted from Gao's 1995 play of the same name, was presented in English on RTHK's Radio 4 on 11 February. Gao has lived in exile for 13 years and was awarded the Nobel Prize in 2000. RTHK producers say that while his works are banned on the mainland, there is nothing critical of the Chinese Government in the play, which tells of an encounter between an elderly artist and his wife and a young couple in their country home that ends in romantic entanglement. (*South China Morning Post*)

Three years after he was arrested for sneaking back into China to help an opposition party, US-educated activist **Wang Ce** was freed a year early for good behaviour, the government-run Xinhua News Agency said on 14 January. Wang, 52, left China in 1984 to earn a doctorate in political science at the University of Hawaii. He settled in Spain and led a group of Chinese exiles, the Freedom and Democracy Party. Wang secretly crossed into China from Vietnam in October 1998 after authorities refused to renew his passport and was subsequently arrested. (*Nando Times*)

Writers in Prison Committee (WiPC) and International PEN are increasingly concerned about the health of Chinese writer, editor and veteran activist **Xu Wenli**, which, according to his family, has been steadily deteriorating since his imprisonment in December 1998. He is now believed to be in critical condition. International PEN again calls upon the Chinese authorities to ensure that Xu Wenli receives the medication and dietary requirements necessary for the treatment of his condition as a matter of urgency. (WiPC/PEN)

Historian **Xu Zerong**, research associate professor at the South-East Asia Institute, Zhongshan University, Guangzhou, was sentenced in January 2002 by a Shenzhen court to 13 years in prison, three years for 'economic crimes' and ten years on charges of 'leaking state secrets'. The charges relate in part to his use of allegedly classified documents concerning Chinese military operations in the Korean War (1950–53), gathered in the course of his research. Xu is appealing against his sentence. Xu's research specialised in Chinese Communist Party history, military history and China's relations with Southeast Asia. He received his doctorate from St Antony's College, Oxford, in 1999. (NEAR)

COLOMBIA

Colombian journalist **Claudia Gurisatti** fled the country after renewed death threats from one of the warring sides in the country's long-running civil conflict. Last year she was warned by then attorney-general Alfonso Gómez Méndez that members of the Revolutionary Armed Forces of Colombia (FARC) guerrillas planned to assassinate her. The FARC dismissed the threat as a fake. Recent editions of her TV news programme *La Noche* included footage of meetings between members of the FARC and Venezuelan military officials, while past threats have been linked to her interviews with Carlos Castano, head of the paramilitary United Self-Defence Forces of Colombia (AUC). (IPYS)

The death toll among Colombian journalists continued to rise. Journalist **Alvaro Alonso Escobar**, owner of *Región* newspaper in the town of Fundación, Magdalena state, was murdered on 23 December. Escobar's news beat covered towns that are high-risk areas for guerrilla and paramilitary attacks. A month later, on 23 January, **Marco Antonio Ayala Cárdenas**, a photographer with the daily *El Caleño* in Cali, was shot dead by gunmen on a motorcycle outside the newspaper's offices. Ayala Cárdenas had been working on sports and social issues but had recently joined the paper's legal matters team. On 30 January, journalist **Orlando Sierra Hernández**, assistant editor of the daily *La Patria* in Manizales in Caldas department, was gunned down outside his office. He later died in hospital. On 8 February Luis Fernando Soto Zapata was charged with Hernández's killing. The Attorney-General's Office also revealed details of Soto Zapata's capture. IPYS also reported the murder of veteran basketball reporter **Esaú Jaramillo**, apparently by a thief, at his home in Bogotá in January. (IPYS)

The Inter American Press Association has called on the Colombian authorities to review its investigation into the case of journalist and satirist **Jaime Garzón**, murdered in 1999. IAPA says the Colombian attorney ageneral has refused to consider evidence that links the military to Garzón's murder and will only look at evidence against Carlos Castaño, head of the para-military group AUC and the actual alleged killer. Garzón was murdered in Bogotá in August 1999. At the time of his murder he combined his work as a journalist with negotiations for the release of kidnapped hostages and the peace process. (IFEX/IAPA)

DEMOCRATIC REPUBLIC OF CONGO

More than 400 protesting **students from the University of Kinshasa** were detained at police headquarters

on 14 December. Most were released the next day but, according to Amnesty International, some were forced to walk on their hands and knees around the HQ courtyard. Seven students were injured and at least one shot in a separate protest at the University of Lubumshasi against tuition fees and increased accommodation fees. (AI)

The editor of satirical publication *Pot-pourri* **Guy Kasagaembwe** and secretary **Vicky Bolingwa** were detained between 31 December and 3 January, in connection with an article about President Joseph Kabila and his government. Intially accused of endangering state security, the charges were later dropped. (AI)

CROATIA

Zagreb Radio 101 was again refused a licence to broadcast beyond the Croatian capital by the Croatian Radio and Television Council. 'The decision not to grant a regional licence to Radio 101 is merely the first step in eradicating the station,' said **Zeljko Matic**, one of the station's editors. The former regime of Croatian president Franjo Tudjman tried to close the station down on several occasions. As in Serbia, Croatian independent broadcasters want the licences reassigned, as the present holders were all beneficiaries of the former regimes in both countries. (ANEM)

CUBA

Bernardo Arévalo Padrón, journalist and director of independent press agency Linea Sur Press, was widely

but incorrectly reported in mid-January to have been released four years into a six-year sentence handed down in 1997 on charges of having produced 'enemy propaganda'. Padrón, who was held in El Diamante prison in Rodas, Cienfuegos Province, had suffered acutely from high blood pressure and bronchitis. He remains in jail with economist **Vladimiro Roca Antúnez**, serving a five-year prison term handed down in 1999 for 'sedition and other acts against state security'. (WiPC/PEN)

Marta Beatriz Roque, leader of the Cuban Institute of Independent Economists (ICEI), announced the launch of a new website chronicling day-to-day life in Cuba at www.cubaicei.org in January. The site will contain news from roughly 130 dissident groups, as well as monthly news reports, opinion pieces and photos. The site also lists contact information for 60 independent libraries and over 20 alternative news sources and, according to Roque, represents about 75% of Cuba's dissident groups. (DFN)

CYPRUS

The Turkish Cypriot newspaper *Avrupa*, noted for its criticism of Northern Cyprus leader Rauf Denktash, was closed down in December after years of violence and threats against the paper. The final straw appeared to be its publication of an article by a Turkish Cypriot secondary school teacher in which she describes Turkey as 'an occupying force in Cyprus'. The woman, a 34-year-old history teacher, was dismissed and the offices of *Avrupa* were raided and stripped of its furniture and equipment. The newspaper managed to keep going for a few days with the help of liberal rival paper Ortam but *Avrupa* owner and editor **Sener Levent** said the 16 December edition would be the last 'until further notice'. An alternative paper, *Afrika*, opened the next day.

CZECH REPUBLIC

The trial of former Security Information Service (BIS) agent **Vladimir Hucin** began in Prerov, northern Moravia, on 13 February, but was immediately adjourned until a higher court could rule on the defence's complaint of court bias against the defendant. The judge had already decided to conduct the trial behind closed doors, as the case involved state-security secrets, which prompted protests among those in attendance. Hucin, a former anticommunist dissident, is charged with fraud, bearing arms without authorisation, scaremongering, failure to obey orders, and the unauthorised handling of classified data. If convicted, he faces ten years in prison. (RFE/RL)

EAST TIMOR

East Timorese journalists have expressed dismay at an agreement that may leave their newly independent nation without an independent national broadcaster and leave control of television and radio to its former colonial power, Portugal, the *Sydney Morning Herald* reported on 29 December. The protocol of co-operation between East Timor and Portugal provides for Portuguese-language broadcasting in the new nation, where only the minority of older citizens speak or understand the language. The document, which has not been made public, makes no mention of the most widely understood local language, Tetum, or minimum local content requirements or training for East Timorese journalists. Control of the media is an important issue in East Timor which was subjected to strict censorship under Indonesian rule. (*Sydney Morning Herald*)

EGYPT

Wahid Ghazi and **Hossam Wahaballah**, editor-in-chief and journalist with the Cairo weekly *al-Mowagaha*, were sentenced to two years' imprisonment and a fine of 100 Egyptian pounds (approx US$23.50) on 25 November. Egypt's High Council for the Press instigated proceedings against the two following the publication in June of photos showing men and women in 'compromising positions' considered 'offensive to readers'. The article related to the 1996 case of an excommunicated Coptic Christian monk. The photos were taken from one of the monk's videotapes.

Egypt's Court of Cassation has granted imprisoned human rights expert **Saad Eddin Ibrahim** a new trial. Ruling on 6 February, the court rejected six rulings in the original 21 May judgement of the State Security Court, which sentenced Ibrahim and 27 colleagues to up to seven years in prison. All the defendants' appeals were granted as well. The charges related to the Centre's published sociological studies of Egyptian society and accepting a European Union grant for a voter information project. They included spreading false information about Egypt abroad, bribery, fraudulent use of funds, and using donations for his think-tank, the Ibn Khaldun Centre, without explicit permission of the government. (DFN)

A military court began hearing charges on 24 January against 94 defendants accused of forming an illegal Islamist group called **al-Waad** (The Promise). The charges ranged from membership of the group to plotting assassinations of public officials. (*Cairo Times*)

On 4 December, a Cairo court ruled that the American University in Cairo could not prohibit the wearing of the *niqab*, a full face-veil. A visiting doctoral student was told by guards she had to remove her veil because of security concerns, but the court considered it a matter of personal and religious freedom. (*Cairo Times*)

On 18 December, two students were convicted of soliciting gay sex on the Internet, and distributing indecent photographs of themselves. They had been caught by an undercover policeman and both were jailed for a year. In the same month a report was published by Amnesty International, criticising the authorities' persecution of homosexuals in the wake of the Queen Boat nightclub case. (*Cairo Times*)

On 24 December, a military court began trying alleged

1/1972: FROM THE FIRST INDEX INDEX

BRAZIL
The film *Zabriskie Point*, directed by **Michelangelo Antonioni**, has been banned on the grounds of 'insulting a friendly country'. The country in question, the USA, has not banned *Zabriskie Point*.

BULGARIA
Boris Krumov, editor-in-chief of the Sofia newspaper *Anteni*, was dismissed at the end of 1971 for publishing articles that were out of line with the foreign policy of the government.

CAMBODIA
Pre-censorship of the press was reintroduced in December 1971 after having been abolished. Press offenders will now be tried by military courts 'to stop the anarchy reigning in the press' and no new journals will be permitted.

CYPRUS
Bambis Avdellopoulos, a Greek journalist resident in Cyprus for the past 12 years and co-publisher of the Greek language bi-monthly *Kosmos Simera* was expelled.

CZECHOSLOVAKIA
Any person purchasing a typewriter in Czechoslovakia has to have his name and address and a sample of the type registered with the secret police (STB). The penalty for typing out clandestine journals or documents is 18 months to two years.

In January 1972, an unknown number of Czech citizens were arrested for printing and disseminating 'anti-state leaflets'. They are being charged under paragraphs of the Criminal Code dealing with 'subversion', 'hostility to the Socialist system', the 'mass distribution of anti-state material' and 'attempting to overthrow the government'. Those said to be included are: **Ludek Pachman**, the chess grand master, who was jailed for more than a year in 1969 and then released without trial; **Karel Kyncl**, former New York correspondent; **Milan Huebl**, an economist and sociologist at the Communist Party University in Prague; **Jaroslav Sabata**, a former party leader from Brno; **Dr Jan Tesar**, a historian; **Dr Ladislav Hejdanek**, a philosopher; **Dr Rudolf Battek**, a sociologist and former deputy to the Czech national council; one Evangelical minister, **Miroslav Dus**, and two members of his church council, **Dr Jirasek** and **Mr Novak**.

GREAT BRITAIN
An assistant director of the Welsh Arts Council, **Peter Jones**, was found guilty and fined £20 (US$30) in December 1971 for procuring through the post from Holland a magazine called *Suck*. The package apparently broke open in a sorting office, 'horrifying' staff there. Jones explained that he was organising a public exhibition on 'Sex and Society', for which quotes from *Suck* would be used, and that no one else would see the magazine. The magistrate said on passing sentence: 'This is the crudest filth I have ever seen,' and George Thomas, Labour's shadow Welsh affairs spokesman, said he would challenge the government on spending public money on 'pornographic literature'.

GREECE

The professor of classics at Yannina University, **Professor Theophanis Kakridis**, was suspended from his post for the last six months of 1971 after the newspaper *Vima* published his letter in July advocating an amnesty for political prisoners. His suspension was for 'publicly expressing opinions on a political question ... thereby behaving in a way incompatible with his status as a university teacher.'

A civil court in Athens refused in February to apply Law 509, which has been criticised by the International Federation for Human Rights for being drafted in such vague terms as to permit arbitrary abuse and excessive punishments for expression of opinion. The law, which allows sentences of up to the death penalty for 'seeking the application of ideas aiming at overthrowing by force the regime, or the prevailing social order, or for attempting to convert others to their application,' was first introduced 25 years ago during the civil war.

INDONESIA

TD Hafas, the editor-in-chief of the daily newspaper *Nusantara*, is to appeal against his sentence of one year's imprisonment passed in December 1971 for publishing articles that were said to have insulted President Suharto and members of the government.

LEBANON

Ghassan Kanatani, the editor-in-chief of *Al Hadaf,* was imprisoned in November 1971 for 'libelling King Feisal of Saudi Arabia'.

PORTUGAL

The secretary-general of the Portuguese Union of Journalists, **Antonio Dos Santos**, was arrested last August after his union had rejected some of the government's proposals for a new law on censorship to replace the old law of 45 years' standing, providing greater reliance on self-censorship. The union took particular exception to all journalists having to register with the government. The government rejected the union's alternative suggestions and in February Dos Santos was sentenced to 12 months' imprisonment and five years' loss of civil rights for 'activities endangering the security of the state'.

SOUTH AFRICA

At his trial on 29 November 1971, **Benjamin Pogrund**, night editor of the *Rand Daily Mail*, pleaded not guilty to charges of theft and possessing documents banned under the Suppression of Communism Act. Pogrund was working on a PhD thesis concerning the development of South African nationalism. Many of the confiscated documents are 20-year-old publications which have only recently been banned and which represent the bulk of his research material. Also produced as evidence were Pogrund's notes on the forbidden African National Congress which Pogrund claimed to have been part of his thesis work.

Donald Woods, the editor of the *East London Daily Despatch*, is to sue the head of South Africa's Bureau Of State Security (BOSS), General Hennie van den Bergh, for defamation because the latter has implied that within the English-language press 'enemies of public safety' have been organising criticism of the South African government.

more on p120

members of the proscribed **Muslim Brotherhood** on a range of charges, including possessing promotional publications about the group. Later, in the aftermath of the 20 February train disaster in which nearly 400 people were burned to death, it was reported that the government had barred the Muslim Brotherhood from offering its traditional humanitarian aid to disaster victims. (*Cairo Times/ Independent*)

Nile TV began trial broadcasts in Hebrew in January, the first Arab channel to do so, beaming two hours of news, politics, culture, documentaries and drama into Israeli homes via satellite. Officials say the channel will not shy away from controversy and may include Israeli guests on talk shows, which Nile TV does not normally allow. Israel's public Channel One and Three already show one to two hours of Arabic programmes daily for the country's large Arab-speaking community. (*Cairo Times*)

ETHIOPIA

On 25 January, **Zekarias Tesfaye**, publisher of the Amharic private weekly *Netsanet*, was arrested while having lunch with friends at a hotel. He was later released on bail of 5,000 birr (approx US$600). The journalist has been accused of 'defamation and publishing fabricated news' in his newspaper in relation to business tycoon and investor Sheikh Mohammed al-Amoudi. (EFJA)

On 21 February **Amare Aregawi**, editor-in-chief of the Amharic private weekly *The Reporter*, was fined 500

birr by the country's supreme court for contempt and reporting that 'jeopardised the credibility of the court among the public'. But minority opinion Justice Tegene Getaneh argued that though the reporting was inaccurate, he worried that the fine would handicap the development of 'the budding practice of court reporting'. He was outvoted four to one. (www.sudan.net)

Academic **Mesfin Wolde-Mariam**, 71, returned to Ethiopia in late January to voluntarily face charges of inciting students at the University of Addis Ababa to violence. The charges are widely regarded as a trumped-up response to his address to a seminar in May 2001 on human rights and academic freedom. The day after this discussion, students protested against the banning of their newspaper and the outlawing of student council meetings by the university administration. Police and soldiers reacted with a crackdown in which about 40 people were killed and thousands of students arrested. Professor Mesfin, former head of the Ethiopian Human Rights Council, was arrested by armed police officers along with a colleague, **Dr Berhanu Nega**, an economist who also addressed the seminar, and only released on bail after a month in prison. (NEAR)

FRANCE

A French judge investigating the activities of **François 'The Iguana' Santoni**, main opponent of the Corsican peace process, ordered phone taps on six journalists working

on the story, detaining some for questioning. Santoni was then killed by an unknown assassin. The case raises fears for the right of journalists to preserve the confidentiality of their sources when covering wars on terrorism. Three lawyers and six journalists were targeted at the request of Jean-Louis Bruguière, the magistrate leading anti-terrorist investigations. Another three lawyers were also targeted the same way. (Index on Censorship)

GUATEMALA

Guatemala's radio licensing body (SIT) has announced plans to reopen cash bidding for new radio broadcasting frequencies. The plan flies in the face of the efforts of Guatemalan civil society groups to have the law changed so that small community broadcasters and those serving indigenous populations can get on air. The World Association of Community Radio Broadcasters' (AMARC) Legal Programme in Latin America have expressed concern at the plan, confirmed on 24 January. It warns that the auction will hinder efforts to pass a new Community Media Law to democratise the media, as backed by the country's peace accords and international treaties. (AMARC)

A new law requiring practising professionals to be officially recognised by guild associations was passed on 30 November 2001 amid protests from media groups, including the **Guatemalan Association of Journalists (APG)**, which say the rule could be used to bar certain journalists from publishing, though the law is not targeted at the journalism profession specifically. A modified version of the professional-isation law was passed on 20 December. But APG president Victor Hugo de León points out that before approving the law the ruling National Republican Front (FRG) omitted a specific clause that would guarantee the constitutional rights of free speech and access to information. On 3 January, human rights attorney Julio Arango Escobar filed an offi-cial objection before the Constitutional Court. (Meso-America)

HAITI

On 3 December, a gang armed with stones and machetes killed **Brignol Lindor**, news editor at Radio Echo 2000, a private station in Petit-Goâve. Three days before, the town's deputy mayor Dumay Bony had named him and demanded 'zero tolerance' of opposition activities. The Association of Haitian Journalists (AJH) claimed members of the pro-government Domi Nan Bwa group admit murdering Lindor. The public prosecutor in Petit Goâve issued warrants for the arrest of nine members of the group, though none has been carried out. (RSF)

On 21 January, five local jour-nalists, including **Guyler Delva**, secretary-general of the AJH, were threatened by the pro-government Youth People's Power (JPP). It gave Delva 48 hours to withdraw an 18 January legal complaint against JPP leader René Civil, whom he accused of threat-ening him on the radio three

days before. Civil had accused him of being 'in the pay of foreigners'. Delva said that Civil's words on the air — 'Thank you Guyler Delva, thank you, thank you, Guyler Delva' — contained hidden threats in the Haitian Creole language. The AJH began negotiating with foreign embassies to aid journalists facing death threats to leave the country. (*Herald*, St Vincent)

HUNGARY

A target list of foreign jour-nalists in Budapest was printed in the pro-govern-ment daily *Magyar Nemzet* on 9 January, singling out jour-nalists from leading British, German, Austria, Dutch and French newspapers, for alleged 'negatively biased' reporting on Hungary. (RFE/RL)

British management from the Tesco International group have ordered its Hungarian outlets not to sell translated copies of *The International Jew*, an anti-semitic tract by the 20th-century industrialist Henry Ford. (RFE/RL)

On 19 February, the National Radio and Television Board (ORTT) took Pannon Radio to task after discovering that the Istvan Bocskai Founda-tion for an Open University, an organisation founded by Hungarian Justice and Life Party (MIEP) Chairman Istvan Csurka, had obtained a 26% stake in the radio station's operator, Gido Media Ltd, on August 2000. The media law bans political parties from obtaining direct influence in a broadcaster and under Gido Media's statutes, the Bocskai Foundation's 26% stake gives

it effective veto power. The ORTT had earlier ruled that Pannon Radio promoted hatred against Roma and homosexuals, anti-semitism and xenophobia. It violated the media law and the consti-tution and ignores its obliga-tion to provide balanced information. The report recommended a 2–3 million forint (US$8–12,000) fine. (RFE/RL, CJR)

INDIA

On 29 December, as tension between New Delhi and Islamabad deepened, the Pakistan Telecommunication Authority (PTA) ordered the country's cable TV operators to block transmission of Indian channels, 'in view of the one-sided, poisonous Indian propaganda by that country's channels aimed at tarnishing Pakistan's image'. During the 1999 stand-off in Kashmir, India pulled the plug on Pakistani TV programmes run by Indian cable operators, though this time there was no rush to repeat the trick. However, according to the BBC, the authorities in Indian-administered Kashmir did suspend long-distance national and international call facilities from public phone offices. (BBC)

Shankar Sharma, the director of First Global, accused the federal govern-ment on 27 November of using the income tax and stock exchange authorities to repeatedly harass him and his company for having a 14.5% stake in the investigative news website Tehelka.com — which embarrassed the government in March 2001 by breaking a story about army and govern-ment officials taking bribes to ensure arms contracts (*Index* 3/2001). The Enforcement Directorate, which took Sharma into custody on 17 December, argues that Sharma's involvement with Tehelka has nothing to do with its investigation into how First Global's dealings on the stock and foreign exchange markets may have precipitated a stock market crash on 2 March 2001. (*Frontline*)

On 29 December, the government in New Delhi banned a planned visit to Pakistan by a four-member peace mission headed by retired Navy admiral **Ram Das**. The private group, named Soldiers for Peace, was due to meet with Pakistan's leader General Pervez Musharraf. The Human Rights Commission of Pakistan said that the mission had been aimed at promoting peace between the two states. (AFP)

In its 4 January issue, the magazine *Frontline* reported that a five-member fact-finding committee set up by the Press Council of India (PCI) had substantiated allegations that media personnel were deliberately attacked by police at an opposition political rally in Chennai on 12 August 2001. According to the PCI report, the police were ordered to attack media personnel and destroy their equipment because the televised arrest of a Tamil Nadu opposition leader last July had embarrassed the state's government. (*Frontline*)

Award-winning novelist **Arundhati Roy** was jailed for a token one day on 6 March for suggesting that

the panel wanted to 'muzzle dissent' and opposition to the development of a giant dam over the objections of local farmers. 'I stand by what I said. I am prepared to suffer the consequences,' Roy said as she was taken away. 'The message is clear. Any citizen who dares to criticise the court does so at his or her peril.' Justice RP Sethi said in his ruling that freedom of speech did not grant anyone licence to scandalise the court or lower its dignity. Many of the protesters are Narmada Valley residents whose homes could be flooded when the dam is built. They displayed placards and banners with slogans such as 'Free speech is not contempt.' (*Frontline*, BBC)

On 27 February, a train full of mainly Hindu hardline members of the **Vishnu Hindu Parishad (VHP)** was set alight by Muslims in the town of Godra, in western Gujarat. The train had been travelling back from the northern town of Ayodhya, in Uttar Pradesh, where the VHP wants to revive the furore that surrounded the destruction of the Ayodhya Mosque by extremists in December. Scores of deaths followed in retaliatory assaults on innocent Muslims. In an ironic twist Home Minister LK Advan – who whipped Hindu cadres into a frenzy with his fiery rhetoric about Ayodhya ten years ago, and whose right-wing Hindu Bharatiya Janata Party subsequently rose to prominence on the back of the issue – had his ministry order the authorities in Uttar Pradesh to stop VHP activists from travelling to Ayodhya, and placed a ban on the movement of stone

pillars and other construction materials to the town. (*Hindu*, BBC News Online, *Frontline*)

On 26 February 11 **Shi'ite Muslims** were murdered at a Mosque in Rawalpindi by suspected cadres of the hard-line Sunni Muslim group Sipah-e-Sahaba. The military government of General Pervez Musharraf has blamed the attack on 'groups opposed to . . . [its] policy of fighting terrorism'. About 85% of Muslims in the country are Sunni, but there has been conflict between the two branches of Islam for many years. (*New York Times*)

Recent publication: 'India: Briefing on the Prevention of Terrorism Ordinance', AI, November 2001, 18pp.

INDONESIA

Indonesia's state minister for communications and information, Syamsul Muarif, raised the spectre of a return to press censorship on 28 December by suggesting that he was considering ways of reining in the press, which he described as being 'out of control'. The old ministry of information – armed with powers to suppress media rights under the Suharto regime – was disbanded by President Abdurrahman Wahid on taking office in October 1999. But his successor, President Megawati Soekarnoputri, is preparing to restore some of its powers and place them under Syamsul's direction. Syamsul said the government would soon submit bills regulating cyber-law and electronic transactions. His office was also drafting bills on access to information and broadcasting. (*Jakarta Post*)

Police ransacked the offices of the paper *Waspada* in Medan, North Sumatra, on 23 January, destroying equipment and injuring reporter **Setia Budi Siregar**. Local journalists said the incident started as riot police tried to disperse a gang brawl near their office. After mistaking the building's janitor for a gang member, the police broke into the paper's newsroom and attacked journalists for several minutes until the officers were persuaded that all present were *Waspada* staff. Deputy Police Chief Ishak Robinson Sampe apologised but refused to charge the involved officers. (SEAPA)

IRAN

A clampdown on the media that began in April 2000 was revived and intensified in November. On 10 November RSF reported that clergy court officials had that day arrested **Issa Khandan**, a social affairs editor on the dailies *Khordad* and *Fath*. His wife said she did not know the reason for his arrest. On 24 November, **Siamak Pourzand**, 70, a diabetic with a weak heart, also went missing in custody. Amnesty International linked his disappearance to his work as manager of Majmue-ye Farrhangi-ye Honari-ye Tehran, a leading cultural centre in Tehran. Known for his articles against the Islamic regime, he is married to human rights lawyer Mehrangiz Kar, now living in the US. The courts then closed the pro-reform *Mellat* newspaper on 30 November. According to official Iranian press agency IRNA, Judge Saeed Mortazavi said the order was designed to prevent

'offensive measures aimed at creating tension and insecurity in the climate of the country's press'. The reformist weekly *Asr-e-Ma* was shut down by the authorities on 15 December and its publisher**, Mohammad Salamati**, sentenced to 26 months' imprisonment. He was still free pending appeal at time of going to press. The same week **Gholam-Hossein Ataiee**, editor of *Neda-ye-hormozgan*, a reformist weekly in the southern province of Hormozgan, was given a five-year suspended jail sentence and fined 15 million rials (US$8,600). On 16 December the Iranian authorities released **Reza Alijani**, editor-in-chief of the suspended reformist monthly *Iran-e-Farda*, after he had spent nine months in prison. He was arrested in February, ten months after his magazine was banned, and accused of acting 'against state security'. He was awarded the 2001 Reporters Sans Frontières–Fondation de France Prize in November. But the most overt blow against the reformists was struck on 3 December with the appearance in court of **Mohsen Mirdamadi**, 42, director of the reformists' party organ *Nowrooz* and chairman of the national security and foreign affairs commission of parliament. The charges, also levelled against the newspaper, include 'propaganda against Iran's Islamic regime', 'supporting counter-revolutionaries and other opponents of the regime', 'offending religious beliefs' and 'spreading corrupted western culture'. (Index on Censorship)

Two cinema magazines were suspended on 24 and 27 Jan-

uary, in an apparent response to the prominence of Iranian film-makers – almost all sympathetic to liberal reform – at home and abroad. The two, *Gozarech-é-Film* and *Cinema Jahan* were accused of 'untrue reporting' and publishing 'obscene' photographs. Staff at *Gozarech-é-Film* were said to be 'counter-revolutionaries' and 'communists' and *Cinema Jahan* was 'disturbing public opinion and creating an atmosphere of tension and insecurity in the press sector'. (RSF)

Publications: Amnesty International, *Iran: A Legal System That Fails to Protect Freedom of Expression and Association*, December 2001

IRAQ

Iraqi security forces tightened already restricted access to the Internet. There are only a few Internet cafés in Baghdad and some of the larger provinces; the first was opened in 1999 in Baghdad. For the whole population of around 19 million people, there are just 200 computers with Internet access. The state-controlled Internetfirma, the only provider in Iraq, blocks access to sites and employees monitor computers linked to the Internet. Visiting sites with anti-Iraqi content which have escaped the censor is dangerous. Private access to the Internet is forbidden but universities offer courses on using it. However, in northern Iraq, in the provinces of Dohuk, Arbil and Suleymaniya, there is Internet access with no government control. (IMK, Iraq Press)

Iraqi authorities in Baghdad have instructed registry offices in the city of Kirkuk (South Kurdistan) not to permit the registration of Kurdish names to newborn babies. Registrars are pressuring Kurdish inhabitants to give their babies Arabic names by threatening not to have the children registered. If the parents still refuse, they are then forced to take first names such as Saddam or Uday (Saddam's son) as their official names. (IMK, Kurdistan Newsline)

The Kurdish literary figure, writer and journalist **Akram Ali** has died in Sweden, where he lived for nearly two decades. Akram, known as Akram-i Mam Ali in the Kurdish intellectual circle, lived in Suleymania, Iraq, where he started writing in the 1970s. He left in fear of prosecution by the Iraqi Baath regime. He was a columnist on the monthly Kurdish-language newspapers *Jini Niwe* and *Payam*. Both were published in London and are now out of circulation. (Kurdish-Media.com)

JORDAN

The chief editor of the weekly *al-Shahid*, **Hussein Emoush**, was detained overnight on 7 January in connection with a complaint from former president of the higher judiciary council Farouq Kilani claiming that *al-Shahid* misquoted a court ruling on a lawsuit subject to a counter-suit involving Kilani and another plaintiff. (Middle East News Online)

Fahd al-Rimawi, editor of the Amman weekly *al-Majd*, was arrested and detained for

15 days on 13 January, accused of publishing 'false information', an offence under Jordan's Penal Code. Several *al-Majd* articles had criticised the government of Prime Minister Ali Aboul Ragheb and one had quoted local sources who claimed, correctly, that the government would soon be replaced. (CPJ)

Recent publications: 'Jordan: Security Measures Violate Human Rights', AI, February 2002

KENYA

On 2 February it was reported that the government had rescinded a decision to increase duty on newsprint by up to 40% and was to reinstate the old rate of 25%. (*East African Standard*)

Hundreds of primary school children were sent home after Catholic Bishop John Njue ordered the closure of six church-sponsored primary schools in Mbeere in Nairobi in a dispute with the state educational authorities about the appointment of head teachers. (*East African Standard*)

On 1 February, the World Space Corporation and Capital FM signed a deal that will allow the station to broadcast digitally via satellite to Eastern, Central and Southern Africa. World Space Managing Director, Isaiah Okoth, claims the company has sold 30,000 digital receivers in Kenya alone and plans sales of up to 100,000 units by the end of the year. (*East African Standard*)

KUWAIT

Four Kuwaiti lawyers said they planned to sue the al-Jazeera satellite news channel for broadcasting a programme they say insulted Kuwait and its people on 5 February. The four lawyers claim that Egyptian researcher and writer **Sayed Nassar** made 'false and slanderous statements' about Kuwait during the show, which also featured Kuwaiti columnist **Nabil al-Fadhel**. Al-Jazeera, which cut short the live programme because it was so tense, reran an edited version of the show the next day. (Middle East News Online)

In January, **Dr Shafeeq Ghabra**, director of the Kuwaiti Information Office, Washington, DC, was recalled by his government to answer for his participation in a panel at the World Economic Forum summit held in the US this year, which featured a former Israeli foreign minister. He defended his participation as purely academic and not in the name of the Kuwaiti government. (Index on Censorship)

KYRGYZSTAN

Seventy demonstrators picketed a two-day international conference on terrorism jointly sponsored by the OSCE and the UN Office for Drug Control and Crime Prevention, opened in Bishkek on 13 December. The demonstrators called for the release of political prisoners, including former **Vice-President Feliks Kulov**. (RFE/RL)

The Kyrgyz government issued a decree on 14 January

stipulating that the interior and justice ministries make an inventory of publishing houses and publishing equipment and control the import of such equipment. US Ambassador John O'Keefe recommended that the decree be rescinded. However, the Kyrgyz authorities argued that the new measures would contribute to the fight against radical religious parties, such as **Hizb ut-Tahrir**, which spread unauthorised leaflets. (TOL)

ResPublica, one of the leading independent weeklies in Kyrgyzstan, is now available only online after the Uchkun state-owned printing house refused to print it following a decision by a Bishkek court in January. Uchkun applied a similar ban on the magazine *Moya Stolitsa-Novosti*. The same month the Interior Ministry was told to make an inventory of printing presses in Kyrgyzstan. Opponents of the move, which is aimed at preventing 'subversive activities by extremist religious centres', launched an appeal in February, fearing a clamp-down on the independent media outlets. (TOL, RFE/RL)

Poet **Asanbai Jusupbekov** appeared in court on 21 February charged with 'spreading false information', after visiting jailed parliamentarian **Azimbek Beknazarov**. The same day three Kyrgyz parliament deputies said they had written statements from persons who spoke to Beknazarov in detention confirming that he had been mistreated. (RFE/RL)

LATVIA

The Latvian National Radio and Television Council voted on 14 February to dismiss Rolands Tjarve as the director-general of Latvia's public Latvijas Televizija (LTV), for his approval of a trilateral agreement between LTV, Hansa Lizings and Media Bridge media agency, which LTV was to be a guarantor to a 354,000 lats (US$553,000) bank loan. The agreement was considered to be a direct violation of the law On Radio and Television, which bans the pledging or sale of LTV assets. (RFE/RL)

LEBANON

Lebanese police cited morality laws, legislation banning links with Israel and 'incitement to commit suicide' when justifying their 4 January raid on a Beirut branch of **Virgin Megastore**. They confiscated 600 DVD films including *The Great Escape*, *Rush Hour*, *Key Largo* and comedies such as *Some Like It Hot* and *The Nutty Professor*. The store manager was detained for two days. (Agencies)

Two Lebanese journalists appeared before a military court on 12 December, charged with having links with Israel, offences that may carry the death penalty. **Habib Yunes**, an editor at the Lebanon office of the London-based Arabic daily *al-Hayat*, and **Antoine Basil**, correspondent for MBC, were arrested in August during a sweep against opposition activists. Basil has also been accused of facilitating contacts between an Israeli official and **Tufiq Hindi**, political adviser

to the banned Christian anti-Syrian Lebanese Forces (LF) militia. Hindi was also arrested in August. (Middle East News Online)

Elie Hobeika, a prime witness in the Belgian war crimes case against Israeli Prime Minister Ariel Sharon, was assassinated on 24 January by a remote-controlled bomb. He had just told Lebanese TV that he was ready to go to Brussels to testify about the 1982 Sabra and Shatila massacre, where Hobeika's Christian militiamen slaughtered hundreds of unarmed refugees under the eyes of the occupying Israeli army, then headed by Sharon. The Belgian judges were expected to decide on 15 May whether they would seek to put Sharon on trial. (*Independent*, *Jerusalem Post*)

MOROCCO

On 21 November the Court of Appeal acquitted 36 human rights protesters who had been sentenced earlier in 2001 to three months' imprisonment for 'participating in the organisation of an unauthorised demonstration' on 9 December 2000. The rally in question called for an end to the impunity for perpetrators of human rights abuses in recent Moroccan history. (AI)

The interior minister banned a large-scale demonstration in support of the Palestinian people set for 20 January in Rabat. The various secular human rights groups responsible for the event unsuccessfully challenged the decision in court. (*El País*)

Moulay Hicham al-Alaoui, cousin of King Mohammed

VI and second in line to the throne, left for exile in the USA on 23 January. He criticised the secret services for attempts to discredit him, leading to the November announcement of a commission to investigate his alleged clandestine links with top army officials. Sometimes known as the 'Red Prince' for his outspoken support of democracy in Morocco, he denied attempting to destabilise the current regime and blamed those against change for undermining him. (*El País*)

MALAWI

On 10 December, Blantyre daily newspaper the *Chronicle* was barred from publication by its own printers. Editor-in-chief **Rob Jamieson** said the printers wanted him to remove an article investigating local reggae star Evison Matafale's death in police custody. 'They said that they could only print for us if we removed the offending article and put new, acceptable articles in their place,' Jamieson said. He refused and the paper did not appear. (MISA)

MALAYSIA

The Malaysian government on 16 January rejected allegations of a 'plot' to discredit journalists on the Kuala Lumpur English-language daily, the *Sun*, to justify censorship. Media rights groups allege that the journalists were given bogus information about a supposed plot to assassinate the Malaysian prime minister, Mahathir Mohamed. The publication of the story and its quick discrediting resulted in the dismissal of 40 members of staff and the appointment of special editorial advisers to vet all sensitive stories before publication. (BBC Online)

The Malaysian Minister of Home Affairs **Abdullah Haji Ahmad Badawi** has been criticised for his actions to rein in the country's daily *Sun* newspaper, which had published an article about an alleged plot to assassinate him and the prime minister. Under his pressure, the *Sun* retracted the story and suspended four staff members. Andrew Puddephatt, executive director of Article 19, commented that this kind of direct government interference 'exerts an unacceptable chilling effect on freedom of expression' in Malaysia. (A19)

MALDIVES

On 5 December, **Mohamed Nasheed**, politician, writer and historian, began a sentence of two and a half years' exile on the island of Angol-hitheemu in Raa atoll. He was found guilty on 8 November of the theft of unspecified government property from the home of ex-president Ibrahim Nasir. Local observers and Amnesty International believe that Nasheed has been exiled for his support of the introduction of a political party system, and for his attempts to make government ministers accountable to the country's parliament (Majlis). (AI, Maldivesculture.com)

According to Maldivesculture.com, the National Security Service (NSS) has launched a crackdown against **Sandhannu**, an underground anti-government Dhivehi-language publication distributed by email. On 9 December, cartoonist **Naushad Waheed** and two unnamed students were arrested by the NSS for alleged connections to Sandhannu. These arrests were followed by the detention of brothers **Mohamed and Ismail Zaki**, and **Ibrahim Luthfee** on 31 January. Amnesty International issued an urgent action about the safety of the six detainees in early February. (AI, Maldivesculture.com)

MEXICO

Fernández García, editor of the weekly *Nueva Opción*, based in Tamaulipas in north-east Mexico, was shot dead on 18 January in the city of Miguel Alemán. According to Reporters Sans Frontières, he had recently published an article on alleged relations between the former mayor of Miguel Alemán, Raúl Rodríguez Barrera, and drug traffickers. A few days before his death, García had accused the former mayor of wanting to kill him. The unknown killer was able to kill him despite the presence of two bodyguards. Ironically he had worked for a daily newspaper owned by Barrera before joining *Nueva Opción*. (RSF)

Journalist **Francisco Castellanos**, correspondent for the weekly magazine *Proceso* and contributor to the daily newspaper *El Mañana* in north-east Mexico, was threatened by Gabriel Herrera Trujillo, a municipal police chief in the western Mexican state of Michoacán. On 4 November, *El Mañana* published an article by Castellanos alleging that a former state prosecutor and a number of members of the Michoacán state police were involved in cases of embezzlement and racket-eering. (RSF)

There are still no clues as to the identity of the killer of **Morales Ferrón**, found with his throat cut on 1 February. The body was found in the offices of the Mexican Radio and Television Association (AMRT), of which he was president. The 79-year-old journalist wrote for the daily *El Sol de Medio Día* under the pen-name Severo Mirón (Tough Onlooker). Police reported signs of a struggle but the motive remains unclear. (RSF)

Mexican army general **José Francísco Gallardo Rod-ríguez** was unexpectedly freed on 7 February, two weeks before his case was to go before the Inter-American Court of Human Rights. Gallardo was arrested in October 1993, one week after his master's thesis entitled 'The Need for a Military Ombudsman in Mexico' was excerpted in the Mexican magazine *Forum*. In 1996, the Inter-American Commission on Human Rights (IACHR) said he was being imprisoned 'without reason and legal justification'. (International PEN)

NEPAL

In January, the *Kathmandu Post* said that more than 54 jour-nalists had been arrested since the government imposed a state of emergency in November and that many of them had been tortured while in custody. Among the arrested were **Bandhu Thapa**, publisher of the weekly *Deshantar*, and **Gopal Budhathoki**, editor and publisher of the weekly *Saanghu*, held for a day on

17 December in Kathmandu, and BBC stringer **Sharad KC**, detained for a day on 5 January in western Nepal. On 29 January, **Kishore Shrestha**, the editor and publisher of the left-wing weekly *Jana Astha*, was arrested at his offices by police. The Federation of Nepalese Journalists de-manded that journalists still in detention should be released immediately. (BBC News Online, the *Kathmandu Post*, CEHURDES)

NICARAGUA

Pablo A Cuadra, a well-known and respected poet, writer, intellectual and jour-nalist, died in his home on 3 January from respiratory illness. Born in Managua in 1912, Cuadra, often known by the initials PAC, was the co-director of the Nicaraguan daily newspaper *La Prensa* until 1987 and was instrumental in the fight for press freedom. As a press activist and a vocal member of the Sandinasta opposition his activities ultimately cost him a short term in jail. The day following his passing the government declared three days of national mourning during which flags were flown at half-mast. (Meso-America)

NORTHERN IRELAND

The US has named five para-military groups in Northern Ireland as illegal organisations – the **Continuity IRA**, **Loyalist Volunteer Force**, **Orange Volunteers**, **Red Hand Defenders** and the **Ulster Defence Associa-tion**. The five had been put on a European Union list of suspected terrorists published

after Christmas. Inclusion in the US treasury department list empowers US agencies to seize assets, investigate activi-ties and prevent fund-raising. (*Guardian*)

PAKISTAN

General Pervez Musharraf took a rare and politically risky stand against influential nationalist and Islamist right-wing activists, ordering the arrest of more than 600 people in 13 January raids on five banned militant groups. Pakistani officials also im-posed a 30-day ban on the daily *Dopehar*, after it pub-lished a news item headlined 'Differences in Federal Cab-inet' on 2 January. APNS secretary-general Kazi Asad Abid said that if the news item was not correct the authori-ties had the right to contradict it. (APNS)

Daniel Pearl, South Asia bureau chief for the *Wall Street Journal*, was kidnapped in Pakistan on 23 January while researching links between Pakistani extremists and Richard C Reid, who was arrested in December on a Paris–Miami flight he allegedly boarded with ex-plosives in his sneakers. A videotape received on 22 February showed Pearl dead. His body has not been found. The chief suspect in the case, British-born Islamic militant Ahmed Omar Saeed Sheikh, admitted in a 14 Feb-ruary court hearing his role in the kidnapping, but his state-ment is not admissible be-cause it was not made under oath. The Bush administration has sought to extradite Saeed, reportedly on a warrant for the 1994 kidnapping of an American in India who was freed unharmed. But Pakistan says it will try him in its courts before considering sending him to face charges in the United States. The government's case against Saeed appears based primarily on the statement of accomplice Fahad Naseem, who says Saeed told him of plans to kidnap someone who was 'anti-Islam and a Jew'. Police are looking for several other suspects in the case, including one Amjad Hussain Faruqi, the man police believe actually abducted and held Pearl. (RSF, AP, CPJ)

Amid the rising tension between New Delhi and Islamabad that followed the 13 December suicide attack on the Indian parliament, police in the border town of Wagah broke up a peaceful anti-war demonstration on New Year's Eve by baton-charging the 500-strong crowd. Eight of the demonstrators were injured in the attack. (AFP)

On 1 February, General Pervez Musharraf responded to diplomatic pressure from Washington to crack down on Islamic extremists by issuing a special order that allowed his military regime to establish special anti-terrorism courts headed by a High Court or Sessions Court judge, a magistrate and a high-ranking military officer. Under the new law all terrorism cases will be transferred to these new courts, people who aid and abet terrorists could face the death penalty. Anyone convicted will have a right to appeal. The anti-terrorism courts will function until 30 November this year, but can be extended. (BBC News Online)

PALESTINE

On 13 December, Israeli helicopters heavily bombed the **Voice of Palestine** (VOP) broadcasting centre in Ramallah run by the **Palestine Broadcasting Corporation** (PBC). The following morning, bulldozers moved in and ploughed the remains into the ground. Israeli army sappers then blew up the antenna used to transmit programmes across the West Bank. On 19 January, Israeli forces destroyed a second PBC building in Ramallah, which housed administrative offices and the broadcasting facilities for the VOP, as well as studios for the official Palestine TV. The occupying forces confiscated equipment and later detonated explosives, setting the building on fire and causing half of it to collapse. The Israeli military termed the action a response to the killing in Hadera of six Israelis, claiming that Palestine TV and radio incites violence against Israelis, a charge the PBC strongly denies. The PBC was set up in 1994 following the signing of the Oslo peace accords giving the Palestinians limited authority. (AFP, CPJ)

Israeli-Arab Knesset member **Azmi Bishara** remained charged under Israeli anti-terrorism laws, over a speech he gave in Syria praising the resistance against the Israeli occupation of southern Lebanon. He is also charged under a 1948 ordinance on foreign travel, in connection with his work co-ordinating humanitarian visits to Syria for hundreds of Israeli Palestinians, mostly elderly, who had been separated from their families since Israel seized the

Syrian Golan Heights in 1967. In an unprecedented move, the Knesset voted to lift his parliamentary immunity on 7 November to allow his prosecution. (Adalah)

On 2 January, **Dr Mustafa Barghouti**, director of the Union of Palestinian Medical Relief Committees, was arrested after giving a press conference on the disastrous impact which Israeli security closures were having on medical care in the Occupied Territories. The conference included members of the European Parliament and delegates from the US and Europe. Israeli authorities claimed Barghouti did not have permission to enter Jerusalem, his birthplace. After his release he was greeted by a group of journalists, and in a scuffle with police, he was re-arrested. He suffered a fractured kneecap and various lacerations and bruises on his face and body. Several others were injured including Italian MEP **Luisa Morgantini**. Several hours later Barghouti was released again. (AI, LAW)

At least two other human rights defenders remain under administrative detention orders which allow indefinite detention without charge or trial. These include **Abed al-Rahman al-Ahmar**, a field-worker for the Palestinian Human Rights Monitoring Group, who was arrested in Jerusalem in May 2001 because he had no pass, and **Daoud al-Dar'awi**, a staff member of the Palestinian Independent Commission for Citizens' Rights, arrested in September 2001, who was placed under administrative detention in October immediately after a judge ordered his release on bail. (AI, LAW)

On 4 January, the Palestinian Authority closed down the offices of the *Hebron Times*, an independent weekly newspaper published in Hebron in the occupied West Bank. The paper's editor, **Walid Amayreh**, said more than 30 Palestinian security operatives arrived at the paper's offices with an order to close the publication. The week before the editors were summoned to the Hebron Governor's office where they were told to tone down the paper's criticisms of US policy. The PA recently closed more than 40 charities, offices and youth clubs which Israeli intelligence and the CIA claimed were associated with Hamas. (*Middle East Realities*)

On 18 January, Israeli occupation forces opened fire on Palestinian demonstrators in Ramallah and injured LAW researcher **Thoraya Alayan**, who was hit on her chin by a rubber bullet. Four other Palestinians and a Spanish journalist were also injured. On 3 November, Alayan and another LAW field researcher, **Hosam Rajab**, were hit by rubber-coated metal bullets while monitoring a demonstration in Ramallah. On 11 December, she was shot at while filming a Palestinian vehicle that had been stoned by Jewish settlers near Ramallah and her tapes were confiscated. (LAW)

In February, the Israeli authorities extended the closure of Orient House, the headquarters of the Palestine Liberation Organisation in East Jerusalem, for another six months. The Israelis shut the building in August and confiscated the PLO's archives. (*New York Times*)

PHILIPPINES

The Committee to Protect Journalists (CPJ) expressed concern about reported threats to journalists from the Abu Sayyaf, an armed group active in the southern Philippines that US and Filipino officials have linked to the al-Qaeda network. More than 600 American troops had recently arrived on the southern island of Basilan to help the Philippine army in its efforts to crush the Abu Sayyaf, which claims to be fighting for a separate Islamic state. On 9 February, Captain Harold Cabunoc, who commands Philippine Scout Ranger troops operating on Basilan, warned all foreign journalists about the risk of kidnapping by the Abu Sayyaf and advised them against travelling to the island alone. (CPJ)

POLAND

Warsaw prosecutors charged Self-Defence Party leader **Andrzej Lepper** on seven counts of slander on 19 February. On a local radio station in November 2001, Lepper called Foreign Minister Wlodzimierz Cimoszewicz a scoundrel and Cimoszewicz's father a criminal who killed Poles. Addressing the parliament in December, Lepper accused five prominent politicians of taking bribes and having contacts with the mafia. Because of these pronouncements, Lepper was stripped of the post of deputy speaker and of his parliamentary immunity. Lepper pleaded not guilty and said the charges were unfounded. No trial date has been set. (RFE/RL)

RUSSIA

A **website run by Russian monks** was briefly shut down in January because of their over-zealous spamming. The monks of the St Trinity and St Nicholas monastery in Shmakovka sent emails asking for donations to thousands of inboxes. The monks said they were new to the Web and didn't realise they were doing anything wrong. (RFE/RL)

Russia's highest court of appeal upheld the liquidation of the Moscow Independent Broadcasting Company (MNVK) in mid-January, dooming Russia's last surviving independent nationwide television channel, TV-6. It followed a suit brought by the pension fund of state-run oil conglomerate LUKoil-Garant, a minority shareholder in TV-6. The objective of the suit, say TV-6 staff, was to silence the last station owned by industrial magnate **Boris Berezovskii**, a bitter opponent of President Vladimir Putin and indirect owner of 75% of the station. An unprecedented political alliance — Communist Party leader Gennadii Zyuganov, Yabloko leader Grigorii Yavlinskii, and Union of Rightist Forces head Boris Nemtsov — later signed a joint declaration in defence of the embattled station. They said the disappearance of TV-6 would give the government an effective monopoly over television programming and neuter public discussion of the authorities' actions and the struggle against corruption. (CPJ, Radio Echo Moscow)

After months of court dispute and international protest, a military court in Vladivostok *continued from p109*

1/1972: FROM THE FIRST INDEX INDEX

SOUTH VIETNAM

In October 1971, the government suspended the news agency **Tin Mien Nam** for publishing an article entitled 'The government has taken measures to encourage people to vote on 3 October'. On 19 October, police seized editions of 14 out of Saigon's 43 Vietnamese-language newspapers, accusing them of publishing articles 'likely to sow confusion among the masses and harm national security'. In February 1971 the news agency **Tin Viet** was closed down indefinitely.

SOVIET UNION

Vladimir Bukovsky, a publicist and former secretary to the writer Vladimir Maximov, was sentenced to two years in prison, five years in a labour camp and five years of exile on 5 January on charges of 'anti-Soviet agitation and propaganda'. He is thought to have been sentenced for giving interviews to foreign correspondents about the imprisonment of dissenters in mental hospitals and for sending materials on this subject abroad together with an appeal to foreign psychiatrists to study this practice. Bukovsky had earlier served 15 months in prison for distributing copies of *The New Class* by Milovan Djilas, and endured mental hospital and labour camps for defending *The White Book*.

Annasoltan Kekilova, a young Turk-menian poet, was confined to a psychiatric hospital last September after protesting to the Communist Party about conditions in the Turkmenian Soviet Republic. After her complaints, she was dismissed from her job, her books were withdrawn from sale and her poems ceased to be read on the radio.

SPAIN

On 2 December 1971, the novelist and film critic **Luciano Rincon** was to have been tried *in camera* for 'insulting the head of state'. Rincon was arrested the previous May after the appearance of an article in Paris about the succession to General Franco. The article was published in the Spanish-language journal, *Cuardernos de Ruedo Iberico*, under the pseudonym Luis Ramirez, and as a regular contributor Rincon was suspected of being the author. A group of Spanish writers living in Paris subsequently swore an oath that it was they, not Rincon, who had used this pseudonym and that Rincon's contributions invariably appeared under his own name. Nevertheless, the trial was rearranged for 29 February 1972 when he was sentenced to five years' imprisonment.

Over **300 Spanish intellectuals** sent a letter to the Ministry of Information last November protesting over the ban on a lecture to commemorate Picasso's 90th birthday, and demanding the release of the art critic **Jose Maria Moreno Galvan**, arrested with two others after giving an impromptu speech to students in the Madrid University cafeteria. He was not released from prison to attend his own trial, at which the public prosecutor demanded two-year sentences for Galvan and the two students. The latter described the ban and the arrest as 'an insult to freedom of expression and a violation of basic human rights'.

The February issue of the magazine *Mundo Social*, published by the Company of Jesus, was seized by order of the Ministry of

Information and Tourism before it had been distributed. The company announced that two articles were the cause of the seizure: 'We Go to Europe or We Stay at Home' by **Dr Emilio Manrique** and 'Extended Disorder in the University' by **Fr Fernando Prieto**, SJ. The February number of the magazine, 'Discusion y Convivencia', was also seized, but it is not known which articles were responsible.

SWITZERLAND

The publisher of a satirical magazine, *La Pilule*, was fined S. Fr. 500 in January for printing an article insulting a 'head of state', namely the Shah of Persia.

TAIWAN

Quintin Yuyitung and his brother **Rizel**, publisher and editor of Manila's *Chinese Commercial News*, have been sentenced in Taiwan respectively to two and three years' 'reformatory education' for allegedly spreading Chinese communist propaganda in the Philippines. Although the brothers are not citizens of nor had ever visited Taiwan, they were forcibly deported from the Philippines and the Nationalist Chinese government has insisted on its right to try them.

TURKEY

Yasar Kemal, the well-known novelist, was recently released from jail after having been sentenced in July 1971 for translating *Introduction to Marxism* by Emile Burns into Turkish.

USA

Angela Davis, formerly assistant professor of philosophy at the University of California, Los Angeles, has been released on $100,000 bail while the jury is selected for her trial of murder, conspiracy and kidnapping. Miss Davis was dismissed from the university by Governor Reagan and the university regents in June 1970 for 'extramural activities' incompatible with her profession as a teacher. An earlier attempt to dismiss her for being a Communist Party member in 1969 failed. Miss Davis contends she is being tried for her political beliefs.

New charges of stealing government documents were preferred in December against **Dr Daniel Ellsberg**, who in June 1971 was accused of having unauthorised possession of papers (the 'Pentagon Paper') which he gave to the press for publication. The new charges are more serious and carry a maximum penalty of 115 years' imprisonment.

A recent report from the American Civil Liberties Union stated that 'attacks on the press by government officers have become so widespread and all-pervasive that they constitute a massive federal attempt to subvert the letter and the spirit of the First Amendment'.

WEST GERMANY

Professor Ernest Mendel, a Marxist economist from Belgium, was deported from Frankfurt airport in March a short while after arriving there on his way to a lecture in Berlin. Professor Mendel had earlier been offered a post at the Free University of West Berlin, but this was rejected by the West Berlin Senate. He was then invited to address a student conference in West Berlin and it was while on his way there that he was banned from entry to West Germany and deported. ❏

*Compiled by **Robin Tudge***

found journalist **Grigory Pasko** guilty of treason and sentenced him to four years' imprisonment on 25 December. The 20 months he has so far spent in custody cut the overall term to two years and four months. Pasko, an investigative reporter with *Boyevaia Vakhta* (Battle Watch), an in-house newspaper published by the Russian Navy's Pacific Fleet, was well known for his work on exposing the environmental dangers posed by the fleet's under-maintained nuclear-powered vessels. He was arrested in October 1997 and charged with passing classified documents to Japanese journalists. The allegedly 'secret' papers included agricultural ministry papers on Korean farm labourers and the court eventuallyconcluded that the only 'secret' papers on his possession were some handwritten notes Pasko took at a meeting of the Military Council of the Pacific Fleet, which he had routinely covered as a reporter for *Boyevaia Vakhta*. In the end the court ruled that Pasko intended to pass secret documents to Japanese journalists, even if he could not be proven to have actually done so, and was thus still guilty of treason. Pasko's attorneys have already appealed the verdict to the Russian Supreme Court in hope and expectation that it will again reverse the verdict but he must stay in jail until the appeal is heard, in up to a year's time. (*Dos'e na tsenzuru*, Index on Censorship)

Skinheads in St Petersburg went on a rampage on Prospekt Kultury, beating up passers-by and smashing shop windows and advertising billboards on 17 February. On the same day in Moscow, a

tenth-grade Azerbaijani student was beaten up by skinheads. (RFE/RL)

A draft law on cable TV services poses a danger for the independent mass media, Alexei Samohvalov of the Council of Europe said on 10 December. The draft was prepared by the Liberal Democratic Party and by former TV news reader Alexander Burataeva, leader of the youth wing of the pro-presidential Yedinstvo Party. The 12th article of the draft states that there should be no more than three cable channels in one broadcasting territory. (Glasnost Media)

The *Novye Izvestia* newspaper reported on 8 February that Russia's Interior Ministry was looking at controls on Internet users, including a requirement to apply for a police licence before buying a modem or an internet link. The ministry denied the reports. (Glasnost Media)

In an interview with Ekho Moskvy radio on 13 February, Russian journalist **Anna Politkovskaia** accused government officials of a smear campaign following her latest trip to Chechnya to investigate human rights abuses and the killing of civilians. One reported special forces attack on a village in Shatoi Raion killed six civilians and orphaned 28 children. But Ilya Shabalkin, a public relations man with the Federal Security Service (FSB), said Politkovskaia's trips aroused 'unhealthy sensationalism'. He said that her paper, *Novaia gazeta*, had been paid US$55,000 by the Soros Fund for the reports and that she was a self-publicist. Sergei

Sokolov, *Novaia gazeta* deputy editor-in-chief, said that she had been clearly threatened by members of federal and special forces units in Chechnya and Moscow and had been forced to leave the country for a while. Soros officials said on 21 February that Politkovskaia's work had nothing to do with its grant to the paper. *Novaia gazeta* says it will sue the FSB for libel. (RFE/RL, *Guardian*)

In Chechnya, 3,000 people from Tsotsan Yurt took to the streets on 13 February to protest the bombardment of their village, blocking roads with the corpses of family members killed in the raids the night before. District administrators, local prosecutors and even local TV crews avoided meetings with the protestors, who said they could not guarantee their safety. Local residents, mostly women, climbed on to army vehicles and attacked soldiers. However, the protesters later described the action, not as a rally, but as *mekhtezet* (mourning). According to witnesses, the protestors disassociated themselves from Chechen separatists. (Glasnost Media)

RWANDA

Human Rights Watch called on the Rwandan authorities in February to make public its charges against two detained Catholic Church figures or release them. The two, **Laurien Ntezimana**, who worked for reconciliation between Hutu and Tutsi before and after the 1994 genocide, and **Didace Muremangingo**, a young survivor of the genocide, published a local journal called *Ubuntu*.

Ubuntu has used the term *ubuyanja*, meaning rebirth of strength or energy, in some of its articles, but the word is also used by a banned political party founded by former Rwandan president Pasteur Bizimungu in June 2001. (HRW)

SAUDI ARABIA

The US State Department's latest annual report on International Religious Freedom states that Saudi Arabia is 'an Islamic monarchy without legal protection for freedom of religion, and such protection does not exist in practice'. (US State Department)

On 12 January, it was reported that identity cards are being issued for women for the first time. The cards include a picture of the cardholder's uncovered face. (*The Times*)

SERBIA

The Synod of the Serbian Orthodox Church condemned anti-semitic remarks made by a retired Orthodox priest in a New Year's broadcast, AP and Yugoslav agencies reported on 5 February. The remarks by **Zarko Gavrilovic**, in which he said Jews are 'born defective because of incest', drew protests from Israel and Yugoslav Foreign Minister Goran Svilanovic. In a statement, the church said it 'rejects and condemns [anti-semitic remarks and actions] resolutely' and also denounced the 'language of hatred' heard recently in Yugoslavia. (RFE/RL)

Belgrade's independent Radio B92 reported in early January that its signals to listeners in the capital were being interrupted by a reportedly unlicensed radio station called Radio Perper. Station chief **Veran Matic** filed a complaint with the Federal Ministry of Traffic and Telecommunications that he was threatened by people claiming to be from the new station. Matic says the situation underlines the need to pass legislation to regulate the present chaotic situation caused by the lack of a proper broadcast licensing law. (ANEM)

SINGAPORE

On 15 January, Foo Shyang Piau, Singapore's UN delegate, praised the US Administration's widely reported call to US networks and newspapers to restrict coverage of remarks by Osama bin Laden. 'This was healthy guided censorship, Singapore too has worked out its own formula,' Piau said. (WiPC)

SLOVAKIA

Article 19 has congratulated Slovak MP **Frantisek Sebej** and colleagues for taking Slovakia's criminal libel provisions to the country's Constitutional Court. The step resulted in February in the temporary suspension of the provisions pending a final ruling that may strike them out. Articles 102, 103, 154(2) and 206 of the code restrict free speech, says Article 19, by imposing jail sentences for gross insult or defamation of state bodies or officals. The group says that in the interest of public debate and government accountability, public bodies of all kinds should be prohibited from bringing defamation actions. (Article 19)

SRI LANKA

TamilNet reported on 17 December that the ban on presenting the Governor's Award to **P Manickavasagam**, president of the Sri Lanka Tamil Media Alliance, and **A Nadesan**, Batticaloa correspondent for the Tamil daily *Virakesari*, at the annual Northeast Provincial Tamil Literary Festival, had been lifted. The governor had suspended the festival last September, and removed the names of the two journalists from the awards list, after the Eelam People's Democratic Party had accused the men of writing anti-government articles. (TamilNet)

Dharmaratnam Sivaram, the editor of the TamilNet website, and **M Wijetharan**, correspondent for the independent Tamil daily *Thinakathir*, were attacked on 26 December by five men armed with clubs and knives in the offices of *Thinakathir* in the eastern town of Batticaloa. Both men suffered minor injuries in the attack and the paper's offices were ransacked. Three men, one of whom is allegedly a member of the government's Counter Subversive Unit, were subsequently arrested by police. Sivaram was accused in the state media last June (*Index 4/2001*) of being a spy for the Liberation Tigers of Tamil Eelam. (*The Times of India, Lanka Academic, The Hindu*, RSF)

Ninety-seven thousand copies of the 6 January edition of the state-run **Sunday Observer** newspaper were destroyed by the government after the paper published an article that questioned the authenticity of the Buddha's tooth relic housed in a temple in Kandy. Kumar Abeysinghe, acting chairman of the state's publishing arm and secretary of the Ministry of Mass Communications, launched an inquiry, allegedly to find out whether the article had deliberately aimed to discredit Prime Minister Ranil Wickremasinghe's new government and raise religious tensions in the country. (Gulf News Online)

Shantha Premaratne, former deputy minister of tourism and aviation under the People's Alliance regime, surrendered to the Anuradhapura Magistrates' Court on 17 January in connection with threatening a Buddhist monk during the campaign for the 5 December parliamentary elections. John Amaratunga, minister of the interior, had earlier ordered Premaratne arrested after the complainant had accused the police of inaction in the case. (Gulf News Online)

On 22 January the government announced plans to abolish the law of criminal defamation, set up an independent press complaints commission, and introduce a freedom of information act, as part of a series of media reforms. Both the repeal of the law of criminal defamation and a new freedom of information act are already in draft form and will likely be presented to parliament this year, after press and civil society groups have studied them. According to Prime Minister Wickremasinghe, the other reforms will take longer to implement because the government is currently cash-strapped. (Gulf News Online)

Two air force officers were sent to prison on 7 February for an attack on **Iqbal Athas**, defence correspondent for the *Sunday Times*, in February 1998 (*Index* 2/1998, 5/1998, 2/2001). The High Court in Colombo sentenced each man to nine years' hard labour and fined them 10,000 rupees each (US$107.50) for invading Athas' home, holding a gun to his head, and scaring his daughter in connection with a critical series of articles about the air force. (BBC News Online, Reuters)

Frederica Janz, a *Sunday Leader* staff writer, alleged on 15 February that she had received a death threat in the post for causing 'irreparable damage to the special unit of the army'. Janz has embarrassed high-ranking people connected with the military in a recent series of articles. (Lanka Academic)

Recent publications: *Sri Lanka: The Arrogance of Power – Myths, Decadence and Murder* by Rajan Hoole (University Teachers for Human Rights [Jaffna], July 2001, 504pp); *Norway and the Peace Process in Sri Lanka* by Allan Bullion (Civil Wars, Vol. 4, No. 3, Autumn 2001, pp70–92); *The Will to Freedom: An Inside View of Tamil Resistance* by Adele Balasingham (Fairfax Publishing, 2001, 380pp); *Sri Lanka: Human Rights and Return of Refugees by the Sri Lanka Project* (British Refugee Council, December 2001); 'Sri Lanka: Rape in custody' (AI, January 2002, 16pp).

SUDAN

In November, Sudanese authorities detained 30 journalists and other employees of an independent daily after the individuals marched to the Information Ministry to protest the censoring of a story on corruption. Thirty journalists from the daily *al-Watan* were arrested and loaded on to three trucks after they delivered a protest note to an official at the ministry. There was no word on the arrests from the government, which has been increasingly annoyed with criticism in the local media. Sudanese law punishes the publication of unsubstantiated accusations of corruption by fines and jail terms. (IFEX)

Editor **Nhial Bol** of the English-language daily *Khartoum Monitor* was fined 5 million Sudan pounds (approx US$1,950) and the paper an extra 15 million (US$5,800) on 16 January over an article linking the state to the slave trade in the country. In the article, Bol wrote that 'slavery is practised because the government facilitates it by allowing Arab raiders to use government-owned trains for ferrying the abducted people'. Bol was briefly jailed when he could not pay the fine, but was loaned the money by a local businessman. The *Khartoum Monitor* faces four different trials on public security law charges. It is feared that, if money cannot be found both to cover the fines and to pay legal defence fees, the newspaper will go out of business. (Sudan Online)

SYRIA

On 21 January, the satirical weekly *Addomari* suspended publication after the government demanded that it handle the distribution of the magazine, presently handled privately. Though known for its cautious criticism of the government, the state's main interest appeared to be profit. State distributors want 40% of the newspaper's earnings from sales and to distribute fewer copies. Fearful of bankruptcy, owner **Ali Farzat** suspended publication. Farzat says the publications law does not require private newspapers to be distributed through the state company.

THAILAND

The 10 January issue of the Hong Kong-based *Far Eastern Economic Review* was banned from sale in Thailand on the orders of Major-General Treethos Ronlitthi-wichai, chief of a police department that oversees press affairs. The issue, which had already been on sale in Thailand since 3 January, was banned under the 1941 Publishing Act, which allows authorities to censor statements or articles that 'might lead to social and national disorder'. The order related to a one-paragraph item citing based on a 5 December 2001 speech by King Bhumibol Adulyadej which reportedly included criticism of Thaksin Shinawatra's performance as prime minister. (CPJ)

TUNISIA

Tunisia's Judiciary Disciplinary Council suspended **Judge Mokhtar al-Yeh-yawy** on 29 December on charges of breaches of professional duty and undermining the reputation of the judiciary, reported the Cairo-based Arab Programme For Human Rights Activists. The decision of the council,

convened by the Tunisian Constitutional Court, upheld a 14 July 2001 order by the government suspending him from the courts after he published an open letter on 6 July urging the government to respect the courts' constitutional right to independence. Al-Yehyawy said that Tunisian judges were being forced to deliver verdicts to suit the wishes of government. He was temporarily returned to office in August after widespread objections by Arab and international NGOs. The suspension coincided with the launch in Tunisia of an association campaigning for the independence of the judiciary and the bar, in which al-Yeh-yawy was due to play a key role, added Amnesty International. (Amnesty)

On 2 February, four members of the Tunisian Workers' Communist Party (PCOT) were arrested and imprisoned. Three of the men, **Hamma Hammami**, **Abdeljabbar Madouri** and **Samir Taa-mallah** had been in hiding for four years. Neither the defendants nor their lawyers were allowed to address the court, and the police interrupted proceedings, taking the defendants away for several hours without explanation. Madouri failed to return with the others and then had his sentence increased by two years to over 11 years in jail. A foreign journalist was assaulted by police and had his camera destroyed. (AI)

TURKEY

The Higher Education Council (YÖK) is to punish students who campaign to add Kurdish subjects to

university courses for 'separatist activities'. Penalties will range from a disciplinary hearing to expulsion. According to the Turkish daily *Radikal*, 10,608 students have already applied to their college authorities to enquire after possible Kurdish-language courses as an optional subject. Of these, 6,425 were flatly refused and 4,233 had their requests officially recorded by the universities concerned. (*Cumhuriyet*, *Radikal*, IHD-Istanbul)

The Turkish newspaper *Milliyet* reports that the provincial governor of Bolu, **Mehmet Ali Turker**, attending a reception to celebrate the 75th Anniversary of the Turkish Republic, refused to cut a cake shaped to represent Turkey saying: 'That's a fine piece of work but I can't cut a cake representing Turkish territory with a picture of Ataturk in the middle. I cannot divide my country!' The paper reported that 'he liked the cake but didn't cut it for fear of committing treason'. The cake (to the accompaniment of cheers from the guests) was returned to the kitchen intact. (*Milliyet*, *Cildekt*)

Turkish publisher **Fatih Tas**, accused of disseminating separatist propaganda, was acquitted on 13 February after one of his authors – the celebrated American linguist and philosopher Noam Chomsky – appeared in an Istanbul court and asked to be tried alongside him. Tas escaped the one-year jail sentence he had been anticipating. 'The prosecutor clearly made the right decision,' said Professor Chomsky, who had petitioned to be named as a co-defendant. 'I hope it will be a step toward establishing the freedom of speech in Turkey that we all want to see.' Tas, who last year published *American Interventionism*, a Turkish translation of Chomsky's essays, declared after the trial: 'If [he] hadn't been here we wouldn't have expected such a verdict.' Tas still faces charges over books that question Turkey's human rights record. But the National Security Court of Diyarbakir also started an investigation into Chomsky's speech at the city's theatre hall. The investigation focuses on his comment: 'I have been monitoring the noble and tragic history of the Kurds for years. Throughout history, oppression has always given birth to resistance and violence. But I hope that an autonomous Kurdistan will happen.' (KurdishMedia.com)

The director of Belge International Publishers in Istanbul, **Ayse Nur Zarakolu**, (*Index* 4/1995, 6/1995, 2/1996, 3/1997) died on 28 January. Ms Zarakolu was an active defender of human rights and freedom of expression, and had a case pending at the European Court of Human Rights. The case, Ayse Zarakolu v Turkey, concerns the prohibition of a book, *Our Ferhat – Anatomy of a Murder*, and the prosecution of Ms Zarakolu as the book's publisher. The book was an account of the killing of Ferhat Tepe by Turkish state security forces. (KHRP)

On 11 February, the Turkish High Audiovisual Council (RTUK) banned Diyarbakir-based **GUN TV** for a year for broadcasting a love song by the Kurdish musician **Siwan**

Perwer. Since its creation in 1994, the RTUK has, according to official figures, already been suspended for varying periods over 500 radio and TV networks. (IMK)

UGANDA

Plans to grant Colonel Muammar Ghadafi an honorary degree from Uganda's Makerere University, stymied by the opposition of the **University Senate** last October, were still blocked in January, despite a bid to force members of the senate to reveal their positions by requiring them to sign their 'secret ballots'. The senators simply declined to return them. (www.allafrica.com)

President Yoweri Museveni will formally write to the Ministry of Education officials instructing them to implement the teaching of sex education in schools in Kampala, reported *New Vision* on 4 February. Museveni said this would help with the decline of the spread of HIV/Aids in Uganda. 'I want to write to them formally to ensure that every fortnight, headmasters or headmistresses gather all the pupils and teac' them how Aids is spread and how it can be prevented,' Museveni said. (AllAfrica.com)

UKRAINE

Kyiv Mayor **Oleksandr Omelchenko** has confirmed the authenticity of a recording of a phone conversation with Our Ukraine election bloc leader Viktor Yushchenko on their efforts to secure the dismissal of parliamentary deputy speaker Viktor Medvedchuk. According to RFE/RL reports, Omelchenko said

his comments were neither new or scandalous, but the bugging of his telephone was a crime and he wanted the courts to act. (RFE/RL)

The Ukraine government has responded to a wave of violent attacks on the media, not by stepping up police activity but by providing them with weapons – an offer that angered the International Federation of Journalists (IFJ). The Ukrainian Interior Ministry plans to allow journalists reporting on politics, crime and corruption to carry guns that fire rubber bullets, to protect themselves. 'Even under controlled conditions, this policy is an admission by the authorities that they are powerless to defend the press,' said Aidan White, General Secretary of the IFJ.

The Committee of Voters of Ukraine is concerned about mass irregularities in the election campaign, such as ignoring the ban on campaigning before 9 February, candidates abusing their official positions, breach of procedure in the formation of election commissions, and violence against candidates. According to the outcome of the committee's January monitoring, none of the culprits was punished. According to the committee, 70% of irregularities in January were linked to the pro-presidential For a United Ukraine bloc. (RFE/RL)

A Ukrainian MP with audio tapes said to contain recordings of President Leonid Kuchma obliquely ordering the silencing of Ukrainian journalist **Georgy Gongadze** sent them to a former FBI audio expert for authentication. The results were positive. Kuchma denies any wrongdoing. Gongadze's torso was found in 2000. (*Guardian*)

UNITED STATES

A federal judge threw out a ban on babies' dummies, tubs of vapour rub and glow sticks at 'rave' parties in New Orleans, saying the restrictions violated the **party-goers'** First Amendment rights to free expression. Federal prosecutors said the items were associated with use of the drug ecstasy. US District Judge Thomas Porteous said in a 1 February ruling that the government could not keep legal items out of places because they were associated with illegal activities. (Freedom Forum)

A group of **3,500 residents of Anniston, Alabama**, are suing chemicals giant Monsanto for allegedly covering up the contamination of their local rivers and land over 50 years. Monsanto has already paid $80m on previous legal settlements related to the case but the new case rests on secret internal company memos that reportedly claim that Monsanto was aware more than 30 years ago that its chemicals factory, producing the now-banned industrial coolants PCBs, were contaminating fish in local rivers. Action was allegedly not taken to deal with the problem until the 1990s. (*Guardian*)

A Muslim woman has sued the US state of Florida for suspending her driver's licence after she refused to remove her face-covering veil for the photograph. State offi-

cials demanded **Sultaana Freeman**, 34, pose without her veil following checks of records after 11 September. Florida law states that licences should bear a full-face photograph, but civil rights lawyer Howard Marks cited another Florida law stating the 'government shall not substantially burden a person's exercise of religion'. (AP)

After more than five months, freelance journalist **Vanessa Leggett** was freed on 4 January from a US jail where she was held for refusing to reveal her sources to federal authorities in Texas. Leggett, 33, is currently writing a book about the 1997 murder of Houston socialite Doris Angleton. Her research includes taped interviews with murder suspect Roger Angleton, the victim's brother-in-law, shortly before he committed suicide. On 6 July 2001, US District Judge Melinda Harmon asked Leggett to turn over her materials to a federal grand jury and jailed her for contempt of court. A three-judge panel of the US Court of Appeals for the 5th Circuit upheld Judge Harmon's ruling on 17 August. The Committee to Protect Journalists (CPJ) said they hoped her release would end her 'unjust persecution'. 'The press cannot be free unless journalists are able to protect the confidentiality of their sources. Leggett was clearly investigating a news story for public dissemination and should never have been jailed in the first place.' (CPJ)

Armed federal agents raided the home of Los Angeles teenager **Sherman Austin** on 24 January, seizing

computers and files relating to his website www.raisethefist.com and his past hacks into a US government website. The FBI say that he used the site to publish bomb-making information and supply code to hack into US army websites. The post-11 September USA Patriot Act expands the ability of law enforcement agents to hunt for terrorists. The agents seized several computers and documents, according to an FBI spokesperson quoted by the *Washington Post*. All of the site's files, which were dedicated to 'the anti-corporate globalisation movement', were lost as a result of the raid, Austin told the same paper. The website is now offline. (*Washington Post*)

Free-speech groups led by the San Francisco-based Electronic Frontier Foundation (EFF) asked a federal judge on 4 February to toss out a case brought against the employers of a Russian software developer under a controversial US copyright law. The EFF and others have filed a 'friend of the court brief' in support of Elcomsoft, employers of programmer **Dmitry Sklyarov**, who wrote a program capable of circumventing security features built into AdobeBooks. Sklyarov, a Russian citizen, was arrested on a visit to the States and charged along with Elcomsoft under the Digital Millennium Copyright Act (DMCA). Federal prosecutors dropped their case against Sklyarov in December. (*Washington Post*)

New York poet and performance artist **Sarah Jones** filed a suit against the US Federal Communications Commission on 22 January, charging that it violated her First

Amendment rights to free speech by fining a radio station that played one of her songs. The 1999 song 'Your Revolution' critiques the degradation of women in mainstream hip-hop music. It contains no obscene words by FCC standards but has some sexual imagery. The FCC fined KBOO-FM, a listener-supported station in Oregon, $7,000. 'My name was hanging in the air with "indecent" attached to it in this really problematic way, especially since my work is concerned with social justice and feminist issues,' she said. (*New York Times*)

The American Society of Newspaper Editors asked US Secretary of Defense Donald Rumsfeld to lift a ban on news organisation photos taken of the arrival of detainees from Afghanistan in Cuba on 10 January. While Rumsfeld maintained that the detainees, all suspected members of the al-Qaida group, were not entitled to the rights guaranteed to prisoners of war under the Geneva Convention, the Pentagon barred news organisations from transmitting pictures of detainees in hoods and shackles on the alleged grounds of Red Cross objections that the images might violate the prisoner's dignity under the Convention. A Red Cross spokesman said the organisation had not raised this issue. 'The explanation provided for restricting the release of the photographs not only appears to contradict the facts, but is a fundamental infringement of the work of the photographers and camera crews involved,' Tim J McGuire, ASNE president and editor of the *Star Tribune*

in Minneapolis, wrote in a letter to Rumsfeld. (ASNE)

The US Congress cannot wall off part of the Internet just because many Americans might think it contains material harmful to children, a lawyer for operators of sexually explicit websites argued to the Supreme Court on 28 November. 'There is no such thing as an objective nationwide standard to judge what is damaging for youngsters but might have artistic, educational or other value for adults,' said American Civil Liberties Union lawyer Ann Beeson. 'A national standard would be an exercise in futility,' she said as the justices examined whether Congress went too far with a 1998 law intended to shield children from online smut. (Freedom Forum)

Unhappy with the determination of the state-funded **Voice of America** to maintain attempts at balance in its existing Dari- and Pashto-language broadcasts to Afghanistan, the Democrat chairman of the Senate Foreign Relations Committee, Senator Joseph Biden, and the committee's senior Republican minority arch-conservative senator, Jesse Helms, submitted a bill to the Senate on 6 December to authorise the establishment of a 'Radio Free Afghanistan' to provide its own news broadcasts in Dari and Pashto. The statute would provide $8m for operations in fiscal year 2002, which began on 1 October 2001, and $9m for capital spending. During the early stages of the conflict, the US State Department had attempted to prevent an interview with the leader of

Afghanistan's ruling Taliban militia, Mullah Mohammed Omar, being broadcast to Arabic audiences on the US radio station Voice of America. Among the many critics of these efforts was the International Press Institute, which argued that the US could not permit 'balanced news stories to be reported in western countries while trying to prevent similar news stories being aired in the Middle East'. (Agencies)

In January, two radio Internet programmes produced by Cosmic Entertainment were forced offline when their ISP, Hypervine, received a call from an alleged federal agent saying that their assets could be frozen for carrying pro-terrorist materials. IRA Radio's **A1 Lewis Live** broadcast Irish news and politics including interviews with presumed terrorists, and Net Radio's **Our Americas** dealt with Latin America's rebels in Spanish. Cosmic's chairman admits to self-censorship while the FBI decline to comment. (USA Today)

On 30 January, law professors challenged President George W Bush's unilateral proposal to try foreigners accused of terrorism in military tribunals. Military tribunals lack the right to choose one's own solicitor, the presence of a jury and the possibility of appeal. In addition, they do not require a unanimous verdict of guilty beyond doubt. The lawyer's petition forced a re-draft of the proposal which now needs a unanimous verdict for the death penalty, and grants the rights to appeal and to choose a solicitor. (News Censorship)

'They that can give up essential liberty to obtain a little temporary safety deserve neither liberty nor safety' Benjamin Franklin

NOAM CHOMSKY ON
ROGUE STATES

EDWARD SAID ON
IRAQI SANCTIONS

LYNNE SEGAL ON
PORNOGRAPHY

... all in INDEX

SUBSCRIBE & SAVE

UK and overseas

○ **Yes! I want to subscribe to *Index*.**

❑ 1 year (4 issues)	£32	Save 16%
❑ 2 years (8 issues)	£60	Save 21%
❑ 3 years (12 issues)	£84	**You save 26%**

Name

Address

B0B5

£ _____ enclosed. ❑ Cheque (£) ❑ Visa/MC ❑ Am Ex ❑ Bill me
(Outside of the UK, add £10 a year for foreign postage)

Card No.

Expiry   Signature

❑ I do not wish to receive mail from other companies.

INDEX ✉ Freepost: INDEX, 33 Islington High Street, London N1 9BR
☎ (44) 171 278 2313   Fax: (44) 171 278 1878
@ tony@indexoncensorship.org

SUBSCRIBE & SAVE

North America

○ **Yes! I want to subscribe to *Index*.**

❑ 1 year (4 issues)	$48	Save 12%
❑ 2 years (8 issues)	$88	Save 19%
❑ 3 years (12 issues)	$120	**You save 26%**

Name

Address

B0B5

$ _____ enclosed. ❑ Cheque ($) ❑ Visa/MC ❑ Am Ex ❑ Bill me

Card No.

Expiry   Signature

❑ I do not wish to receive mail from other companies.

INDEX ✉ Freepost: INDEX, 708 Third Avenue, 8th Floor, New York, NY 10017
☎ (44) 171 278 2313   Fax: (44) 171 278 1878
@ tony@indexoncensorship.org

Following a parent's complaint, the book *Sophie's Choice* by William Styron has been withdrawn from La Miranda High School library for containing sexual references. The National Coalition Against Censorship (NCAC) is appealing to the school official on the ground of students' First Amendment right.

On 17 January, in St Paul Minnesota, **Elliot Chambers**, a sixth-grade student, had his right to wear a T-shirt with the logo 'straight pride' upheld by Judge Donovan under the First Amendment. The T-shirt offended a group of homosexual students and their complaints led to the principal forbidding Elliot to wear it. (*Telegraph*)

The International Skating Union (ISU) has instructed judges of the Olympic Games in Salt Lake to deduct 0.1 to ice-skaters who held poses deemed undignified. The ruling follows a series of complaints by the general public. Judge Nancy Meiss says that some dancers are pornographic while the Italian duo **Fusar Poli** and **Maurizio Margaglio** claim that the threat is nothing more than censorship. (BBC Online)

UZBEKISTAN

A Czech court ruled on 14 December against the extradition of Uzbek dissident **Mohammad Solih** to Tashkent, local and western agencies reported. The Prague municipal court cited the international outcry following Solih's arrest on an Interpol warrant in late November and expressed doubt as to whether the poet and human rights activist would receive a fair trial in Uzbekistan. The court also noted that the Czech Republic does not have an extradition treaty with Uzbekistan. Solih, who left Uzbekistan in 1993, was sentenced *in absentia* for his alleged involvement in bombings blamed on Islamic militants in Tashkent in 1999. Solih claims the charges are part of the Uzbek government's efforts to discredit him and his political party, ERK. (RFE/RL)

Jailed Uzbek poet **Yusuf Dzhumaev**, detained since October 2001, was freed on 8 January. Dzhumaev had appeared in court in Bukhara on 29 December at an open trial. He is a member of the banned secular opposition movement Birlik (Unity) and was charged with planning to overthrow the government. Details are sketchy, but it is believed that he was freed under a presidential pardon. (International PEN/WiPC)

VATICAN CITY

The Internet needs regulation to stop depravity flooding cyberspace, says Pope John Paul. The 81-year-old Pontiff warned that while it offered access to immense knowledge, the Internet did not necessarily provide wisdom and could easily be perverted to demean human dignity. 'Public authorities surely have a responsibility to guarantee that this marvellous instrument serves the common good and does not become a source of harm,' the Pope said in a message prepared for World Communications Day on 22 January. The Pope does not have an email address, Reuters report, but the Church is reportedly searching for a patron saint of Internet users. (Reuters)

VENEZUELA

On 15 February, the Committee to Protect Journalists (CPJ) wrote to President Hugo Chávez to protest against the harassment of the Venezuelan press, noting Chávez's 'verbal attacks' as a cause of the problem. On 6 January, Chávez criticised the Caracas daily *El Nacional* on radio and accused one of its journalists, **Yelitza Izaya Yanez**, of 'disrespect' and 'lying' when covering anti-Chávez protesters in the Caracas area of Catia. The following day, the offices of *El Nacional* were surrounded by some 100 supporters of Chávez's Fifth Republic Movement (MVR) who prevented employees from leaving the building.

On 20 January, a group of journalists from Globovisión Televisión — reporter **Mayela Leon**, cameraman **Jorge Manuel Paz** and assistant **Jhan Bernal** — were attacked by MVR supporters while covering a story for the weekly radio programme. The journalists, forced to abandon their work, were escorted from the areas as soldiers intervened. A team from Radio Caracas Televisión were also forced to abandon their report during a broadcast on the same day, according to local press reports. On 31 January, two men threw a home-made bomb at the offices of the daily *Asíes la Noticia* – part of the publishing house CA Editora El Noticia that owns

El Nacional – shattering the glass doors. Flyers left at the scene accused **Ibéyise Pacheco**, editor of *Asíes la Noticia*, and three other journalists of plotting to thwart the 'process of change' in Venezuela. Chávez, who has called on Venezuelans to 'overthrow the dictatorship of the communications media', has been urged by the CPJ to condemn the attacks and work to create a less volatile climate in which journalists can work 'without fear of reprisal'. (CPJ, LAP)

VIETNAM

An 8 January decree instructs Vietnam's police to confiscate and destroy publications that do not have official approval, especially those expressing dissenting political viewpoints. According to the Associated Press, a government official named several publications that were targeted for confiscation, including the memoirs of **Lt.-Gen. Tran Do**, Vietnam's most famous dissident. Other banned documents include transcripts of a 1999 Internet forum run by Ho Chi Minh City-based dissident scholars **Tran Khue** and **Nguyen Thi Thanh Xuan** and 'Meditation and Aspiration', an essay by dissident geophysicist **Nguyen Thanh Giang**. (CPJ)

ZAMBIA

On 18 January, Zambia's chief opposition party, the United Party for National Development, petitioned the Supreme Court to declare the results of the 27 December presidential election invalid, claiming electoral fraud. Opposition leader **Anderson Mazoka** claims that polling stations in

the Southern Province closed earlier than most of those in the rest of the country, making it impossible for thousands of his supporters to vote, and that not enough ballot papers were sent to some areas known as opposition strongholds. He also claims that ballot boxes were stuffed with ballot papers that did not bear the official stamp. ('Southern Africa Report')

ZIMBABWE

The president of South Africa, Thabo Mbeki, warned in November that civil conflict could explode in Zimbabwe if full press freedom is not ensured in the run-up to presidential elections in March. In a private meeting in Pretoria with board members of the World Association of Newspapers on 27 November, Mbeki said: 'The people of Zimbabwe need to say this was a fair election contest. The press freedom issue is getting worse and exacerbates as we get closer to these elections. If the outcome is not accepted by the people of Zimbabwe, the situation will be even worse and you have the danger of civil conflict.'

The board of WAN, meeting in South Africa, awarded its annual Golden Pen of Freedom prize to Zimbabwe's most prominent press freedom advocate, **Geoffrey Nyarota**, editor of the *Daily News*, on 27 November. The award, announced by the board of the Paris-based WAN at its meeting in South Africa on 27 November, was made in recognition of Nyarota's outstanding defence of press freedom in the face of constant persecution. In a

statement, the board said: 'Geoffrey Nyarota has with great courage stood firm and resolute in the face of repeated attempts to silence him and his newspaper. He has continued to edit a newspaper which has gained the trust of his readers by fearlessly providing them with the truth about government corruption and the country's economic and social upheaval. His fierce devotion to free, honest and independent journalism is an inspiration to his colleagues everywhere.' (WAN)

On 29 January, BBC correspondent **Thabo Kunene** was arrested and detained for one hour in Lupane, 100km outside Bulawayo, along with a visitor from Holland and a driver. They were arrested at a roadblock. 'They separated us on arrival at the police station and we were continually told that we were a security risk,' Kunene told the *Daily News*. (BBC)

The Zimbabwean authorities will not be prosecuting journalist **Basildon Peta**, local correspondent of the London *Independent* and secretary-general of the Zimbabwean Union of Journalists, *Index on Censorship*, IFEX and others report. Held overnight in Harare central prison, Peta's detention was the first high-profile arrest under the new Public Order & Security Act, brought in by Zimbabwe leader Robert Mugabe to restrain political opposition and the independent media during his re-election campaign. The charges against Peta were dropped the next day. Amid some dispute about the detail of his account of his arrest, Peta soon after went into exile in South Africa. He had faced charges of failing to notify authorities about a demonstration by more than 60 journalists outside parliament, called to protest against the Access to Information and Protection of Privacy Bill. During the demonstration, armed riot police broke up the protest and arrested *Daily News* reporters **Rhoda Mashavave** and **Foster Dongozi**, and **Cornelius Nduna** of the *Standard*. (MISA, *Financial Gazette*, Harare)

Press freedom came under attack in virtually every region of the world in 2001, with an alarming number of journalists killed or imprisoned, and an increasing threat of censorship and repression in many countries, the World Association of Newspapers (WAN) said in its annual half-year review of press freedom worldwide, published on 26 November. 'The global press freedom situation has deteriorated in several countries over the past six months; the number of murdered journalists, particularly, is rising dramatically,' WAN wrote in a report to its board, meeting in South Africa. Fifty-six journalists were killed worldwide, 41 of them between June and November, and seven in Afghanistan in the two weeks preceding the report. The total had already exceeded the 53 killed in the whole of 2000. 'Several European countries and the United States are among the countries where journalists have been killed: terrorism of one kind or another is definitely a threat that must be taken into account in every nation,' concluded the report. The events of 11 September were raising concerns of increasing censorship in the United States and elsewhere. Latin America remains the most dangerous place for journalists: nine have been killed in Colombia alone, and journalists have also died violently in Brazil, Paraguay, Bolivia, Ecuador, Mexico, Guatemala and Costa Rica. One hundred and five journalists were in prison at the time of the report, with Iran (19), Burma (18) and China (15) jailing the most. (WAN)

Compiled by: James Badcock (North Africa); Hanna Gezelius (South-East Asia); Andrew Kendle (India and subcontinent); Carly Lake (South America); Agustina Lattanzi (South and Central America); Gill Newsham (Turkey and Kurdish areas); Ruairi Patterson (UK and Ireland); Shifa Rahman (East Africa); Neil Sammonds (Gulf States and Middle East); Fabio Scarpello (Western Europe, North America, Pacific and Australasia); Katy Sheppard (Russia, Poland, Ukraine and Baltic States); Mike Yeoman (Central America and Caribbean), with contributions from Tony Callaghan, Rohan Jayasekera, Agustina Lattanzi and Vera Rich. Co-ordinated by Natasha Schmidt

ENDURING WARS

OBSCURED BY BUSH'S GLOBAL
WAR ON TERRORISM, THE VICIOUS
LITTLE DOMESTIC WARS BETWEEN
NEIGHBOURS GO ON: IRELAND,
ISRAEL–PALESTINE, TURKEY –
AND NOW NIGERIA AND INDIA

Gaza, Palestine: Shati Refugee Camp and its 'child martyrs'
Credit: Larry Towell / © Magnum Photos, Inc.

NONE SO BLIND

RONAN BENNETT

WHEN IT COMES TO ASKING WHY THE
IRISH PEACE PROGRESS HAS MADE
SUCH SLOW PROGRESS SINCE ITS
INCEPTION IN 1994, THE MEDIA HAS
A LOT TO ANSWER FOR

If we take the IRA ceasefire of 1994 as its beginning, the peace process in the north of Ireland is now almost eight years old, and yet only the most optimistic would claim that anything like a real peace has been established. There have been obvious gains: the death toll is down, some republican guns have been 'put beyond use', the political parties talk to one another – even if it is through clenched teeth – in newly created institutions of government unimaginable only a short time ago. But the conflict continues to simmer. In recent months, Belfast has seen the worst sectarian rioting for a generation; there have been sectarian assassinations by Loyalist paramilitaries; punishment beatings and 'exiling' are common occurrences; republican irreconcilables continue to bomb; the parties are still deeply divided over crucial constitutional issues and questions of reform; and – ominously for the long term – the atmosphere both among the politicians and people on the streets remains charged with suspicion and hostility. Belfast may not be Jerusalem and Derry is not Ramallah, but the peace process has yet to evolve from nervous stand-off to fully fledged settlement.

Why has there not been greater progress? The British media, particularly the print media, have not been slow to apportion blame. Despite occasional differences of emphasis among the titles, reflecting the broader political allegiances of proprietors, staff and readers, there has been an underlying consensus: 'tribal' intransigence among the disputing factions is frequently cited, as are the supposed shortcomings of some of the key players. Thus Gerry Adams, the Sinn Fein president, is regularly upbraided for playing a double game – talking peace but secretly planning for war. John Hume, the former leader of the Social Democratic and Labour Party, is criticised for failing to tame the beast he unleashed when he, with the help of successive Dublin governments and the Clinton administration, brought Adams and Sinn Fein in from the political wilderness. Tony Blair has attracted criticism for conceding too much too quickly to the 'men of violence' (though this has been nothing compared with the sustained abuse heaped on the head of Mo Mowlam, Labour's first secretary of state for Northern Ireland in the Blair government).

Unusually, the voters themselves have been berated – 'unusually' because the depiction of 'ordinary people' in such conflicts is typically that of long-suffering, traumatised victims yearning for their leaders to put aside their bellicosity and get on with the serious business of making peace. But in recent elections voters everywhere from Newry to Ballycastle, Antrim to Fermanagh, have been deserting the centre ground, represented in the media as Hume's SDLP and David Trimble's Ulster Unionists, by casting their ballots for the parties of the so-called extremes, notably Sinn Fein and Ian Paisley's Democratic Unionist Party. As a columnist in the *Daily Telegraph* put it after the 2001 general election in which Sinn Fein won four seats and the DUP came close to unseating Trimble, Irish voters reversed an axiom of political life. Normally we speak of political leaders letting down the electorate. This was a case, the *Telegraph* claimed, of the electorate letting down the political leaders.

But what of the media's own role in this? Does the media itself bear any responsibility for the way things have turned out since the IRA announcement on 31 August 1994 of a 'complete cessation of military operations'? Media opinion as expressed in leading articles and comment pieces in the period leading up to and immediately after the IRA announcement throws some interesting light on how journalists were able to react to sudden and unexpected change in a long-running conflict, and how their response in turn helped influence the course of events.

Though rumours of a ceasefire had been in the wind for some time, when the IRA announcement did come it seemed to take many by surprise. Albert Reynolds, the Irish Taoiseach at the time, has said that when he telephoned John Major to tell him, the British prime minister simply did not believe it. Major was not alone. It was, after all, a development that British politicians and commentators of all political colours had confidently predicted would never happen, *could* never happen. Between the early 1970s and 1994, certain orthodoxies had become established in British media commentary on the north of Ireland, and they became more firmly entrenched with every passing atrocity. Central to the orthodoxy was that the 'men of violence' (Loyalist gunmen were included in this, but really only in passing: when the media spoke of the men of violence they meant first and foremost republicans – the IRA and Sinn Fein) were addicted to violence, gangsterism and bloodlust. It was unimaginable that they could break their dependency on the gun, for without the gun they were nothing. Over the years, a number of journalists – among them Peter Taylor, Jonathan Dimbleby, David McKitterick and John Pilger – have challenged the orthodoxies or expressed concern at growing censorship problems, and in 1995 journalists staged a 24-hour strike over the *Real Lives* controversy – but on the whole media comment has been remarkably homogenous.

More than anyone else, Gerry Adams, as republicanism's most prominent public face, embodied this orthodoxy. By the early 1990s, Adams was secretly talking to John Hume about how the conflict might be brought to an end. News of their meetings was broken by the Derry-based journalist Eamon McCann. It might have been supposed that the development would find at least a cautious welcome. But no. The reaction was uniformly negative in the British, and for that matter in the Irish, media. Hume – a man of impeccably democratic standing, one of the very few in the north of Ireland who has consistently and unambiguously championed exclusively democratic and peaceful means to end the conflict – was denounced as a fool, a dupe or worse.

As for Adams, the levels of vitriol he attracted appeared to be in direct proportion to the frequency he talked of peace. A few examples will illustrate the point. Typical is the *Sunday Telegraph*'s description of Adams in October 1993, by which time the Hume–Adams talks were public knowledge, as 'one of the coldest, cleverest, least lovable and most formidable enemies to peace in Ireland's bloodstained history'. The *Observer*, reviewing the prospects for a ceasefire, concluded: 'Even if Gerry Adams's heart is in peace, his words and actions suggest a man who has neither the confidence nor the courage to drive events.' Over the summer of 1994, with rumours that an IRA announcement was imminent, the attacks intensified, became almost hysterical. One commentator in the *Guardian* expressed his view that 'Gerry Adams is a drab little schoolteacher who had the operation for his conscience, a pedantic little psychopath peering through thick glasses at 20 years of handfuls of earth thrown into the ground.' There was much, much more of the same, not all of it delivered with quite the same coolness or detachment.

A question here. Let us assume for the sake of argument that republicans were genuine, in 1993–94, in wanting to call a ceasefire (subsequent events make this a not unreasonable assumption). Like any politicians, Sinn Fein's

*Washington March 2000: St Patrick's Day in the White House.
(l–r) Adams, Hume, Clinton, Trimble. Credit: Camera Press / Mark Wilson*

leaders would have been scanning the media for straws in the wind. How would the British respond to such a gesture? At that time, John Major's government was under intense pressure, its Commons majority virtually non-existent and right-wing enemies circling like vultures. Adams and his key lieutenants are very aware of the role of the modern media in political life, and they must have noted the tenor of comment and calculated that the unremitting hostility would not make it easy for the beleaguered prime minister to respond with sufficient flexibility to take advantage of the new situation. In such circumstances, it is not difficult to imagine hardline republicans saying it simply wasn't worth the candle. To Adams's credit, he pressed on, even when Major said in response to media goading about the possibility of negotiating with republicans that it would 'sicken him to his stomach' to have to shake Gerry Adams's hand. The statement went down well in the media, but hardly did much to advance the prospects of peace.

The difficulty here was that by 1994, many British commentators and editors simply loathed Adams and the IRA. This was hardly surprising. As the IRA found it harder to carry out attacks on military targets, they went for softer, civilian ones with the inevitable result of horrific civilian carnage. It was entirely right that the media responded with outrage to these atrocities.

But it was wrong that commentators allowed themselves to be blinded to significant developments then taking place in Adams's thinking and in republican strategy. In this, the 1988 broadcasting ban imposed on republican and Loyalist spokespeople had a part to play, as did the intermittent banning of radio plays, television documentaries, reports and other miscellaneous items over the years (*Index* 2/1995).

But state censorship in this instance had much less impact than the media's own fixation with maintaining the orthodoxies. It is illustrative of just how entrenched these were that when I wrote a piece in 1992 for the *Guardian* suggesting that Adams was looking for a way to bring about a ceasefire and that any settlement would necessarily involve negotiations with the Sinn Fein leader, it led to denunciation by MPs, in other newspapers, on radio and in the letters columns of the *Guardian* itself.

Given the nature of media comment, one might think that after the unthinkable did occur – the 1994 ceasefire – there would have been a long queue of people lining up to acknowledge that they had misread the story and would now have to work out the best way to respond to this radical and unforeseen new development. Nothing of the sort happened. With few exceptions, the British media followed the line of Unionists and Loyalists. Trimble said Adams was 'not a fit person to sit at the table. I don't envisage a situation of personal contact with this gentleman.' Paisley, ever more colourful, asked: 'Will we permit Ulster to be chloroformed into accepting this peace as a real peace? It is not a peace process. It is a surrender process, which we must resist.' And that was the media line in a nutshell: it was not a peace process. And since it was not a peace process, no political response, no reciprocal gesture, was necessary.

The right-wing papers were united in their rejection of the republican initiative and they supported Major when he said that republicans would have to prove the ceasefire was real by surrendering their weapons before there could be political movement. The prime minister found support in other newspapers more usually critical of him and his government. Adams was depicted on the cover of the *New Statesman*, hands dripping in blood, crawling out of a primordial sea to take his first faltering footsteps on the long evolutionary road to human being. According to the *Guardian* just a month after the ceasefire, Adams was as 'a coffin-filler strategically deciding to desist from filling coffins . . . The advantage of killing people is that if you stop killing, you become a man of peace and Gerry Adams has the appropriate banality for the part.'

When Adams travelled to the USA – the British government had vigorously opposed the granting of a visa – to rally support and put pressure on Major to begin all-party talks, the print media erupted in fury. In an unsympathetic review of the trip, *Vanity Fair* quoted the former Conservative minister Michael Mates on Adams: 'He's extremely clever and extremely devious. He looks you straight in the face and gives you bare-faced lies. Of course, that's what terrorists do.' The *Guardian* found not only Adams but all of Irish America repellent: 'The East Coast Irish political circus . . . is posturing, tribal, self-indulgent and unhelpful. It's old-fashioned and it's lazy . . . The lionising of Gerry Adams by American politicians has got to stop . . . He makes no concessions and offers no compromises. He claims dignity and respect and yet offers and behaves with neither. You do not have to be any sort of unionist to feel pretty lousy about human beings who argue in the dishonest way that Mr Adams does or about human beings who fall over themselves to ignore it the way that President Clinton did again yesterday.' When Adams blamed the Major government for stalling progress, the *Guardian* rounded on him. 'Gerry Adams says everything but the truth about his movement, offers the peace process everything except the things which would really help and places the blame for any difficulties on everyone except his own people. His evasions are transparent and offensive.'

As time passed and the IRA ceasefire held firm in spite of there being no progress on all-party talks, a certain amount of finessing was required. Adams may have delivered what had previously been thought impossible but that was as far as he could go. The ghost of Michael Collins was spied walking the land, the visions in part inspired by Neil Jordan's 1996 eponymous film. In this revised scenario, even if Adams was genuine in wanting peace, something by now that some commentators were conceding, the hard men in the shadows would never let him compromise. Time and again in editorial columns it was suggested that Adams's position was hopeless: if he dared shift from the traditional republican position of Brits Out he would end up with a bullet in the back of his head just as Collins had.

In February 1996, the IRA, angered by the lack of political progress, exploded a massive bomb in London's Docklands, killing two people and causing millions of pounds' worth of damage. The media responded with something akin to relief. At last they no longer had to pretend to be in favour of the peace process and could fall back on the orthodoxies that had sustained them for so long. 'The terrorists and their weasel-mouthed spokesmen, led by Gerry Adams, have reverted to type,' the *Sunday Times* wrote. 'Dublin and Washington must now see Adams for what he is – a jet-setting sham and a glib-tongued frontman for murderers.' The *Guardian* decided Adams was an irrelevance. 'Gerry Adams is part of the Troubles. By treating him as if he is essential to a permanent settlement, we glorify and glamorise intransigence, bigotry and extremism.' The *Daily Express* was outraged by Adams 'drinking champagne with the US President in the White House, fêted in Europe's capitals, courted and grovelled to by the bouffant transatlantic interviewers. After Friday's bombing, perhaps even they will ask whether they want to be seen in such odious company again.' Few asked the question that seemed most pertinent at the time: could this have been avoided?

While Major remained in power, propped up by Unionist votes, there could be no meaningful progress, and this was one area in which Major did not have to defend himself against a media onslaught. It took the election of a Labour government under Tony Blair, in May 1997, for British politicians to take advantage of the by now demonstrable republican willingness to make politics work. There have been reverses – some, like the Omagh bombing, near catastrophic; others, like the temporary suspension of the institutions created by the Good Friday Agreement, part and parcel of polit-ical life. With the IRA ceasefire intact and with the decommissioning of IRA weapons, some sections of the British media have been prepared to accept that Adams and Sinn Fein are doing what they can to deliver their part of the bargain. Others remain hostile to the whole project, unable to reconcile themselves to something that began as a republican initiative. Charles Moore, editor of the *Daily Telegraph*, for example, makes no bones about his continued antipathy to the peace process as it is presently constructed; and as the recent media fuss about Adams and his three Sinn Fein MP colleagues being given offices in the Palace of Westminster shows, British editors and leader writers still have a long way to go before they are convinced that the peace process is worth their support. The point is: when the peace process next hits the buffers, what attitude will they take? Will they, as they have in the past, leap on the opportunity to bury Ireland's chance for peace? Or will they say, let's leave aside what happened in the past and ask who is working to keep the settlement and who is working to undermine it? Perhaps then we might have reason to be more optimistic. ❏

Ronan Bennett grew up in Ireland and now lives in London. His latest book is The Catastrophist *(Review, 1998)*

New Internationalist Magazine
www.newint.org

STANCEXISTENCERÉSISTANCEXISTENC

Globalisation
The battle for the 21st century.
Everybody's talking about it...

But the **New Internationalist** brings you the *real* stories from globalisation's frontlines. From **Seattle** to **Soweto**, from **Genoa** to **Chiapas** people's movements are on the streets to take back democracy and declare that:

'we are a people not a market, and our world is not for sale'.

The **New Internationalist** explores the issues and stories behind buzzwords like globalisation. We take one subject a month; debt, corporate power, the WTO, fair trade, slavery, resistance or big oil to give you the complete picture. If you want to keep on top of the issues that matter you need the **New Internationalist**.

FREE
3 MAGAZINES & COLOUR WORLD MAP

POST TO: NEW INTERNATIONALIST, FREEPOST MID17880, MARKET HARBOROUGH LE87 4JF

YES I wish to take up your offer of a free trial to the **New Internationalist** magazine. Please send me copies of the next three issues of the magazine and my free gifts. If I decide not to subscribe I will write and let you know within ten days of receiving my third issue. If I wish to continue I need do nothing. Starting from the first of the following month my account will be debited quarterly, until I cancel in writing, with the **NI** subscription price – currently £7.85 (or £9.85 if delivery outside UK).

Name _____

Address _____

Postcode _____

INSTRUCTION TO YOUR BANK OR BUILDING SOCIETY TO PAY BY DIRECT DEBIT
Please fill in the form and send to New Internationalist FREEPOST MID17880 Market Harborough LE87 4JF

DIRECT Debit

Name and full postal address of your Bank or Building Society

To: The Manager _____ Bank/Building Society

Address _____

Postcode _____

Name(s) of Account Holder(s) _____

Bank/Building Society account number

Branch Sort Code

Banks and Building Societies may not accept Direct Debit Instructions for some type of accounts.

Originator's Identification Number

9	8	4	4	4	2

Reference Number – to be completed by New Internationalist

Instruction to your Bank or Building Society
Please pay **New Internationalist Publications** Direct Debits from the account detailed on this instruction subject to the safeguards assured by the Direct Debit Guarantee. I understand that this instruction may remain with NI and, if so, details will be passed electronically to my Bank/Building Society.

Signature(s)

Date

☐ Occasionally we allow carefully screened organisations to mail our subscribers. If you would prefer not to be mailed by anyone else please tick this box. This free trial offer only applies to direct debits. Annual subscriptions for £28.85 UK/£34.85 Overseas may also be paid by cheque, Visa or Mastercard. New Internationalist Publications Ltd. Reg. in England No. 1005239. Reg. Office 55 Rectory Road, Oxford OX4 1BW.

6698

WHY SO FEW?

MICHAEL FOLEY

THE MURDER OF IRISH
JOURNALIST MARTIN O'HAGAN
RAISES IMPORTANT QUESTIONS

Many years ago I was travelling with a Belfast-based journalist through the city when we were stopped by armed men in balaclavas and told to get out of the car. My driver was outraged. 'How dare you. I'm a journalist,' he said, waving his NUJ card. 'If you don't let us through I will report you to Danny Morrison,' the then Sinn Fein press officer. The armed man mumbled an apology and his comrades let us through. Behind us, other drivers were not so lucky and ended up with their cars being used as barricades.

The story illustrates the 'unwritten rule' that journalists were not to be shot, and is one reason why so many were shocked, even puzzled, at the shooting of journalist Martin O'Hagan. Why now? How was it that Martin O'Hagan was the first journalist to be killed? How was it that journalists, some working for sectarian media outlets, worked as if their press card was a shield? In other areas of conflict, killing journalists has become commonplace.

The reasons why Northern Ireland's combatants rarely targeted journalists are many and complex. Civil society in Northern Ireland never collapsed despite all the pressures it was under. Institutions such as schools, libraries, social security, to name a few, always functioned. Throughout direct rule elections were contested. From local authorities to Westminster and the European Parliament, elections were fought with enthusiasm and passion and were covered by committed journalists as obsessed with politics as journalists anywhere.

Northern Ireland was never totally without a democratic culture, albeit an imperfect one, where the media had a place. Throughout the 30 years of conflict, someone was always working on some peace initiative or politicians were seeking to influence public opinion; they all needed the media.

Northern Ireland's divided nature conferred a special role on journalists, especially print journalists. Newspapers felt no need to be impartial and balanced: in a divided society, nationalists need the *Irish News* or the *Derry Journal* and Loyalists the *Newsletter* or the *Portadown Times*.

Journalists were and are necessary in a society where there was only limited forum for debate but where public opinion was always an important ingredient. Whether Taoiseach, prime minister, Loyalist or nationalist, SDLP or DUP – or the British Army – all needed journalists to speak to their own side or even the other; sometimes to propagandise. Journalists, even when working for sectarian outlets, could demonstrate a professional detachment, allowing them to be viewed as somewhere between a necessary evil and a trusted conduit.

This has never made working in Northern Ireland easy. Journalists learned a form of tradecraft or street skills. Covering Loyalist events meant contacting whoever was the big man in an area. Journalists, especially photographers, learned how to cover funerals, marches and demonstrations in ways that got them the pictures without getting thumped. Journalists were often scared, but their press card was a shield.

So why Martin O'Hagan? One suggestion was that his death was the result of the collapse of leadership and discipline in certain paramilitary organisations. Some are now solely involved in criminal activities and have nothing but contempt for public opinion. This has to do with developments within Northern Ireland, especially within working-class Loyalist communities, the areas Martin O'Hagan wrote about, over the years since the peace process took hold.

Martin O'Hagan's death conforms to a worldwide trend, of which crime reporter Veronica Guerin's death outside Dublin a few years ago was a part. The most vulnerable journalist is a local journalist, not a star foreign correspondent wearing designer fatigues and body armour. The journalists most likely to be killed for their work are those whose revelations are read by those immediately affected within the community, not by an audience half a world away. They write for ordinary people, telling them what is happening in their own communities, challenging criminals and violent people at great risk to themselves.

There is one last question raised by Martin O'Hagan's death: the lack of reaction in Britain and Ireland. His death was covered; leading politicians and others voiced their disgust. And then: silence.

Why? Some have suggested it was because Martin O'Hagan worked for a tabloid newspaper, without a high profile outside the local community; that O'Hagan was nothing more than a decent hack.

Another reason is Northern Ireland itself. The combination of widespread boredom with its problems and the fear that too much analysis of exactly why he died might force awkward conclusions. ❏

Michael Foley is a lecturer in journalism at the Dublin Institute of Technology

EVERY STONE IS BEAUTIFUL

NEIL SAMMONDS & LALEH KHALILI

TWENTY YEARS AGO, THE MASSACRE OF
PALESTINIAN REFUGEES IN THE SABRA AND
CHATILA CAMPS IN BEIRUT SHOCKED THE WORLD.
TODAY, OVER 3 MILLION PALESTINIAN REFUGEES,
350,000 OF THEM IN LEBANON, DREAM OF
RETURN, A RIGHT THAT, UNLIKE OTHER REFUGEE
GROUPS AND DESPITE UN RESOLUTIONS, IS NOT UP
FOR DISCUSSION SO FAR AS ISRAEL IS CONCERNED

IM FAROUQ *(68) Bourj al-Barajneh Camp, Beirut, Lebanon*
I was born in 1933 in what is now Lebanon, but when I was five months old
we moved to Al-Bassa, near Acca, in Palestine.

We left Palestine in 1948 because there was bombing all around. So we
crossed the border to Naqoura. We lost Palestine because all the Arab countries were stupid. How they betrayed us. They opened their borders to us, and
the Arab Army of Salvation said they were going to defend us. But they gave
us damaged weapons, so we couldn't fight the Israelis who had heavy
weapons. Then the Arab leaders made the Arab Army of Salvation leave
Palestine and the Jews took it over. From Naqoura, Lebanese army trucks
took people to different parts of Syria and Jordan. We spent the nights under
Naqoura's olive trees for 28 days, then we were taken to Barja'. After four
years in Barja' we came here to Beirut.

My sister and I married two brothers and we lived in tents. I had our first
child in a tent, and there was mud everywhere, even over our mattresses and
pillows. Women would wait hours at the water pipe, sometimes a whole day.

I lost my son during the Israeli occupation. One day we were told he had
died but we don't know where his body is. When the PLO left Lebanon at
the end of August 1982 things got worse. The Sabra and Shatila massacres
happened two weeks later and the Lebanese army could come to the camps,
arrest the men and put them in jails.

During the War of the Camps there wasn't anything to drink or to eat.
We spent the time in the shelters. And there was this woman whose three
sons were killed in front of her and even now she is almost crazy. It is very
hard to lose your son.

Before we left Palestine, our life was beautiful, I remember the waters, small pebbles and plants and trees. We had a nice, happy life and it was most beautiful. I will go back if God wishes it. Palestine was paradise on earth. I want to go to our home in Palestine, even if I could just put a tent there. I wish, I wish. When I was there I was taken to Jebel Amel near al-Quds [Jerusalem]. Every stone in there is beautiful.

IM HAMID *(68) Bourj al-Barajneh Camp*
I was born in Lazaza in 1934. In 1948, Lazaza was destroyed with tanks; it is now called Beit Halad. I was married and had a son. We walked across the border and stayed at Marieh. We lived there for four years under a house made with sticks, among the Gypsies. In 1952, the Lebanese government moved us to Nabatiyah and the International Red Cross gave us tents. But there was no work, so we moved to Tel el-Za'ater. But we left because of the siege and massacre in January 1976 [when right-wing Christian Maronites killed several thousand Palestinians – Ed]. My brothers disappeared and my husband was killed.

Then we moved to Damour where there were empty houses since Palestinians had killed hundreds of Christians there in the same month. Three years later, the Israelis invaded so we moved to Tariq Jadidah. We lived there until a year ago when we were given US$5,000 to vacate our home, and we bought this house in the camp.

Life was terrible in Tel el-Za'ater. My oldest son was killed by the Syrian-backed Amal militia while praying in the mosque. There were three of them and they tortured him. If you were Palestinian, they would kill you. They could tell we were Palestinian from our accents but we said we were Palestinian anyway.

I don't have any sweet memories. Except of when I was in Palestine. Everything in my life is a black memory. I had my second child at night and the next morning my husband died. After six years as a widow, I got married and then that husband died in Tel el-Za'ater. I had to leave his body right there on the street without any place to bury him.

ABDELMA'TA HUSSEIN *(52) shopkeeper, Bourj al-Barajneh Camp*
I am from Sidna Ali, Yaffa, but was born in Tulkarem camp in the West Bank, where we lived in tents given by the UN. I joined Fatah in 1966 and, when Israel occupied the West Bank in 1967, I moved to Jordan. I joined Fatah

because I wanted to return to my country by any means and because it was the most inclusive Palestinian movement – for socialists, Islamists, Ba'athists, Christians, whatever. There is a love of martyrdom, of dying for one's country. Every night we were sneaking across the border between Jordan and Palestine, doing operations, and we would bring back a little bit of the dirt of our country. It didn't matter whether we lived or died: to die as a martyr in the Palestinian lands was better.

But the Jordanians prevented the PLO from fighting and I ended up here after we were kicked out in 1970 following Black September [when Arafat and the PLO were driven out of Jordan – Ed].

The Jordanian system was much harder than the Lebanese because you couldn't speak about politics. In Jordan, Palestinians can go anywhere they want, as they have Jordanian identity cards, and they can take any job they want, but they can't be involved in politics. We are forced to take Jordanian nationality.

We were supposed to forget something called Palestine. If I get hungry, I won't recognise my hunger, but forgetting my cause is a crime.

I was injured for a third time in Lebanon in July 1971 at the Jordan–Palestine border; and in 1974 I was hit in Kfar Shouba in Lebanon during the invasion. When I was injured, the Jordanians took me prisoner and tortured me worse than the Israelis would.

But I loved my life as a military man. There is a cactus and it hurts when you pick it but when you eat it you like it. It was the same for me. I am not happy as a civilian. Civilians don't do anything. You are lazy, sit around, drink coffee and visit people. I even bring my children up in military style.

Our life in Lebanon is a life of hardship. We are surrounded. We cannot work, we cannot do anything. We have the freedom to go out but we don't have the freedom to work. Even doctors or engineers can't work. There are two jobs open: garbage men or construction workers. I couldn't legally open this shop outside the camp.

I will only go back to Palestine if it is free, not if it's under Israeli occupation. My return has to be dignified and as a recognised ex-fighter. I have been fighting for more than 30 years and don't want to go back for nothing.

I have been inside the 1948 and the 1967 borders. I have seen al-Quds, Khalil [Hebron], Tulkarem and Jenin. The views inside Palestine are amazing. Near the Jordanian border, on the way to Nablus, is a beautiful place called Wadi Bidan. And near the Dead Sea is a place with sweet water and trees . . . Palestine is heaven.

YOUSSEF IBRAHIM *(37) second-hand fridge and TV salesman,*
Wavell Camp, Baalbek, Lebanon

My family's from Na'imi village, near Haifa. Now we are among the 5,000 refugees in Wavell. The houses are too close together; services from UNRWA (United Nations Relief and Works Agency) are inadequate. If someone needs an operation, UNRWA might give one-sixth of the money. Since 1972, we've been forbidden to work but the authorities usually turn a blind eye – how else would we live?

Why should I give up my right of return? If a stranger from another continent came and kicked you out of your house, would you let them stay? If I was offered all of Lebanon I'd say no: I want my land. All the Jews who lived in Palestine before 1917, fine, they can stay. The others should go. They can live in any country they want. The ones from Europe and America, why do they come? They've got houses and other nationalities.

Arafat is an historic leader. No one else could have made peace with Israel. But 22% [the whole of the West Bank, Gaza Strip and East Jerusalem] isn't enough. And it's divided. The Zionists take 78% and they still want more. I'm not against Jews, just Zionists.

I support the operations of the martyrs. The Zionists smash our houses, kill our brothers and sisters, keep us at checkpoints for five hours. They use F-16s, Apaches. Should I just watch? Women and children shouldn't be killed, but settlers are legitimate targets. There are UN resolutions – 194, 242, 338, 425 – but Israel rejects them. The West only enforces the resolutions against the Arabs – Sudan, Libya, Iraq. Israel killed 25,000 Lebanese, has 200 nuclear weapons and 20 Lebanese in Israeli prisons – who in the West talks about that? But Hizbullah captures three occupying Israeli soldiers and Madeleine Albright and the UN complain. It wasn't UN resolution 425 [calling for Israel's withdrawal from South Lebanon] that forced them out, it was the resistance.

TAREQ MOHAMMED *(27) maths teacher, Wavell Camp*

I'm from Lubni village, near Tiberia. I don't have a work permit. I have to leave the classroom whenever inspectors come, though sometimes they don't mind. The Lebanese government makes problems for us. We can't move around freely or get proper work. We were deprived of our land and now of our rights as humans. But we do what we can to make it better, to help each other.

I want to get married so I need an apartment. But if I marry a Palestinian and I die, the flat is given to the government.

Now we really wish we were helping our brothers and sisters in Palestine. Not because I want to kill Israelis but because it's a duty. They're fighting the whole world. I respect the suicide bombers. We consider them martyrs. They are prepared to die so that others can live. The Jews have a right to live but not on my land. We may in time accept Israel. People are fighting for the Bank, Strip and Jerusalem, but I want my land, my Lubni.

Sari Nusseibeh [former PA spokesman for Jerusalem Affairs] is a traitor for saying we will compromise on our right of return and resolution 194. He has a right to his own opinion, but that's all it is. If I was given Lebanese citizenship I would only take it as a temporary measure. Why should I deny my own identity? One day, maybe, I might get citizenship of another country. Then I may be able to visit my own land.

KHOLOUD HUSSEIN (33) homemaker and part-time translator, *Bourj el-Barajneh Camp*

My mother's family is originally from Fara village near Safad. My father's is from Rashidiye, a camp on the south-west coast, but originally from Kwika. When the Zionists came with their guns, the Arab Army of Salvation told the families to leave for a few days. My dad was only nine. Actually, when I was young I stopped saying I was from Fara because people used to tease me [*fara* means 'mouse' in Arabic] and instead I said I was from Kwika.

Generally, life is quite nice here – relatives always pop round to see each other. The only thing I don't like about this camp is that there is nowhere for the children to play; there's not even a playground in the school. And work opportunities are very poor. We can't work in offices or for the government. Also, the Lebanese look down on us, despite us being here 53 years. Lebanese politicians don't want us here, and we don't want to be Lebanese. They think we want to be naturalised but we only want to return.

Politicians in Palestine can't do anything. Even Arafat is under siege. It's the US and UK who can make decisions. The US could stop Israel immediately but it doesn't try. They see the numbers of Palestinian civilians killed and numbers of houses destroyed and yet say we are the terrorists.

In the beginning I was against the armed struggle but now I agree that more than stones are needed. Maybe it's a way for the Israelis to realise they should stop killing.

I didn't go to the border after the liberation of the south. My friends advised me that it would be too dangerous and, anyhow, my husband forbade me. And now Palestinians need permission from the government to visit the border area. Although Hizbullah was the main resistance group, they learned from the Palestinians. Palestinians were part of the Lebanese resistance.

I don't know if I will return to Palestine. Only God knows. I hope I will. In my dreams I see myself in Palestine. ❏

Neil Sammonds is a freelance writer and activist. He monitors freedom of expression in the Middle East for Index on Censorship *and is the editor of* Palestine News *(www.palestinecampaign.org).* **Laleh Khalili** *is a Columbia University postgraduate student researching Palestinian memory among the refugees in Lebanon. All interviews January/February 2002*

IDENTITY, IDENTITY

AMARTYA SEN

THERE ARE MORE WAYS OF SEEING PEOPLE
THAN IN THE STRAITJACKET OF RACE, CREED OR
WHATEVER WE MEAN BY 'CIVILISATION'. VARIETY
IS THE NAME OF THE IDENTITY GAME — AND A
SAFER WAY TO GO THAN CONFRONTATION IN THE
NAME OF DIFFERENCE

The basic weakness of the thesis of a 'clash of civilisations', which has been much championed recently, lies in its programme of categorising people of the world according to a unique, allegedly commanding, system of classification. This is deeply problematic because the civilisational categories are crude and inconsistent; and also because there are many other ways of seeing people (linked to politics, language, literature, class, occupation and other affiliations).

The inadequacy of the thesis of clashing civilisations thus begins well before we get to the point of asking whether civilisations must clash. No matter what answer is given to this question, addressing it in this coarse form tends, in itself, to push us into an illusive way of thinking about the people of the world. The befuddling influence of a singular classification traps those who (like many senior statesmen in Europe and the US) dispute the thesis of a clash but respond within its pre-specified terms of reference. To talk about 'the Islamic world' or 'the western world' (as is increasingly common, in line with Samuel Huntington's categories) is already to reduce people into this one dimension. The same impoverished vision of the world — divided into boxes of civilisations — is shared by those who preach amity among civilisations and those who see them clashing.

In fact, civilisations are hard to partition in this way, given the diversities within each society as well as the historical linkages between different countries and cultures. For example, in describing India as a 'Hindu civilisation', Samuel Huntington's exposition of the alleged clash of civilisations has to downplay the fact that India has many more Muslims (about 125 million, more than the entire British and French populations put together) than any

Madras, India: 'Welcome' to religious harmony –
Hindu, Muslim and Christian images share a wall
Credit: Mark Henley

other country in the world with the exception of Indonesia and marginally Pakistan. Also, it is futile to try to have an understanding of the nature and range of Indian art, literature, music, food or politics without seeing the extensive interactions across barriers of religious communities. This includes Hindus and Muslims, Buddhists, Jains, Sikhs, Parsees, Christians (who have been in India since at least the fourth century, before there was a single Christian in Britain), Jews (present in south India since the fall of Jerusalem) and even atheists and agnostics. Sanskrit has a larger atheistic literature than exists in any other classical language. Huntington's categorisation may be comforting to the Hindu fundamentalist but it is an odd reading of India.

A similar coarseness can be seen in the other categories invoked. How homogeneous should the 'Islamic' box be? Consider Akbar and Aurangzeb, two Muslim emperors of the Mughal dynasty in India. Aurangzeb tried hard to convert Hindus into Muslims and instituted various policies in that direction, of which taxing non-Muslims was only one example. In contrast, Akbar revelled in his multi-ethnic court and pluralist laws, and issued official proclamations insisting that no one 'should be interfered with on account of religion, and anyone is to be allowed to go over to a religion that pleases him'. If a homogeneous view of Islam were to be taken, then only one of them could count as a true Muslim. The Islamic fundamentalist would have no time for Akbar; and UK Prime Minister Tony Blair, given his insistence that tolerance is a defining characteristic of Islam, would have to consider excommunicating Aurangzeb from the community of Muslims. I expect both Akbar and Aurangzeb would protest, and so would I.

A similar crudity is present in the characterisation of what is called 'the western civilisation'. Samuel Huntington gives good examples of the importance of tolerance and individual freedom in European history, and insists that the 'West was West long before it was modern'. But there is no dearth of diversity here either. For example, when Akbar was making his pronouncements on religious tolerance in Agra in the 1590s, the Christian Inquisition was in full flow: in 1600, Giordano Bruno was burned at the stake for heresy in the Campo dei Fiori in Rome.

The first problem with reliance on civilisational partitioning is, therefore, its extraordinary crudity. This is supplemented by a second problem: the absurdity of the implicit presumption that this partitioning is natural and necessary and must overwhelm all other ways of identifying people. That imperious view goes not only against the old-fashioned belief that 'we human beings are all much the same' but also against the more plausible understanding that we are diversely different. For example, Bangladesh's split from Pakistan was not connected with religion but with language, literature and politics. Each of us has many features in our self-conception. Our religion, important as it may be, cannot be an all-engulfing identity. Even a shared poverty can be a source of solidarity across borders. The kind of division highlighted by, say, the so-called 'anti-globalisation' protesters – whose movement is, incidentally, one of the most globalised in the world – tries to unite the underdogs of the world economy. Its programme goes firmly against religious, national or 'civilisational' lines of division.

The main hope of harmony in the contemporary world lies not in any imagined uniformity but in the plurality of our identities, which cut across each other and work against sharp divisions around one uniquely hardened impenetrable faultline. The political leaders who dispute the clash of civilisations but think and act in terms of a unique partitioning of humanity into 'the western world', 'the Muslim world', 'the Hindu world', and so on, make the world not only more divisive but also much more flammable. They also end up privileging the voice of religious authorities (who become the *ex officio* spokesmen), while muffling other voices and silencing other concerns.

The robbing of our plural identities not only reduces us, it impoverishes the world. ❏

Amartya Sen won the Nobel Prize for Economics in 1998 and is now Master of Trinity College, Cambridge. This piece is based on a speech he gave in New Delhi at the inaugural meeting of South Asians for Human Rights – a new nongovernmental forum co-chaired by Asma Jahangir (Pakistan) and IK Gujral (India) – and originally published in Frontline *(Madras), January 2002*

4/1975: PETER HAZELHURST, INDIA

INDIAN CUT-UPS

Following the national state of emergency declared by Prime Minister Indira Gandhi on 26 June 1975, and imposition of censorship, Delhi was almost without newspapers for two days. This had more to do with the protracted power cuts that had started the night before than with the emergency measures but the coincidence was striking. The one newspaper to appear in the capital, the Motherland *of the Hindu nationalist party, defied the censorship and published the names of the principal figures then under arrest; its presses were immediately sealed and its editor, HKR Malkani, was arrested. When the government imposed strict pre-censorship, editors could ridicule the authorities by leaving white spaces to indicate censored material. One Calcutta editor used this technique to particularly good effect when he left a white space under the headline 'Jawaharlal Nehru's Letter to his Daughter while in British Prison' – the letter itself having been censored. The new minister of information and broadcasting, VC Shukla, banned the blank spaces as a 'form of protest'. He installed government officials in all the major newspaper offices and Indian press agencies to delete criticism of Gandhi's actions. Others were left to send their copy for the censors to the Press and Information Bureau, as the India correspondent for* The Times *describes.*

While I waited to submit my report to the censor in Delhi, a junior Indian official toyed with a blue pencil, suddenly frowned, and began scoring out one line after another of an American reporter's work. The reporter protested, 'Why have you deleted the report suggesting that demonstrations against Mrs Gandhi have fizzled out?'

'Because nobody would want to plan a demonstration against the prime minister. Nor can you inform your editor that this report has been censored,' the official said.

The frustrated correspondent asked why the phrase 'Mrs Gandhi was found guilty of corrupt practices during the 1971 elections' was being deleted, when it was simply repeating the court's verdict.

'Well, all right, I will pass that if you change "corrupt practices" to "minor irregularities",' the censor said.

'No,' said our colleague adamantly, 'just leave a blank space.'

'But it will be senseless and the readers will know it has been censored. Change it or the entire report will be held back,' the censor snapped.

Once-helpful press officers in India's Information Bureau were implementing one of the most rigorous forms of censorship. ❏

EXPLOSIONS GALORE

ADEWALE MAJA-PEARCE

ETHNIC CONFLICT, THE RELIGIOUS DIVIDE
AND A GREEDY AND INCOMPETENT
GOVERNMENT THAT HAS YET TO DELIVER
ON ITS DEMOCRATIC PROMISE THREATEN
NIGERIA'S FUTURE

Nigeria is exploding, with worse to come as we approach the elections early next year. First the armoury at the Ikeja military cantonment in the middle of busy Lagos caught fire early one Sunday evening and all hell was let loose; and then the city erupted in yet another round of ethnic clashes that took the army three days to quell. There was no particular connection between the two events unless both were caused by *agents provocateurs* intent on undermining the stability of our nascent democracy. If so, we shall never know. The government has already signalled its intention to censor the official report on the explosions in case it really does turn out to have been sabotage, which really would undermine . . . And nobody bothers with the ethnic clashes which are forever erupting all over this fractured country because democracy – however nascent – has yet to be delivered three years after the military ostensibly disengaged from power.

The only other connection between the two events, apart from the obvious physical danger of living in a country so incompetently run, was the person of the president himself, Olusegun Obasanjo, a former military head of state whose administration appears to be 'jinxed', as one mischievous politician quipped. The occasion was Obasanjo's visit to the cantonment, where he proceeded to behave with typical arrogance: 'Shut up! Shut up! You're unruly,' he fumed at the grieving crowd. 'I have talked to the governor, the commander of the cantonment, the police commissioner . . . They all know what to do. I just came here because I happened to be passing by.' That same evening found him in one of the *sharia* states in the far north where women, but not men, can be stoned to death for adultery – 'the man is not a woman, whereby she will have a protruding stomach to show,' according to one stoning judge – before he discovered that over 600 people had been killed (later revised upwards to 1,000) and offered a terse apology:

'It was only on my arrival at Katsina that I received a report on the sheer scale of the tragic incident . . .'

Ironically, most of the victims weren't killed by the rocket-propelled grenades that demolished the 3,000-strong Command School, among other buildings. Passers-by fled in panic, thinking there was a coup in the making, only to be drowned in a canal some distance away, many of them children stampeded from behind in the gathering dusk. Even more ironically, many of those lives might have been saved had the army taken the opportunity to reassure the populace in good time. It happened that an independent film crew were nearby and got their scoop, but soldiers at a checkpoint confiscated their tape in the interests of the national security they were to be called upon to protect a few days later when the country's two largest ethnic groups went for each other. Mercifully, the president held his peace this time round, but any gaffe he might have been inclined to make was pre-empted by the nationwide furore over a CNN report on the clashes, which said that Nigeria was still effectively under military rule and, further, that most Nigerians liked it that way because only the military could contain the disparate forces tearing the nation apart.

The report itself was inaccurate but not altogether misleading. Unfortunately, the correspondent, a Kenyan national, missed the larger picture, which was the scale of the trauma Nigerians suffered during the days of direct military rule that was only brought to an end by a messy – and ultimately unworkable – compromise that allowed the generals to retain the fabulous wealth they looted from the Niger Delta, estimated at US$100 billion, more than three times the national debt, in a country clamouring to be placed among the poorest of the poor. Those were the days when Ken Saro-Wiwa and his fellow Ogoni activists were judicially murdered after a kangaroo trial at the very moment the Commonwealth heads of government were gathering in Auckland, New Zealand, to decide what to do about the troublesome giant of Africa; the days when trade unionists were kidnapped in broad daylight, perhaps on their way to church, and locked away for months on end without access to their families or lawyers; the days when journalists were convicted for coup-plotting by secret military tribunal and then flogged every morning so that 'the incessant beating with horsewhips coupled with long periods of solitary confinement in dark cells has damaged my eyesight,' to quote one of them. Another, who was let out of his cell just nine times in three and a half years, now suffers 'persistent fungi on my fingers, bilateral eye irritations and poorer vision' as a result of his incarceration.

3/1997: KEN SARO-WIWA, NIGERIA

*Nigerian novelist, poet, campaigner against the devastation of Ogoniland
by the oil companies and founder of the Movement for the Survival of the Ogoni
People, Ken Saro-Wiwa was executed with eight other activists by the Nigerian
military government in November 1995 on trumped-up charges of conspiracy to
murder four fellow Ogoni leaders. The following excerpt is from the defence statement
he was prevented from reading in court.*

My Lord, we all stand before history. I am a man of peace, of ideas.
Appalled by the denigrating poverty of my people who live on a richly
endowed land, distressed by their political marginalisation and economic
strangulation, angered by the devastation of their land, anxious to preserve
their right to life and to a decent living, and determined to usher to this
country as a whole a fair and just democratic system, I have devoted all my
intellectual and material resources – my very life – to a cause in which I
have total belief and from which I cannot be blackmailed or intimidated.
I have no doubt at all about the ultimate success of my cause . . . nor
imprisonment nor death can stop our ultimate victory.

I and my colleagues are not the only ones on trial. Shell is on trial
here, and it is as well that it is represented by a counsel said to be holding a
watching brief. . . . the ecological war the company has waged in the delta
will be called to question sooner rather than later and the crimes of that
war be duly punished . . .

On trial also is the Nigerian nation, its present rulers and those who
assist them. The military did not act alone. We all stand on trial, My Lord,
for by our actions we have denigrated our country and jeopardised the
future of our children. . . .

In my innocence of the false charges I face here, in my utter conviction,
I call upon the Ogoni people, the peoples of the Niger Delta, and the
oppressed ethnic minorities of Nigeria to stand up now and fight fearlessly
and peacefully for their rights. History is on their side, God is on their side.
For the Holy Quran says in Sura 42 verse 41: 'All those who fight when
oppressed incur no guilt, but Allah shall punish the oppressor.'

Come the day. ❏

*Safiya Hussaini: condemned to
death by the* sharia *courts
Credit: AP / Saurabh Das*

So it was hardly surprising that journalists themselves should be in the forefront of the outrage over the 'satanic' CNN's 'unbalanced, sensational, malicious, mischievous and insulting report [which is] capable of truncating [our] nascent democracy', according to one front-page editorial. This was music to the ears of the Federal government which quickly summoned the erring brother-African-working-overtime-for-the-western-media (and what about his own despotic country, come to that?) because the authorities 'must be seen to be protecting our airwaves and our national image'. Nor was this the first time that the Federal government had been called upon to defend the nation's honour. Previously, it was the 'otherwise responsible' BBC and Voice of America whose reports on the last round of ethnic clashes in Lagos showed that they were now allowing themselves to be used by 'those who want to destabilise Nigeria'. Clearly, things were simpler in the old days, in the days before the new era of 'social responsibility', the term one hears increasingly at editorial board meetings, where it is also recommended that we substitute 'communal' for 'ethnic' in any reports on the clashes in order to douse the embers of ethnicity that can only be extinguished by the same military that helped us to this pretty pass.

Oddly enough, in all the brouhaha about what the foreign media did or didn't say, and whether any of it even mattered, everybody seemed to forget that the enemies of our nascent democracy were not without but within, as demonstrated by the assassination early one evening last December of the attorney-general and minister of justice, Chief Bola Ige. It seems that all his guards abandoned their posts at the same time in search of food, leaving the coast clear for his assassins to walk straight into his bedroom. Later, it was reported that his killers used a special bullet that dissolved in his body upon impact but this is the kind of detail that is relished in a country that has learned to mythologise astonishingly high levels of violence. The police, themselves responsible for much of that violence, quickly swung into action, promising 'it will not be long before the perpetrators are identified and tracked down', but nobody took them seriously because that was what they always said when prominent citizens were murdered in their beds. Not that anyone blamed them. The assassination was obviously political, although the minister of information and national orientation was quick to distance his boss from culpability in the 'dastardly act' on the grounds that 'the President of the Federal Republic is a responsible leader', which was more or less what he said about Obasanjo's predecessor but one, General Sani Abacha, the dictator who caused Ken Saro-Wiwa to be hanged for a crime that he didn't legally commit.

The allegation of official complicity came a month after the assassination, when a small-town politician known by the nickname 'Fryo' walked into a lawyer's office and signed an affidavit indicting Obasanjo for the murder of the 70-year-old chief in a bid to retain power come April next year.

According to Fryo, the presidency paid the deputy governor of one of the six [out of 36] Yoruba states, which Obasanjo must deliver if he is to stand any chance of a second term, to cross over to his party, promising him unlimited funds to unseat the governor. This triggered a war between the deputy and the governor in the course of which a close aide of the former was murdered as he sat in a beer parlour opposite the local police station. He was apparently fired at several times at close range before his skull was bashed in with a sledgehammer in case he possessed charms against bullets. Fryo then claimed that he was told by the deputy to prepare for 'the battle ahead' and offered US$50,000 to assassinate Chief Ige. He declined the offer. Three days later, the minister was dead anyway.

The lawyer chosen to receive these disturbing allegations was careful to get Fryo's complete statement both in writing and on tape before handing him over to the police in a blaze of publicity that would make it difficult for them to disappear him. This was just as well. He himself was summarily arrested shortly afterwards, whereupon a chastened Fryo suddenly recanted, claiming that his original statement had been doctored by the lawyer. The murder will never be solved and will be superseded by more assassinations as we approach the elections.

Those elections will be only the third supervised by a civilian regime in over four decades of independence. Both previous attempts were charac- terised by mayhem in the Yoruba areas of the country as the then ruling party rigged its way back into power – 'Whether you vote for us or you don't, we are returning to office; we will make sure that invisible bodies vote for us,' in the famous words of one politician – only to be overthrown by the military when it was obvious that the politicians had lost all moral authority to govern. On both those occasions, the populace welcomed the return of 'sanity' before discovering that military rule was really not the answer; quite the reverse, in fact. There is no reason to think that things will be different this time around, except that any soldier foolish enough to seize the airwaves with an appeal to his 'fellow Nigerians' will only embolden the country's disparate parts finally to go their own way.

Those disparate parts are the 350 or so ethnic groups and both major religions that were yoked together less than a century ago by a foreign power for the purpose of the plunder that has continued unabated. The vultures this time are the three major ethnic groups who hold the country in a balance of terror while they enslave the minorities in the oil-producing Niger Delta, who pay in their own blood for the 'fraudulent contraption' called Nigeria.

A foreigner visiting the Niger Delta would wonder at the absence of roads, schools, clinics, electricity and running water, made worse by the unregulated destruction of the environment by transnational companies – Agip, Chevron, Mobil, Shell, Texaco – that take their cue from a Federal government that never hesitates to send in the army to quell the restive natives. This practice reached a peak in the mid-1990s when General Abacha appointed a psychopath to 'sanitise' Ogoni land preparatory to hanging Ken Saro-Wiwa. However, any hope that things were going to be different under the new dispensation were dashed within three months of Obasanjo's Second Coming when a detachment of 2,000 soldiers flattened the second-largest town in oil-producing Bayelsa State as reprisal for the killing of seven police officers. At the end of Operation Hakuri 11, as it was called by the minister of defence, only three buildings were left standing and an unknown number of people were killed.

Worse yet, the police officers were not murdered by the peasant farmers and fisherfolk of Odi but by one of the armed gangs of disaffected youths that have proliferated in the volatile region over the past few years, kidnap- ping, extorting and murdering because they have seen for themselves the futility of peaceful protest, which only gets you hanged. Ironically (so many ironies in Nigeria), this particular gang – the Egbesu Boys – was itself instrumental in Obasanjo's victory in that very town by ensuring that the 'ballot box got filled in 30 minutes when nobody was accredited', according to one of the independent election monitors, who also noticed 'Egbesu Boys with guns and if they don't go away from [there] they would kill all of them'.

Not that it mattered. The results were known before the first vote was cast, largely by ensuring that only officially approved parties were registered by the officially appointed electoral commission. The trick was to base registration on national spread. This actively promoted the 'moneybags' politics of the Big Three at the same time as it excluded special interest and minority groups that between them account for about half the country's 120 million people. It was for this reason that a distinguished constitutional lawyer called the commission the 'undemocratic or anti-democratic octopus on the neck of the country' for assuming a role shirked even by the 'foreign autocratic imposition' that was colonial rule.

This octopus was smuggled into the military-inspired 1999 constitution handed to Obasanjo by the generals at a lavish ceremony in Eagle Square which saw Nelson Mandela rubbing shoulders with Prince Charles. The fact that the excluded are increasingly turning to violence simply to be heard ought to concern those who claim to be jealous of our nascent democracy but who are intent only on business as usual, thereby guaranteeing the very violence that will eventually consume them: the madness that has beggared an oil-rich nation is insupportable. According to the United Nations' Human Development Index, Nigeria is currently one place below Haiti, itself the poorest country in the western hemisphere. That is why there will be many more explosions in the months ahead. Never mind what the foreign media might or might not say about the matter, this is merely a distraction. ❏

Adewale Maja-Pearce is a freelance writer and consultant on Nigerian affairs. He can be reached at majapearce@hotmail.com

AVRUPA ON THE LINE

SENER LEVENT

AS 'GREEK CYPRUS' BLOOMS UNDER THE
PROSPECT OF EU MEMBERSHIP, ANGER IS
BUBBLING OVER ON THE OTHER SIDE AS A NEW
GENERATION OF TURKISH CYPRIOTS RECKON
THEIR LOSSES UNDER THE DEAD HAND OF TURKEY
AND ITS HENCHMEN. THE FOUNDER OF A NEW,
INDEPENDENT NEWSPAPER TELLS THE TALE

For years we have been living under the command of others: Turkish militarism permeates our lives at every level; President Rauf Denktas still dominates the scene as he ever did. Not only the media but even our parliament and government is operated as if by remote control by our real rulers, the government in Ankara. Our claim to be an independent and separate state is a mockery. Even the adoption of a multi-party system in Northern Cyprus failed to open the door to democracy.

Breaking old taboos and replacing them with new realities meant taking the first steps along a dangerous path.

On its first day of publication on 17 September 1997, *Avrupa* made its position as an 'independent' daily clear to its readers. Why? Because most of the existing newspapers published in Northern Cyprus were organs of political parties. Those few that presented themselves as 'neutral' were no more than mouthpieces for the 'official view'.

Avrupa took it on itself to proclaim loud and clear what its rivals had avoided: that our emperor was naked. It was soon getting up the noses of the military and of Denktas, and it took only three months for *Avrupa* to tread on the first landmine.

General Peker Gunal of the island's Turkish Security Force Command singled our paper out at a public ceremony, vowing that we would be made to 'pinch our tails and bow our heads'. Denktas took the cue and opened five cases against *Avrupa* for 'belittling the military'.

The judges found us guilty as charged and fined us a crippling 120 billion TL (cUS$85,000) on 29 December 1999, a record fine in Cyprus. Unable to pay, we were forced to watch it rise to US$200,000 over the

*Nicosia, N Cyprus, January 2002:
Turkish Cypriots demonstrate
in favour of reunification
Credit: AP Photo / Harun Ucar*

course of the following two years. Meanwhile, *Avrupa* found plenty of other landmines strewn in its path.

In June 2000, I, as owner and editor-in-chief, and three other colleagues were arrested and accused of 'espionage'. The hand of the Security Force Command and Denktas were behind the plot. After we had spent 11 days in jail, the judges bowed to heavy public pressure and ordered our release.

Since then, I have yet to be indicted for any crime related to these charges. However, my passport, confiscated on the day of my arrest, has yet to be returned to me, thereby barring me from foreign travel.

Avrupa's offices also came under attack. Our print house was bombed in May and November 2001; to date, there have been no arrests. But that is the case with all those responsible for political crimes in Northern Cyprus.

Denktas, who had claimed to have 'personally seen' the non-existent evidence of our guilt as spies, then added insult to injury by publicly accusing us of bombing our own offices. He even offered a US$3,000 reward to anyone who could prove it.

As I write, all these cases await judgement and carry collective jail sentences of up to 500 years for some defendants.

As the months crept on, *Avrupa* was breaking all records in the field of Cypriot jurisprudence. Literally hundreds of charges have been brought against us, most of them related to our habit of presenting the Turkish presence in Cyprus as an 'occupation' and thus 'belittling' Turkey's Security Forces.

Last year, citing the US$200,000 fine with interest still outstanding, Denktas successfully petitioned the courts to confiscate the paper's assets – its print machinery, computers, office equipment and all that was left of its circulation income.

Avrupa was finally forced to suspend publication. Its 'farewell issue' – no 1,535 – came out on 14 December 2001. Its successor, *Afrika*, hit the streets the next day with barely any drop in circulation. It remains the second biggest seller among the ten dailies published in Northern Cyprus. ❑

Sener Levent *was owner-editor of the Turkish Cypriot daily* Avrupa

6/1998: SIWAN PERWER, TURKEY / KURDISTAN

HEAR MY SONG . . .

The Turkish ban on all things Kurdish – language, culture, simply the mention of the word even in the Turkish language – has resulted in widespread hardship for all Kurds and driven hundreds of thousands of them into exile. Yet the people and the identity survive, articulated nowhere more than in the songs ancient and modern of their homeland.

Born in 1955 in Urfa (south-east Anatolia or Turkish Kurdistan), Siwan Perwer, the foremost Kurdish musician and singer of his generation, came from a family steeped in the culture of his homeland; his grandfather was a renowned classical singer and flute player. Siwan believed in change and that 'with music a community can be changed'. His compositions initiated a new school of Kurdish music.

By the 1970s, Siwan had built up a considerable following and began to suffer from the attentions of the authorities. Police would regularly break up his concerts, but Siwan clandestinely appeared around Turkey singing in the banned Kurdish language. His music became a rallying point for Kurds throughout Kurdistan and farther afield. Since his forced exile in Europe, the popularity of his songs has grown, his audience no longer confined to the Kurdish community. 'Ey Ferat', his ode to the great Euphrates that rises in the mountains of Turkish Kurdistan is a classic. 'Herne Pes' (Go Forward) became an unofficial anthem for the Kurdish people and compositions like 'Naze' (Spoilt Girl) have been copied by Turkish artists and become major hits.

Siwan insists on singing only in Kurdish: 'My music is available in Turkey but there is a *de facto* ban or restriction – people who buy the cassettes can be detained arbitrarily. As a musician I am totally banned in Turkey.'

On 11 February 2002, the Turkish High Audiovisual Council (RTUK) banned a Diyarbekir TV network for one year simply for broadcasting a song by Siwan Perwer. ❑

Gill Newsham

KURDISTAN

Kurdistan, my Kurdistan;
Humbled; by others possessed;
Garden of my roses Kurdistan;
Of our grieving the painful cause.

In your loftiness my Kurdistan
Nestle hamlets, towns embraced by you;
And to die is the reward
For worshippers of this and of mine.

Rivers crossing meadows, spilling
Onto fields like painted silver lines
Between hilly vineyards
And endowing with beauty my Kurdistan.

Paupers are we, walking on your soil,
Pitilessly plundered by foes
Of nature's richness and bounty,
Haunted by seemingly endless poverty.

Your luckless people robbed
Of many splendoured golds
While the tower shrines of Korash and Ardashir
Are defiled by ever-watching stranger's probing eyes.

O, mother of the Tigris and Euphrates!
Shameless with no honour is the Kurd who betrays you;
My heart bleeding with other Kurdish hearts,
Yet still alive for you my Kurdistan. ❏

Lyric by **Cegerxwin**, *sung by* **Siwan Perwer**

1986: *NUNCA MÁS*, ARGENTINA

NEVER AGAIN

During the 1970s, Argentina was torn by terror from both the extreme right and the far left.

The armed forces responded to the terrorists' crime with a terrorism far worse than the one they were combating, and after 24 March 1976 they could count on the power and impunity of an absolute state, which they misused to abduct, torture and kill thousands of human beings.

Every civilised nation, including our own, has laid down in its constitution guarantees which can never been suspended, even in the most catastrophic state of emergency: the right of life, the right to security of person; the right to a trial; the right not to suffer either inhuman conditions of detention, denial of justice or summary execution.

From the huge amount of documentation we have gathered, it can be seen that these human rights were violated at all levels by the Argentine state during the repression carried out by its armed forces. Nor were they violated in a haphazard fashion, but systematically, according to a similar pattern, with identical kidnappings and tortures taking place throughout the country.

The abductions were precisely organised operations, sometimes occurring at the victim's place of work, sometimes in the street in broad daylight. They involved the open deployment of military personnel, who were given a free hand by the local police stations.

When a victim was sought out in his or her home at night, armed units would surround the block and force their way in, terrorising parents and children, who were often gagged and forced to watch. They would seized the persons they had come for, beat them mercilessly, hood them, then drag them off to their cars or trucks, while the rest of the unit almost invariably ransacked the house or looted everything that could be carried. The victims were then taken to a chamber over whose doorway might well have been inscribed the words Dante read on the gates of Hell: 'Abandon hope, all ye who enter here.'

Thus, in the name of national security, thousands upon thousands of human beings, usually young adults or even adolescents, fell into the sinister, ghostly category of the *desaparecidos*, a word (sad privilege for Argentina) frequently left in Spanish by the world's press.

 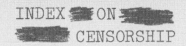 

Seized by force against their will, the victims no longer existed as citizens. Who exactly was responsible for their abduction? Why had they been abducted? Where were they? There were no precise answers to these questions: the authorities had no record of them; they were not being held in jail; justice was unaware of their existence. Silence was the only reply to all the habeas corpus writs, an ominous silence that engulfed them. No kidnapper was ever arrested, not a single detention centre was ever located, there was never news of those responsible being punished for any of the crimes.

A feeling of complete vulnerability spread throughout Argentine society, coupled with the fear that anyone, however innocent, might become a victim of the never-ending witch-hunt.

All sectors fell into the net: trade union leaders fighting for better wages; youngsters in student unions; journalists who did not support the regime; psychologists and sociologists simply for belonging to suspicious professions; young pacifists, nuns and priests who had taken the teachings of Christ to shanty areas; the friends of these people, too, and the friends of friends, plus others whose names were given out of motives of personal vengeance, or by the kidnapped under torture. The vast majority of them were innocent not only of any acts of terrorism but even of belonging to the fighting units of the guerrilla organisations: these latter chose to fight it out, and either died in shoot-outs or committed suicide before they could be captured. Few of them were alive by the time they were in the hands of the repressive forces.

From the moment of their abduction, the victims lost all rights. Deprived of all communication with the outside world, held in unknown places, subjected to barbaric tortures, kept ignorant of their immediate or ultimate fate, they risked being either thrown into the river or the sea, weighed down with blocks of cement, or burned to ashes.

Great catastrophes are always instructive. The tragedy that began with the military dictatorship in March 1976, the most terrible our nation has ever suffered, will undoubtedly serve to help us understand that it is only democracy that can save a people from horror on this scale, only democracy that can keep and safeguard the sacred, essential rights of man. Only with democracy we will be certain that NEVER AGAIN will events such as these be repeated in our nation. ❏

From the prologue to Nunca más: the report of the Argentine National Commission on the Disappeared *by Erneto Sábato (*Index on Censorship *in association with Farrar, Straus & Giroux, New York & London, 1986)*

THE PERSISTENCE OF MEMORY

ALEJANDRA MATUS

I was watching the news on television the other night with my friend, Gabriela. In a brief aside, offered in passing, the newscaster informed us that some 50 people had protested in front of the courts of justice against its failure to advance cases concerning the violation of human rights committed under Augusto Pinochet's military regime, lasting from 1973 to 1990.

Gabriela is a journalist of 30-something. Though none of her relatives could be counted among the 'disappeared' or 'politically executed', like virtually every other Chilean journalist she bore the brunt of the dictatorship's attacks. After the news, she was silent for several minutes before saying, 'I'm ashamed to admit it but I've come to find that kind of news boring. It shouldn't be like that but I'm afraid it's the truth'.

Roberto, Gabriela's partner, is a friend of many years. None the less, only now, after spending two and a half years in exile as a result of my book, *The Black Book of Chilean Justice*, being banned, do I realise that his father was executed by Pinochet's regime for his political opinions.

I returned to Chile in November 2001. My book had been banned in April 1999. A Supreme Court judge, Servando Jordan, accused me of infringing the Security Laws, one of whose clauses establishes a penalty of up to five years for anyone offending against the principal authorities of the countries. The book is a journalistic investigation into the conduct of the judicial powers throughout its history, and in particular into its performance during the years of the dictatorship and those that followed in the transition to democracy. It's here that it becomes obvious that our land has never been able to count on a judicial power, properly conceived and executed but that the judicial system has been – other than in a few unusual moments of isolation – the kind of institution that's in hock to minor hierarchy. It is, therefore, in the service of a political power (or, in certain periods, to the military) and to the dictates of the ultra-rich. As I demonstrate in my book, its lack of autonomy is at the heart of the negligence with which the judiciary acts in instances of human rights violations.

In ensuring that my book was banned, the judge was concerned not only to protect the 'honour' of his profession but to forestall any debate on the conduct of the judiciary during the years of human rights abuse. It had, after all, consistently used its powers to protect the elite political class to the detriment of the weakest sector of society.

According to humanitarian organisations, 84 people were tried and condemned for human rights violations after Pinochet's fall in 1990, the majority of them low- to middle-ranking military and civilians. In the one case that might have demonstrated Pinochet's guilt – the 1976 assassination of Orlando Letelier, exiled Chilean diplomat and prominent critic of the Pinochet regime – while US pressure ensured that the case went to a conclusion in 1995, penalties were insignificant and the judge in question, Adolfo Banados, ensured that any question of Pinochet's criminal responsibility for the murder was not pursued. No doubt he was more conscious of the limits of his authority than his judicial responsibility.

From 1990 on, some 20 journalists and political leaders were accused of violating the law of national security in their attempts to get Pinochet's responsibility for the crimes committed under his government publicly recognised. Now, even though the general is back in Santiago, the general's return to Chile, thanks to the ruling of the new minister of justice, Judge Juan Guzman, what could once only be murmured between four walls can now be shouted from the rooftops – and no one has yet been accused of breaking the law for doing so.

Pinochet will probably never be declared guilty of the grave human rights violations that were committed in his name and under his instructions but his name has, at least, lost its power to strike terror into Chilean hearts. While there is no longer the old fear of legal reprisals for speaking out about the past, the debate has ground to a halt. Chile gives the impression that it is possible to confront the past fearlessly and in public; the criminal role Pinochet was accused of playing can be discussed without fear of censorship. Yet there are other ways of ensuring silence when society feels threatened.

For instance, Elizabeth Subercaseaux's short novel, *My Darling Daddy*, deals with the joint responsibility of ordinary civilians and big business during the period of human rights violations. According to her, these are the truths that Chilean society continues to refuse to assimilate. Her book, which was included in the readers' club operated by the conservative and influential daily *El Mercurio*, was withdrawn without explanation; it was subsequently given restricted release for subscribers only.

That night we watched television with Gabriela, we talked for a long time about why this feeling of apathy had overtaken so many Chileans. The news reflected our sentiment: less than a minute on the discovery of further mass graves within a military precinct, plenty of space for sport, traffic accidents and a song festival in Vina del Mar.

We were forced to the conclusion that most of us already knew perfectly well about the attempt under Pinochet to physically eliminate one section of the population and control the rest. And however much more one uncovers, this knowledge is not translated into justice. And, finally, those responsible for what happened remain hidden in the highest places, masked in shadows and silence.

Gabriela argued that the trial of Pinochet was the highest level of justice to which Chilean society could aspire but that since he had been declared too ill to stand trial, the skein of wool had begun to unravel. Chilean democracy, with all its protective limitations, cannot offer anything better. According to what we've been told, the armed forces never really handed over power in 1990: the game is still played by its rules.

This does not equate with oblivion: oblivion cannot be imposed by decree. Our indigenous peoples have never forgotten the barbarities of the Spanish Conquest and it would be hazardous to suggest that Patricia will simply forget about her husband and Adriana her brother, as if memory had been swallowed up in collective resignation. On the contrary and with little hope of success, they went to enormous lengths to bring to light the crimes committed against their loved ones.

Memory has proved more enduring than reasons of state and tends to emerge in the most unexpected manner. Pinochet's sudden arrest in London at the request of the Spanish courts, forced Chileans to look into the mirror of their recent history for the first time. This did not bring the predicted return of chaos and militarism to the country, but the search for political 'stability' seems to have pre-empted further debate. Once again, we are surrounded by silence. Forgetting is another matter. ❏

Alejandra Matus is a journalist and the author of The Black Book of Chilean Justice. *Translated by Amanda Hopkinson*

CULTURE

Kabul 2002: Afghan men try to gatecrash Unfaithful Love, *the first 'sexy movie' in Afghanistan for many years*
Credit: AFP / Anja Nieringhaus

DARING TO DREAM

REMY OURDAN

Four years of the Mujaheddin, five years of the Taliban, 22 years of war. Ten days ago, the Mujaheddin in their pakols, *the legendary headgear of Ahmed Shah Massoud's Northern Alliance, drove the men in black turbans, symbol of the Taliban, out of Kabul. The Afghan capital had lived through five years of the Taliban regime. And, before that, four years of a civil war between rival Mujaheddin factions. And, before that, 13 years of Soviet occupation. Today, in this capital of a divided, chaotic Afghanistan, a heady scent of freedom is in the air. This city, which could have been so lovely were it not for the war, which still manages to be beautiful despite the war, seems to be seized by a fever of excitement. A city launching itself into the unknown but a city which is slow to react, which wearily understands that Afghan revolutions rarely do it any good . . . Kabulis may be pleased, but they're not really sure what the word 'peace' means any more. A cinema projectionist, a bookseller and a schoolgirl, each tell their story: Taliban barbarity, the excesses of those who went before. Stories of broken lives.*

SHAH MUHAMMAD, *bookseller*
'Kabul would be so lovely if it weren't for the war.'
Shah Muhammad is a cultured man who loves to pore over the pages of his yellowing, dog-eared tomes. He opened his first bookshop 30 years ago under the name 'Shah M'. He has lived through all the changing regimes. 'The communists burned my books . . . the Mujaheddin were too busy burning each other to pay me any attention . . . then the Taliban burned my books . . .' There are no illusions behind his smile. The way he sees it: 'They may have preached different ideologies, but they all brought suffering to Kabul just the same.'

Nevertheless, for Shah Muhammad the Taliban were the worst enemies of civilisation because 'they were absolutely determined to destroy Afghanistan's cultural heritage', burning books, records, film, reducing museum pieces to dust – even destroying the celebrated Bamiyan Buddhas. 'When they built a huge bonfire in the square to burn books from my shop I went to see the minister of culture and I told him: "You can destroy my books, you might even destroy me, but you'll never destroy the history of Afghanistan!" They put my brothers in prison. One of them was tortured

and had to flee the country. I stayed behind to fight against these illiterates.'
While he gets on well with the Mujaheddin who have just captured the
Afghan capital, Shah Muhammad has no illusions about some of them and
how they feel about his country's cultural riches. 'At the time of their first
Islamic government [1992–96] a Mujaheddin minister came in to buy a
book on sexual disorders. He asked me how my business was going. I said:
"Thanks very much; that book's doing well anyway; it's a bestseller as far
as I'm concerned. All your colleagues have already bought it. On the other
hand, there hasn't been a single minister in here enquiring about books
on the cultural history of our country." He was embarrassed and said, "I'm
shocked, but you're absolutely right." He left with the book on sex and
three history books.'

In what is otherwise a cultural wilderness, Shah Muhammad's
collection, consisting of 8,000 books on Afghanistan hidden all over Kabul,
is the most impressive in the entire country. One day he wants to open
a public library and give his precious collection to the nation, 'once there
are people in power with a bit of intelligence'. So far, none of them has
qualified as far as he is concerned. There's one exception: the Tadjik rebel
who was murdered two days before the attacks on the USA. 'If Ahmed Shah
Massoud had been a Pashtun, we might have had no more problems in
Afghanistan . . .'

Sometimes the bookseller played along with the Taliban to beat them at
their own game. So, in order to conform with Taliban laws, he stuck visiting
cards on book covers to hide any pictures of living creatures. But, behind
the shelves, where no one could see, Shah Muhammad kept political works
banned by the mullahs, and postcards and posters that he printed himself.
There is a photo of a lightly clad Queen Soraya, pictures dating from the
1970s of young sportswomen in skirts and, of course, the giant Buddhas.
'I sell thousands of those, through Pakistan, to Afghan communities all over
the world. They love them.'

Shah Muhammad may look like a nice, prosperous businessman, but this
man, who is of mixed Tadjik and Pashtun origin, was part of the resistance in
Kabul. He quotes a line from his favourite Afghan book, *Shah Nama* (*Book of
Kings*), by the epic poet Ferdosi: '"In times of great peril, be now the wolf and
now the sheep." Then you will survive so that you may see whether Kabul,
your beloved, will survive also. I love Kabul,' murmurs Shah Muhammad. 'I
love keeping warm, eating next to a wood stove when it's snowing. That is
a delight; one of the most precious moments in my entire life.'

Kabul 2002: Hindi movies return to the Bakhtiar cinema
Credit: AFP / Jewel Samad

EWAZ ALI, *cinema projectionist*
'I was lucky. One day a friend took me along to the cinema and I got a job there straight away. That was 30 years ago and since then I've been showing films.'
Ewaz, the projectionist in the Bakhtiar, the first cinema to re-open, is dressed in rags. He has barely managed to survive for five years by selling fruit for a few afghanis in the town's markets. Now he's back to fiddling with projectors and peering through the little window to watch the audience's enthusiastic responses. 'When the Taliban captured Kabul we all hoped it meant peace in Afghanistan,' he recalls. 'Then they started arresting people and explaining how they wanted us to live. After three days, we realised just how evil they were. They banned cinema for religious reasons. I still don't understand why, even now.'

Not only did Ewaz lose his job, he had to keep quiet about his ungodly past. Although he feels 'liberated' by Ahmed Shah Massoud's fighters, he, too, is without illusions. He remembers how, even before the Taliban, the fundamentalist Mujaheddin leader Gulbuddin Hekmatyar, another one-time friend of Islamabad and Washington, had already banned cinema. What's more, he knows that there has been very little relaxation of censorship. 'There's a commission that views all films and cuts out any anti-Islamic scenes. One kiss between adolescents is OK, but no naked men or women! No sex scenes! Mind you, I agree with that sort of censorship.'

He might agree, but that does not stop this old projectionist being nostalgic for the good old days when Sean Connery was undressing Ursula Andress on the island of Dr No. 'At that time, America had very good relations with Iran and we used to get the James Bond films from Tehran. That was before the jihad. That was three wars ago. That was . . .' Ewaz can't remember exactly when it was. He says that on the morning the Bakhtiar re-opened, his feelings were 'hard to describe'. There was something like a popular uprising in the street.

The projectionist had brought along his son Abdul. He is old enough to learn the trade now; before the Taliban he was just a child. He placed a reel on the carefully dusted projector. It was *Ascension*, an Afghan war film glorifying those who had fought the Soviets. He watched the film run without interruption. 'There's no interval during Ramadan because the audience aren't allowed to drink, eat or smoke.' In Ewaz's view, this new-found freedom is the result of the first five weeks of US bombing raids. 'Of course, we were very frightened; we didn't like it a bit. But then we saw that they were targeting very precisely, So, once we were fairly sure we weren't going to be killed, we were quite happy.' Now this Hazari projectionist is hoping for some foreign aid. 'For 20 years the world has been watching what's been going on in Afghanistan without doing anything. Now the UN has to help us to stabilise this town and this country. *Insh' Allah*!'

AZIZ GHAZNAOUI, *singer*
'*They banned Afghan music because they claimed it was forbidden by Islam.*'
Ever since he left school, Aziz has been an employee of Radio-Television Kabul and has warbled the official choruses to the praise and glory of the successive Afghan regimes. When it came to the Taliban, it was not an enjoyable experience. 'They banned Afghan music because they claimed it was forbidden by Islam. OK, so I stayed at home. All the singers and musicians in Kabul emigrated to Pakistan or somewhere else, apart from a few who had to read or chant patriotic poems on the radio without musical accompaniment. One day, a minister asked me in a threatening way if I'd got anything against the Taliban or if I thought that their regime wouldn't last long. I had no choice. I just had to go back and sing without music.' Aziz claims that during the weeks of US bombing raids, once he'd got over

his fear, he secretly wrote 'songs about loving your country and about the Islamic revolution', of the Mujaheddin variety. So now he's calmly waiting 'for the government to choose which songs and poems are to be recorded', those that are going to 'give Afghans renewed energy'.

He's also hoping to be allowed to sing tunes performed by his favourite western singers, Tom Jones and Enrico Macias. 'An artist is never subject to a government, he is at the service of the people,' he says, albeit without much conviction. 'Your voice comes from your heart. I am a free man.' Free? Well, what Aziz thinks is that: 'Prison is better than five years under the Taliban! When the Mujaheddin arrived I shaved my beard off that same evening. I looked at myself in the mirror. I hadn't laughed so much in 20 years! The next day, as I rode my bike through the streets of Kabul, shaved and wearing western clothes, passers-by shouted greetings and congratulated me.' ❏

Remy Ourdan is a correspondent with Le Monde, *Paris.*
Translated by Mike Routledge

FICTION, RESISTANCE AND THE READING PUBLIC

A L KENNEDY

IN A CULTURE WITH ACCESS TO REPUTABLE
MEDIA AND VIGOROUS FICTION, THE FULL,
HUMANISING FORCE OF IMAGINATION
COULD HELP DEFEND US, OUR RIGHTS
AND PRIVILEGES AND THOSE OF OTHERS —
IF ONLY WE WOULD LET IT

This is an essay in defence of fiction. It begins like this.

It's 18 September 2001, and I'm taking a train from Innsbruck to Zurich, travelling from one reading to another. The day is faultless, the past weekend's rain inconceivable now under a deep, cloudless blue. The Tyrol's peaks glisten impeccably, receding, while the Alps advance, all cabins and white peaks and mouse-coloured cows: one picture-postcard view after another. I'm comfortably installed in a compartment with only two other occupants: a pair of American tourists, husband and wife, whistle-stopping around Europe. He is small and softly spoken, she is louder and apologetically obese. They are both wearing brand new outfits, hers the more audibly colourful. She tells me about her family and her friends in Pennsylvania — that's where they're from. I mention something about it being 'The Quaker State' — I am, after all, a Quaker attender. They look at me slightly uneasily, as if I'm implying they still wear buckled shoes in private and call each other 'thee'.

They graze almost continually through little snacks from a plastic bag, vaguely unsure of the foreign labels, and read from a day-old copy of USA Today. They speak no German and do not completely understand where they are. The wife asks the husband questions about the landscape, about whether people here would have nannies, about architectural features and lakes. He has no answers, but remains just as docile as she is inquisitive. She takes off her shoes so that he can rub her feet — she has trouble with her feet — and wonders how best to describe the Alps in her journal for the people back home. He glances at his paper in spasms and mentions 'the flag' with the air of someone willing himself to feel reassured. If I were not here, hearing them breathing, I would take them to be peripheral extras in a lazy pulp paperback.

But they are, of course, here and, quite naturally, breathing, entirely alive. And every now and then the wife has other things to say: how moved she was to hear of

WWII veterans who've volunteered to fight, who knows what, after what happened in New York. A week ago today – she can't believe it – she and her husband were already over in Europe by then. They flew here and have no other way back. She doesn't pursue the train of thought, rushing, instead, into more questions: how did they get inside the cockpit? Did they just kill people to get inside? Did everyone know they were going to die? How long did they know? How could anyone do it? Why would they do it? She doesn't wait for answers, rather than find them uncomforting.

When a policeman with a sidearm asks for our passports as we cross into Switzer-land, she flinches, although all is well. Then she continues to be absently sociable and no one I'll ever know better: dressed in her cheerful holiday clothes and terrified.

It is difficult to see someone as a caricature when she is clearly, humanly terrified: her husband rubbing her feet, because this is a domestic habit, a small indication of love, and a comfort in the absence of adequate words.

A few weeks before that train journey I delivered a lecture on fiction at the Edinburgh International Book Festival. What follows will be drawn, in part, from that lecture which sought to identify some of the current threats to fiction and the many unique qualities which make it worth defending.

Why drag the American couple into all this? Partly because my description of them represents what often supplants fiction – non-fiction – a form which seems more reliable, less frivolous than fantasy. Although, in this case, you only have my word for it that the couple existed and, given that they did, I have exercised complete control over their portrayal and, therefore, your understanding of them. So they are here to demonstrate that non-fiction is never exactly just fact.

They may also serve to illustrate the way that fiction today is devalued. What was more insulting to our American friends – that I didn't much take to their clothes, or the suggestion that they might have been borrowed from a bad novel?

Above all, I began with them because what follows will also draw upon recent events. It is my contention that a culture with a healthy access to fiction is better equipped to understand and anticipate the actions of factual human beings and the effects of our own actions upon them. Fiction allows us an unparalleled, intimate understanding of the humanity of others: their joys and pains, angers and hopes. There are no adequate answers to questions like *How could anyone do it?* and *Why would they do it?* but I believe that fiction can play a central role in our struggle towards explanations and away from the clichés and silences of horror, bewilderment and loathing.

My definition of fiction embraces both prose and poetry. I am referring here to crafted writing which involves a personal, emotional commitment, an exposure on the part of the author as part of a conscious, creative act. It is a demonstration of imagination and faith within which the author and the reader become united. Beyond this, the author's presence and, indeed, the reader's self-awareness recede in successful fiction, to the point where the reader is able to appreciate the complexity of a personality other than their own. When we enjoy fiction, this is part of what we enjoy – the humanity of others.

If we examine fiction's position in Britain, the results are hardly cheering. We are used to the idea of largely polite but rather effective controls on factual writing and its authors in this country. We are less aware of controls on imaginative writing and their interrelation with other forms of censorship.

Not that authors of fiction aren't welcomed in public life – but not *as* authors of fiction. There is sometimes a passing acknowledgement that the public read their work – but it's their *opinions* that are wanted. What you'll rarely, if ever, encounter in the British media is any mention of the verses that stick like memories of a scent, a kiss, the novels that follow us through weeks, the phrases we hold because they say what we've wanted to.

For at least the last 60 years, writers, perhaps particularly in Britain and the USA, have been called upon to comment in public arenas, often standing in the place of other more formally qualified witnesses. This is partly because experts of one kind or another may not actually be able to string four words together. Experts may also know too much and the majority of those who trade in mass communication live in constant terror of maddening their audience by exposing it to large accumulations of undiluted fact. And experts are generally expected to be bought and paid for by special interests which encourage them to contradict each other, not to mention reality and intuitive common sense. Writers, meanwhile, may offer a few articulate, unbiased phrases and avoid frightening anyone with unnecessary knowledge.

It's even easier to see why you might pick a couple of novelists to discuss current events, rather than using politicians who will simply lambast each other and thrum with the terror of maddening *their* target audience by inadvertently exposing it to large accumulations of embarrassing fact.

More dangerously, authors may be assumed to have deep and wise insights into human nature. As the news media become less interested in news and increasingly hypnotised by gossip and random musings on the population's more violent and erotic quirks, who better to assist them than typists who seem to have a passable grip on fictional characters.

Sadly, this media exposure encourages readers, if not writers, to forget what authors of fiction *do*. Meanwhile, school curricula squeeze out the writing and reading of fiction, the media avoid it, literary criticism and theory drag every text doggedly down to the level of 'context' and auto-biography and the remnants of logical positivism seek to undermine both meaning and communicative potential. This suppression of fiction, however inadvertent, represents a small extinction of what is human in us.

Too large a claim? Then it must be time for a poem.

A DREAM

When I grow up and reach the age of twenty,
I'll set out to see the enchanting world.
I'll take a seat in a bird with a motor;
I'll rise and soar into space.

I'll fly, sail, hover,
Over the lovely, faraway world.
I'll soar over rivers and oceans
Skyward shall I ascend and blossom,
A cloud my sister, the wind my brother.

I'll marvel at the Euphrates and the Nile,
I'll see the pyramids and the sphinx
of ancient Egypt, where the goddess Isis reigned.
I'll fly over Niagara Falls
And immerse myself in a searing Sahara dune.

I'll drift over the cloud-strewn cliffs of Tibet
And the mysterious land of the wizards;
And once I extricate myself
From the scorching, terrifying wave of heat,
I'll meander over the icebergs of the north.

By wing I'll cross the great kangaroo island
And the ruins of Pompeii,
And the Holy Land of the Old Testament,
And over the land of the renowned Homer
I'll fly slowly, slowly, hovering lazily.

And this, basking in the enchantments of this world,
Skyward shall I soar and blossom
A cloud my sister, the wind my brother.

I'm acknowledged to be a bad poet but I'm aware that this isn't a great piece of work. It shows promise. And it is, of course, a fiction, a dream of impossible mobility, pleasurable freedom and an adult future which contains almost nothing but wonder. The poet is an amateur, a child called Avraham Koplowicz. Here, through the imperfect medium of translation, is his voice. Here is the shape of his breath in his lungs, here is the music his mind arranged for his own delight and others' – for that invisible, unencountered Other that authors can't help reaching out for, into a future time and place.

Safe in that future, I don't know if Avraham would ever have become a poet. He wrote his dream of escape sealed inside the Jewish ghetto at Lodz. On 4 September 1942, the last consignment of its living children was transported to Chelmno Extermination Camp where, like all of the previous consignments of human beings – men, women and children – they were gassed to death using carbon monoxide fed into specially converted Renault trucks. It is unclear exactly when Avraham died.

But the ghetto at Lodz was well documented, both by the Nazis and its own Jewish authority and I do know that Avraham was born in Lodz in 1930. I know that in a little over one and a half square miles the ghetto contained up to 250,000 Jews and 5,000 Roma. I know about the ghetto newspaper, the morale-boosting activities, the typhus outbreaks, the break-up of families on to transports. I know that around 43,500 people died there of starvation and despair and that around 800 Jews were left alive when it was liberated by the Soviets. I can subtract the number 800 from the larger number 255,000. This may make me angry, sickened, determined to act – in whatever minor way I can – against anti-Semitism and ethnic cleansing. But I am still, in a way, adopting a Nazi pattern of thought – I am turning people into numbers. The scale of the Nazi crimes, even now, is in danger of dehumanising their victims, their survivors, any individual their facts can touch.

But, at a certain level, numbers are all that can measure the horror of Lodz or, for that matter, Srebrenica, or Trelew prison, or the 20th century's multiple mass murders in Poland, Siberia, Rwanda, Chile, Cambodia, Chechnya, Palestine, China, Afghanistan – the total of countries becomes, in itself, another terrible number. The 21st century already has it own list, growing: Chechnya, Palestine, Zimbabwe, Afghanistan, New York . . . If numbers and facts can only sustain our outrage and our understanding, our reaction and our will so far, if they can become double-edged, and if we do wish to maintain a commitment to preserve our species and its quality of life, then what else is there?

Photographs, along with other written records, can bear witness to crime, even in the absence of justice. Validated, they are factual evidence. Documents were hidden in Lodz by human beings who were certain they were going to die, but who hoped their evidence might outlive them. People all over the world still balance self-preservation against their determination to bring evidence of crime to light. Good journalists still want to amplify this bearing of witness; here and there, newspapers and TV and radio producers will still let them. And this process relies on a wonderful, life-saving type of writing. Its greatest exponents – like Ed Morrow, Marguerite Higgins, Francis Meynell, Isabel Brown, Martha Gellhorn – are also great writers.

Still, there will always be something missing from what they do – because they deal with facts, with numbers. They are supposed to. The larger their emotional presence in their text becomes, the more they risk its effectiveness. The moment they approach any kind of emotional manipulation, they risk tainting every piece of information they are trying to convey. Beyond this, unless presented with great care, the images which accompany their words may seem simply banal – dwarfed by the coming annihilation that the fragments of time they enclose will never see. Or they may be, like the pictures from Lodz, images of people who do not seem human any more. Nazism was relentlessly capable of writing away human beings' humanity – of reclassifying, labelling, shrinking, starving, dressing in rags, until their lies could seem almost true. Terror, violence, imprisonment, emaciation and disease can remove a great deal of who we are. Refugees, the wounded, the starving – they do not look like us. What they say may not make sense, may not even be words any more. They are being forced to fulfil someone else's prophesy. Journalism can tell us their facts, can attempt to remind us that they once had other lives and joys; organisations like PEN and Amnesty International can represent them, even when they have been made to disappear. Fiction – quietly, privately – does that and something deeper, something before, as well as after, the fact.

Kurt Vonnegut, an American author of fiction, sums up this effect when he writes:

> What happens if you credit a bum with human dignity? – a drunken bum with his pants full of shit and snot dangling from his nose? At least you haven't made yourself poorer in a financial sense. And he can't take whatever it is that you have given him and spend it on thunderbird wine.

There is this drawback, though. If you give to that sort of a stranger the uncritical respect that you give to friends and relatives, you will also want to understand and help him. There is no way to avoid this.

Be warned: if you allow yourself to see dignity in someone, you have doomed yourself to wanting to understand and help whoever it is.

Fiction gives dignity. It offers what no other form completely can – the articulated potential, the spoken dreams, the unmistakable beauty and the possibilities of the immense, human interior reality inside that Other; inside all those human beings who are not myself, yourself. Fiction provides the truth that we are all more than what we seem and irreplaceable.

So fiction written by the dead is useful because it makes us sad and angry that they're dead? Of course, but not only that. Fiction written by living authors who are oppressed, imprisoned or under threat – whatever its subject – screams that these authors are human, that any action taken to damage something so precious is irrevocably criminal. Yes, but more than that. So authors, whatever their status, who give voices to the silenced and who deal with injustices, either literally or symbolically, can alter their readers and themselves so they have a little more strength to abhor and resist those injustices? Yes, that too, and more. *Any author, writing any kind of fiction on any topic, resists the forces that deny our common humanity.* They cannot do anything else – that is the nature of their work.

Because fiction is always about someone other than the reader. By agreeing to read it, we agree to collaborate with the authors, we let them put their words into our mouths, our minds – one of the most intimate intrusions possible. In the case of the novel, we may sustain this intrusion for days, if not weeks. We do this because we tacitly acknowledge that their thoughts can be as important as our own and because they address us, uniquely, with the 'uncritical respect that you give to friends and relatives', if not lovers. We believe in the people authors make, whoever they are, whatever they have done. We care about them, help to make them important, and this is enjoyable and feels very natural and is an exercise which can begin to make it harder to murder, or torture, or harm other people, even other people that we don't know. Fiction may also make it more difficult for us to stand by while such murders and tortures and harms are committed.

And fiction makes us not alone. The writer produces it in the most intimate anticipation of the reader. The reader finds in it sheltered, personal voices which mingle with their own. It is a music which is theirs whenever they want it – openly aloud or interior. It has in it the faith to make worlds out of nothing. The reading and writing, especially of fiction, is an exercise in the practice of faith.

Why should we care about that faith? Why should we care about free imagination which wouldn't, for example, require that the oppressed should write solely about their oppression, or that readers in hell should read only about their torments? Because without imagination we cannot believe in a time when a seemingly permanent injustice will have been removed. We cannot plan its removal. We cannot call up the past which nourishes us and makes us ourselves. We cannot *have* a future, because nothing, in reality, exists other than the endless now: tyranny demands an eternal, unrelieved present tense, a forgetting of our own interior lives and those of all others, our cooperation in the process of our own removal, thought by thought.

And, with imagination, we can fit actions together with consequences – even if those consequences are being intentionally obscured. A widow, grieving for her lost husband, showing his picture, reciting his last words, his likes and dislikes, his plans, has an equal, human weight, whether she lives in Palestine or Israel, Afghanistan or the United States. A murderer, of whatever nationality or religion, is equally guilty and equally close to our own faults and weaknesses. Why else arrest 'non-political' novelists? Why else burn poetry books?

When Mordechai Vanunu wrote, 'Don't look at the whole machine . . . Don't concern yourself with things beyond your grasp,' he invited us to realise that imagination would make that impossible. Vanunu, working at Dimona on the then secret Israeli nuclear bomb programme, found he could no longer separate his actions from their consequence, the weapon from its effects. He had to speak.

On 30 September 1986, five days before his revelations were made public, Vanunu was kidnapped and taken back to Israel. He was tried in camera and sentenced to 18 years' imprisonment. Until 12 March 1998, he was kept in solitary confinement – longer than anyone else on record – a punishment condemned by Amnesty International. The Israeli government has suggested a release date of 22 April 2004.

I have tried to imagine a decade and more in a box cell and failed. But, of course, human beings did imagine his prison and make it true. Human beings with a memory of persecution in the Shoah built themselves a future of institutionalised human rights violations and armed siege. Human beings

*Jerusalem, 1986: breaking the silence. Mordechai Vanunu reveals
details of his kidnap on the way to court. Credit: AP*

imagined the possession of a nuclear capacity before they created it. Human
beings imagined how to convert a Renault truck into a gas chamber. As I
write, as you read, human beings on every continent are imagining the
refinement of tortures, the imposition of fear, subordination and destruction.
They are creating the fictions which they hope will make their crimes seem
justified, acts of self-defence; they are keeping themselves distracted from the
realities of other humans' pain. You know the kind of thing: 'All aboriginals
are animals, rapists and drunks.' 'Chile is threatened by a left-wing
conspiracy.' 'Negroes are lazy and ignorant degenerates.' 'Women are essentially immoral and worthless, they cannot be educated, seen in public, or
allowed to work.' 'Bosnian Muslims plan to murder all Serbian children over
the age of three.' 'The civilised world is being bled dry by a secret Jewish
cabal.' 'All immigrants to Britain are criminals and freeloaders' . . .

10/1991: MORDECHAI VANUNU, ISRAEL
IN THE LION'S DEN

'I'm not a traitor. I'm a man with a conscience who did what he did out
of a deep belief after much thought and many doubts. I didn't want to
perform this act. . . . but were I not to do it, no one else would. And there,
I did it, fearful though I was, and ready to pay the price . . . I knew I had
entered a lion's pit.'
Mordechai Vanunu, from solitary confinement in Ashkelon, 20 November 1987

'Revealed: the Secrets of Israel's Nuclear Arsenal', ran the *Sunday Times*
headline of 5 October 1986. The story was based on information obtained
from my brother, Mordechai Vanunu, an Israeli nuclear technician at
Dimona, Israel's nuclear reactor centre, from 1976 to 1985. Scientists
debriefing Mordechai determined that Israel had 100 to 200 nuclear
warheads, making it the sixth largest nuclear power.

But Mordechai was gone, already lured to Rome by Israeli agents,
beaten, drugged, chained and smuggled thence to Israel. Only in November
did Israeli authorities finally admit they had 'legally detained' him. They
charged him with espionage, treason and revealing state secrets with intent
to 'aid the enemy in time of war'. His kidnapping and trial were conducted
in secret, and he was kept in solitary confinement.

On 22 December 1986, Mordechai broke the silence. On his palm, held
up to the window of the car taking him to a Jerusalem court, was written:
'I was hijacked in Rome, ITL 30/9/86 at 2100 hours. Came to Rome on
BA flight 504.'

Hostile pre-trial media coverage and public prejudice within Israel
diverted attention from the issue at stake: Israel's nuclear programme.
The trial was unjust and *in camera*; the sentence, delivered in March 1988,
punitive: 18 years in prison. The confessions signed by Vanunu on arriving
back in Israel had been extorted after he had spent several days chained to
a bench in a pitch-black room and 40 hours on the floor of a blacked-out
Israeli cell.

He has been held in total isolation since his abduction, visitors
restricted to his family – 30 minutes every two weeks – and his lawyer.
The fluorescent lighting is never turned out; he is under constant
surveillance by a video camera in his cell; his mail is intercepted.

The reasons the Israeli authorities kept my brother's kidnapping and trial a total secret are the same as those that keep their nuclear weapons production taboo. Within Israel, a combination of tight military censorship and self-censorship ensures there is no discussion of nuclear matters; Israel's secret services strangled any potential debate in parliament by threatening members of the Knesset and scientists seeking to testify. The evidence Mordechai brought from Dimona was the first to substantiate western intelligence estimates of Israel's nuclear capability.

On the day Mordechai was sentenced, 27 Nobel Prize laureates and leading scientists appealed to the Israeli authorities that the court had to consider the import of the nuclear question. The European Parliament condemned the kidnapping and called upon Israel's president to pardon Mordechai. To no avail.

Why have western countries, particularly Britain and the USA, kept silent? In the US, the Symington amendment forbids aid to any country with a nuclear programme. Can Mordechai's information have endangered the annual US$4 billion Israel receives from the US? Is this the reason for Israel's desperate attempts to silence him?

'National security' justifies Israel's policy of secrecy on both issues, yet Chernobyl proved nuclear fallout is no respecter of national borders. *Sunday Times* editor Andrew Neil wrote: 'It is in the general interest that we know who is a nuclear power ... Vanunu's story was in the interests of the world at large.'

In April 1991, Mordechai wrote from prison, in circumstances Amnesty International described as 'cruel, inhuman or degrading':

> You have to know that no matter what happens, I am proud of my actions, for my revelations, for not cooperating with their lies, for not keeping silent. That is all that a man can do, to not be afraid of the power of the state; to show to all that in the nuclear age a man is obliged to all the human race.

In August 1991, the supreme court rejected outright his petition to end his solitary confinement. [He has now been in solitary for 14 years, the longest such term ever recorded – Ed] ❑

Meir Vanunu

Radovan Karadjic, responsible for thousands of deaths in Omarska, Keraterm, Susica, Prijedor, Srebrenica, describes himself as a poet. He likened the shelling of Sarajevo to poetry. Issie Sagawa, student of literature, now best-selling novelist and restaurant critic, shot Renee Hartwelt while she was reading aloud from Schiller and then ate parts of her body raw. In at least one later interview, he took pains to mention that he hadn't done this simply in order to write a book about it later.

But we can't fight imagination's dark side by suppressing what has come to be called 'hate speech', we cannot drive the fantasies of bigotry underground and give paranoid hatred a comforting dose of martyrdom and darkness to hide its insecurities. We can't fail to call evil evil because that would be judgemental and we want everyone to be more tolerant. We shouldn't all use our minds less because they are dangerous. We must bring the dark imaginings to light. We must re-examine the nature of imagination and recognise that its destructive use relies on such a narrowness of focus and such an ignorance of human nature and reality that it is essentially vulnerable – the more revealed it is, the more loathsome it proves itself to be. In a culture with access to, among other things, reputable media and broad, vigorous fiction, the full, humanising force of imagination can help to defend us, our rights and our privileges – if we allow it to prosper. But, of course, we don't.

We live in just one of many perfectly nice, civilised countries which are systematically destroying the saving graces which our literature, our fictions, can grant us. We've been doing it for years. We haven't collapsed into genocide recently: we only have public services that cripple and murder the public, a peculiar lack of articulated outrage, an often irrelevant press and a moderately sociopathic political and economic structure. We are content to base many of our comforts on miseries we choose not to imagine.

And who am I to say that in ten years' time we'll still be even this lucky? I'm not aware of any psychological testing that hasn't proved that hatred, to the point of violence, can be induced in many perfectly nice, civilised people in a matter of hours, given the proper circumstances. Subject a population to years, or only months, of propaganda and you can lead them to kill their neighbours, torture their family members, bury their souls. Our fictions are part of the lifetime of resistance and vigilance which guards us against that risk of being pathologically misled.

But instead we have allowed the literary and critical establishment to separate literature, ever more severely, from imagination. Novels are allowed to be social documents, proofs of psychopathology, or reprocessed – preferably perverse – reality. If this were accurate, imagination would be unnecessary and the writer would simply supply the reader with cast-offs from another life, closed to them. Fiction would become a puzzle, only truly solved by intermediaries – the critic and the academic – no intimacy, no mind-to-mind collaboration, no uninterrupted communication, no faith, no dreams. This is a theft we accept on an almost daily basis. It is not as great a theft as the removal of life, or liberty, or the imposition of fear and pain, but it is still something we must resist, because it prepares us (however unwittingly) for the dehumanising steps that eventually lead to those urgent, larger crimes.

And we also decide that certain subject matter, certain protagonists are unsuitable, unfit – which is to say, we decide that certain types of human being and certain situations in which they find themselves are not human enough to warrant fictional treatment. I need hardly point out that this both highlights and radically limits the subversive power of fiction. This kind of disapproval is not new. The *Critical Quarterly*'s original review of *Wuthering Heights* complained that 'animals in their native state' 'Catherine and Heathfield' – trust a reviewer to get Heathcliff's name wrong – were 'too odiously and abominably pagan to be palatable even to the most vitiated class of English readers. With all the unscrupulousness of the French school of novels it combines that repulsive vulgarity in the choice of its vice which supplies its own antidote.' Who has kept Dryden's work alive, kept *Wuthering Heights* in print? – readers who can see beyond knee-jerk prejudice and appreciate courageous fiction.

And, since I've mentioned French novels, it would be nice if readers could support fiction by non-British authors because it is, naturally, just as good as British fiction. British publishing prejudices and self-fulfilling prophesies (largely untried) of low sales and low public interest mean that few foreign authors are ever available in translation in Britain. So we close that window on the world and keep it closed.

Robert Louis Stevenson – a firm believer in the transcendent reality of fiction – found himself censored by the same sociopathic culture which had, for centuries, allowed Britons to commit genocide at home and abroad. When he wrote 'The Beach of Falesa' he produced a wonderful fable of squalor, violence, immorality and waste. It was not released in an unexpurgated form until almost 100 years after its initial publication because of its 'profanity'.

'Bad' language is, of course, the perfect red herring under which to hide the class and race prejudice of critics. Writers like James Kelman and Irvine Welsh will always be attacked for the profanity of their prose, the attacks will almost always come from those who actually despise their subject matter and choice of characters. They make the wrong humans human. Only if the portrayal of the underclass is grisly and degrading enough does it become acceptable – the equivalent of a Victorian day trip to the madhouse, a bit of literary rough. Damned for intellectual or actual perversity, or patronised and re-interpreted as confirming social Darwinism's essential truth, authors are left to hope that their work can simply survive its own publicity and reach a reader who can judge it on its own merits.

That's if the work is publicised at all. Work of quality still manages to have some kind of access to the media, however ludicrous or damaging, but non-fiction is simply much easier to place in magazines and newspapers: now, almost exclusively, the natural homes of purportedly non-fictional writing. The conditional, qualified, edited truth of autobiography, travel reminiscence, celebrity reminiscence, sexual reminiscence, is acceptable, simply because it has some of the trappings of reality. And it can be accompanied by an additional, juicy exposé of the 'real truth' about the author, taking up, say, another half-page alongside. If that doesn't tell you something about the current inadequacies of the form, what does? Non-fiction which needs non-fiction to explain it?

The emotional, human, psychological truth of fiction, its mutual commitment, mutual risk, and its ability to break the bounds of reality, is devalued and increasingly ignored. Not that all non-fiction is bad, or untrue, not that all fiction is wonderful and transcendent. They are both valuable and have some congruent but also many quite different roles. Only one of these forms is now adequately represented in our media – non-fiction. Which is why more and more authors are turning to non-fiction. Poets, of course, labour in a particularly silent and economically unsustainable wilderness.

And if fiction is under attack from the right, then don't believe for a moment it's safe from a left eager to suggest that all critical assessment and all notions of quality must be avoided as divisive and a form of censorship. Sadly – and rather obviously – some writing is better than other writing, and bad fiction does its characters and readers no justice at all. Currently, our most vulnerable writers – those without independent incomes, those in difficult circumstances, or with special needs – are being supported by arts organisations determined to take no interest in the quality of work produced. If new authors supported by public funding and what we might broadly call 'community intervention schemes' are given none of the educative, constructive criticism that any good author should expect, if not beg for, then possibly the one chance they might have to find and develop their voice will be lost – social exclusion will be guaranteed. Believe me, we have more good writers in this country than we have available funds. It isn't that hard to identify good work and promising work. Throw all the money in the world at an untalented writer and they will stay untalented and you can bet a promising one will be standing right behind them, on the verge of giving up. If you have an interest in preserving fiction, you might, for example, give serious and vocal thought to how local and national art organisations disburse their funds.

There is, of course, good fiction that you may not personally like. If you want a healthy society you're going to have to let it stay there and love it just as much as the work you keep on your shelves. There is good fiction that deals with unpleasant subjects. This exercises critics no end and, again, I would have to say has done so since literary criticism started. Let me quote from another *Critical Quarterly* review, this time following the publication of George Eliot's *The Mill on the Floss*:

> . . . we believe that the effect of such fictions tends to render those who fall under their influence unfit for practical exertion by intruding on minds which ought to be guarded from impurity the unnecessary knowledge of evil.

When Stevenson wrote *The Ebb-Tide* he included a passage where Herrick – a man maddened to despair by an atmosphere of insanely pursued capitalism and Calvinism – decides to drown himself. He finds he cannot, 'he must stagger on to the end'. If authors are not allowed to deal with such matters, if those in despair are not fit subjects for fiction, then individuals who have faced their own frailty and mortality can never discover others like themselves given the eloquence of art, loved and presented by another. Our literature becomes small, inhuman, lacking in both wisdom and mercy.

And then there is the representation of evil in fiction. Trash fiction will crawl about in all types of sewers to the delight of no one but the irredeemably, or temporarily, sleazy, and receive curiously little attention. Why? Because the figures involved are not intended to be fully human – horrors happen to them in the same way that sex happens to the puppets of pornography. It can depict a seductive, dangerous universe but it is rarely criticised.

Good, disturbing fiction always kicks up a storm – because it is disturbing. It shows us the humanity of those who do wrong, our vulnerability to their weaknesses, our imperfections and their ability to transform into horrors things we would rather not recognise. We are not all monsters under the skin, but we misunderstand ourselves if we believe that evil cannot at least tempt and bewilder us. This is unpleasant news, but we need to hear it.

And sometimes when we hear it, spoken in the safe dark of our minds, fiction will be couched in language which is itself disturbing – possibly obscene per se (and we already know the trouble that can cause an author), possibly shocking in its construction. Once again, I would never say that you must read books which make you unhappy, but they are necessary. If an author of conscience wants to speak to you in the language of hatred and bigotry, it is because she cares. If she describes something to you, using (as the newspapers might say) the language of the gutter, she won't be doing that by mistake – she will be reflecting the passion of a character, the obscenity of the subject, the energy in those words.

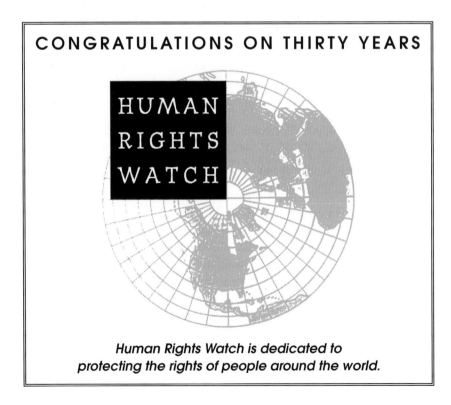

We need strong language. We cannot ever find ourselves in a situation where we have no words for a horror we must face, must understand, must tell to the world. We need the preparation fiction gives us, the full exercise. Fiction is too close to us to be governed by nice manners and it may save our sanity and our lives by ignoring them. I'll quote Kurt Vonnegut again:

> My parents had been taught such nice manners in childhood . . . that they had no simple and practical vocabularies for the parts and functions of their excretory and reproductive systems, and no such vocabularies for treachery and hypocrisy, either. Good manners had made them defenceless against predatory members of their own class.

We need fiction. For the defence of our humanity and for our delight, for the relief of finding ourselves both beautiful and absurd, for mourning, consolation, the sharing and celebration of life, we need fiction. To answer the unanswerable, we need fiction. ❏

AL Kennedy is a novelist and short-story writer; she also writes an occasional column for the Guardian. *Her next book,* Indelible Acts, *will be published in October*

I know them all by sight
in the conservatoire pack
but who'll send me one little word
one little letter from freedom

when I lie on my rough plank-bed
exhausted as a wolf
to whose lips shall I press mine
passionately tenderly

and whose hullo hullo my friend
shall I hear as I freeze
a huge light like a chandelier
and myself – such darkness

Natalya Gorbanevskaia *was a member of the Action Group for the Defence of Human Rights in the USSR. She participated in the demonstration against the invasion of Czechoslovakia in 1968 and was arrested the following year and held in Kazan Special Psychiatric Hospital until 1972. She emigrated in 1975 and now lives in Paris. This poem was written in 1967*

2/1972: ALEXANDER SOLZHENITSYN, USSR

There never was, nor will be, a world of brightness!
A frozen footcloth is the scarf that binds my face.
Fights over porridge, the ganger's constant griping
And day follows day, and no end to this dreary fate.
. . .
My feeble pick strikes sparks from the frozen earth.
And the sun stares down unblinking from the sky.
But the world *is* here! And will be! The daily round
Suffices. But man is not to be imprisoned in the day.
To write! To write now, without delay,
Not in heated wrath, but with cool and clear understanding.
The millstones of my thoughts can hardly turn,
Too rare the flicker of light in my aching soul.
Yes, tight is the circle around us tautly drawn,
But my verses will burst their bonds and freely roam
And I can guard, perhaps, beyond their reach,
In rhythmic harmony this hard-won gift of speech.
And then they can grope my body in vain –
'Here I am. All yours. Look hard. Not a line . . .
Our indestructible memory, by wonder divine,
Is beyond the reach of your butcher's hands!'
. . .
But what if beforehand they give me poisoned bread?
Or if darkness beclouds my mind at last?
Oh, let me die *there*! Let it not be here!
God keep me from going mad!

Translated by Michael Scammell

Alexander Solzhenitsyn *won the Nobel Prize for Literature in 1970 after years
of trouble with the authorities. The publication of this poem in* Index *marked the
first time any of his verse had been published in English. It was written in 1950–53
while he was in the labour camp in Kazakhstan, the experience on which he based
his novel* One Day in the Life of Ivan Denisovich

AND NOW GOODBYE

To all those million verses in the world
I've added just a few.
They probably were no wiser than a cricket's chirrup.
I know. Forgive me.
I'm coming to the end.

They weren't even the first footmarks
in the lunar dust.
If at times they sparkled after all
it was not their light.
I loved the language.

. . .

Poetry is with us from the start.
Like loving,
like hunger, like the plague, like war,
At times my verses were embarrassingly
foolish.

But I make no excuse.
I believe that seeking beautiful words
is better
than killing and murdering.

Translated by Ewald Osers

*Most of **Jaroslav Seifert**'s works were banned and circulated in* samizdat *after his country was invaded by Soviet-led forces in 1968. He was the last president of the Czechoslovak Writers' Union in its days of independence before the authorities closed it down in 1969. In 1977 he was among the first signatories of the Charter 77 human rights manifesto. In 1984 he was awarded the Nobel Prize for Literature*

4/1984: MAHMOUD DARWISH, PALESTINE

WHEN THE MARTYRS GO TO SLEEP

When the martyrs go to sleep I wake up to guard them against
professional mourners.
I say to them: I hope you wake in a country with clouds and
trees, mirage and water.
I congratulate them on their safety from their incredible event,
from the surplus value of the slaughter.
I steal time so they can snatch me from time. Are we all martyrs?
I whisper: friends, leave one wall for the laundry line. Leave
a night for singing.
I will hang your names wherever you want, so sleep awhile, sleep
on the ladder of the sour vine tree
So I can guard your dreams against the daggers of you guards
and the plot of the Book against the prophets,
Be the song of those who have no songs when you go to sleep tonight.
I say to you: I hope you wake in a country packed on a galloping mare.
I whisper: friends, you'll never be like us, the robe of an
unknown gallows!

Translated by Abdullah al-Udhari

Mahmoud Darwish, *probably the best-known Palestinian poet, was born in
Palestine in 1942. His family fled from Israeli occupation in 1948. His political
advocacy on behalf of the Palestinians led to imprisonment and house arrest by the
Israelis. In 1971, Darwish left Israel for Beirut. He returned to Palestine after the
PLO–Israel peace accords in 1993, where he now edits the cultural journal* Karmal

Another Fools' Day
touches down: shush
      For Mercy, Judith, Lunda & Lika

Another Fools' Day touches down, another homecoming.
Shush. Bunting! some anniversary: they'll be preoccupied.
Only a wife, children and a friend, probably waiting.

A PhD, three books, a baby boy, three and half years –
Some feat to put us . . . Shush. Such frivolities no longer
Touch people here. 'So, you decided to come back, eh?'

Rhetorical questions dredge up spastic images. Shush.
In the dusty, brown–grey landscape, the heat unrolls.
Some wizard has locked up his rainbows and thunder again.

Why do the gods hold up the rains?
Don't we praise them enough?
Shush. There are no towers here, no domes or gothic windows.
Only your children, friends, nestling up for a warm story.

Jack Mapanje was imprisoned for three and a half years in Malawi because of his poetry. He now lives and works in the UK

5/1997: OSIP MANDELSTAM, USSR

OLD CRIMEA

It's a cold spring. The Crimea is starving and fearful
and as guilty as it was under Vrangel and the White Guard.
The patched rags are in tatters, the sheepdogs are in a yard,
and the smoke is biting and pungent as ever.

The views are hazy, it is as beautiful as ever.
The trees are in bud, swelling slightly,
and are the real outsiders, and the almond,
blossoming with yesterday's foolishness, arouses pity.

Nature can't recognise her own face:
the refugees from the Kuban and the Ukraine are nightmare shadows.
The hungry villagers in their felt slippers
guard the storehouse gates, never touching the locks.

Translated by Richard McKane

Osip Mandelstam *(1891–1938) went virtually unpublished during his lifetime,
but was not completely silenced until his famous 'Epigram to Stalin' written in
1933 – the same year as this poem – led to his arrest and exile in Voronezh.
'Old Crimea' is based on his interrogation in the Lubianka. He was rearrested
after the expiry of his exile and died of a heart attack on the way back to one of
Stalin's camps*

5/1997: MIN LU, BURMA

QUITE UNFAIR AND CRUEL TO BOOT

I have never heard
That a whole abdomen had to be opened up
Just to cure a mild case of diarrhoea.
I have never heard
That an entire pile of books was burnt
Just because a single termite blighted one.
I have never heard
That a spoilt child was stabbed
Just to scold him for crying for sweets.
I have never heard
That death sentences have been handed down
To minor violators of the Highway Code.
But I have heard that
The odious sentence of a lifetime's transportation
Has been given
For one small offence of rightly being angry
For just one day.

Min Lu, *the Burmese writer and poet, was sentenced in September 1990 to seven years in jail for writing and distributing his poem 'What has become of us?' (Index 5/97), one of the few examples of* samizdat *literature to have been produced in Burma since the May 1990 election. He was released in September 1992*

5/1997: INDAMIRO RESTANO, CUBA

INLE

You learnt that the mystery of the sea
is worth more than language,
when he took you shyly
to the depths of the sands,
You were the love
that foundered on the sea and now begins to appear
riding on a huge cockerel.
The witches take
their spells from the cauldrons
and the sea opens
like a broken mirror;
because your fruits entered
the yellow animals . . .
Guide me in the silence of your love,
guide me, my love . . .

Translated by Mandy Garner

Indamiro Restano, *founder and vice-president of Armonía, a Christian Democrat opposition group in Cuba, was sentenced in May 1992 to ten years in prison for rebellion, disseminating counter-revolutionary propaganda and plotting to overthrow the government. He was released in June 1995 but has since lived in exile*

THE HEARING

The judge was judged.
A question was asked:
'What's the crime?'
'In death's sovereignty,' the judge said,
'living is the crime.'

The gendarme was handcuffed.
A question was asked:
'What is captivity?'
Obeying orders!

The jailer was locked up.
A question was asked:
'What is a cell?'
Man carrying the darkness within him.

THE SENTENCE WAS GIVEN:
THE SYSTEM HAS BEEN ARRESTED
HUMANITY HAS BEEN ACQUITTED OF ALL CRIMES

Winter 1991 Istanbul

Translated by Richard McKane

Recep Marasli *is one of the most eminent activists for the Kurdish cause. First arrested at the age of 16 for his newspaper articles, in 1982 he was sentenced to 36 years' imprisonment but was released in 1991. In 1997, he was arrested on charges of belonging to a pro-Kurdish group but was acquitted and left Turkey*

10/1988: BEI DAO, CHINA

COMET

Come back or leave forever
don't stand like that at the door
like a statue made of stone
discussing everything between us
with a look that expects no answer

in fact what is hard to imagine
is not the darkness but dawn
how long will the lamplight last
perhaps a comet may appear
trailing debris from the ruins
and a list of failures
letting them glitter, burn up and turn into ash

come back, and we'll rebuild our home
or leave forever, like a comet
sparkling and cold like frost
discarding the dark, and sinking back into darkness again
going through the white corridor connecting two evenings
in the valley where echoes arise on all sides
you sing alone ❏

Translated by Bonnie McDougall

Bei Dao, *born in 1949, the year of the Communist Revolution, was one of China's most gifted and controversial younger poets; he moved from the Red Guard in the Cultural Revolution (1966–76) to poet of the Democracy Movement (1978). He was co-publisher and editor of* Jintian (Today), *the leading literary publication of the movement.* Jintian *was banned in 1980 and Bei Dao's work continued be a target of attack. In 1987 he moved to the USA*

POEMS FROM THE POLISH GULAG
BEATA OBERTYÑSKA

In communist Poland, any mention of what were known as 'the deportations' was officially prohibited – and remained so until the restoration of multi-party democracy in 1989. Since then, public interest in the events of 1939–41 has focused primarily on exploring the graves and establishing the identities of Polish officers massacred by the Russians at Katyn and Mednoye. While a substantial body of Polish prose memoirs of the Gulag has appeared in the West – such as Beata Obertyñska's own W domu niewoli (In the House of Slavery) *published in Rome in 1946 – it is only in the last decade or so that such accounts have been published in Poland.*

Od Komi do Kolymy: Gulag Polskich Poetow (From Komi to Kolyma: the Gulag of the Polish Poets), edited and with an introduction by Nina Taylor-Telecka (Polish Cultural Foundation, London 2001) is the first collection of the poetic legacy of the deportations. **VR**

IN THE CATTLE-TRUCK

And they laid him there in the corner
By the wall,
Covered him with a buttonless jacket.
He lay stiffly. Warmth gone.
Who in a transport bothers
His head about corpses at all?
No one.

Even yesterday evening
He murmured he was ailing.
Breathing
He was, still this morning.
Now all is silent.
Into the feet that tramped without haven
The rigor of death is pressing and boring

No one has power any longer
To drag or drive forth to wander
This string-tied raggedness.
Yes.
He has won, in his post-mortal

State, a bed in the corner.
Full-length on his back he now rests.

Kin? For sure, someone is waiting,
Someone prays in the night-time,
That he'll come back, survive it all . . .
But he has lost . . .
How will they know, when we've not the slightest
Idea of his name, what he's called?

JAIL

Jail is not like the storybooks: silence, a gleam
From a small, high-up grating.
Jail is heat, crowding, hubbub and screams,
Water short, and gruel nauseating.

Jail is not loneliness, pitcher and straw,
Rats' feet in silken patter.
Jail is constant awareness that the door
Hides a bayonet and uniform jacket.

Over heaped bodies with floor for bed,
Making a mock of night-time,
A bubble of glass hangs over your head
The blinding glare of the light-bulb.

And the dreams with their unctuous, obliging power,
That through an underground portal
Set you free again for a couple of hours –
Loyally bring you back long before morning.

And those forcefully clamped jaws,
And the will like clenched fist, that ever
In spite of what is there beyond the door –
You'll endure and remember! ❏

*Beata Obertyńska (1898–1980) was the daughter of the poet Maryla Wolska.
Arrested in July 1940, her Siberian odyssey included ten prisons, camp in
Loch-Vorkuta, death barges on the Amu-Daria and a kolkhoz near Bukhara.
Translated by Vera Rich*

THE GUARDED TONGUE
RITU MENON

CENSORSHIP OF WOMEN BY THE USE
OF VIOLENCE AND INTIMIDATION IN
INDIA'S PATRIARCHAL SOCIETY IS MORE
PERVASIVE AND HARDER TO CONFRONT
THAN THE OFFICIAL VARIETY

Ask anyone about censorship and whether there's any in India, and they'll
say, 'No, not really. We're not like Bangladesh or Pakistan, we have freedom
of speech, it's a fundamental right guaranteed by the Constitution.' If you
remind them about Deepa Mehta's *Fire* and *Water* or MF Husain (*Index*
2/1997) and the Gufa in Ahmedabad, or the attack on Ajeet Cour's
Academy of Fine Arts in Delhi or on Sahmat in Ayodhya (*Index* 6/1997)
or even, long ago, on Mushirul Hasan, they'll say those are exceptions, it
was the work of hoodlums. And anyway, all these people went too far, they
should have been careful.

In a way, they're right. There's very little formal censorship in India –
by the state that is – but if this is so, why are we increasingly having to be
'careful', to be mindful of what we say? Is it because street censorship has
usurped the power of the state and taken it on itself to police people's
expression? Or because, as writer Mridula Garg says pithily: 'The more
regressive the state, the more aggressive the mob?' Perhaps, as Nabaneeta
Dev Sen puts it, 'free speech belongs to the mainstream', and if you're on
the margins or if yours is the voice of dissent, your speech is censored.
Could it be that a range of other constraints operate in culture and society,
inhibiting not only one's freedom of speech but of association and mobility
as well? Constraints that obviate the state's need to censor because they're
so effective anyway? Could it be that we need to redefine censorship so
that it encompasses these other myriad forms of silencing, and enables us
to unravel their complex workings?

In July 2001, over 65 women writers from 11 languages met in
Hyderabad, at a most unusual gathering, to discuss not only the many
faces of censorship in India but its peculiarly – and particularly – gendered
dimensions as well. This national colloquium was the culmination of
a unique process: a series of workshops over the last two years with

approximately 200 women – speakers of Urdu, Telugu, Marathi, Malayalam, Hindi, Gujarati, Kannada, Bangla, English and Tamil – that dwelt, not on their writing per se but on the circumstances in which they write, and are read and written about.

Across age and language, caste, creed and community, urban and rural women who write prose and poetry, songs and serials, short stories and novels, essays and autobiographies, talked at length about how and why they write; what they write, and the form they write it in; why they can't write what they'd like to – or why they don't; where and how they publish, and how they relate to the literary establishment and the market in their particular language or regional context. And how almost anything or everything they write is filtered through family, community, society, culture and politics.

'A woman's writing is her gesture,' said Nabaneeta Dev Sen, 'and like all women's gestures it is subject to all sorts of social codes.' Not everyone agreed. Shashi Deshpande says she's a feminist but not a feminist writer: one must be gender-conscious, not gender-bound. Others said they were not subjected to any kind of censorship or curbs on their expression *as women*. They are writers and, like other writers, are free to choose what they write about and how they write about it. They are preoccupied with form and content; with language; with meaning and metaphor; with being read and critically appraised. And yet, when one of them said: 'A woman's life is censored from start to finish, and if not censored then severely edited,' no one thought it either incorrect or exaggerated.

Hindi writer Anamika's comment got to the heart of the matter: 'Scissors to cut with, a needle and thread to sew my lips with. If I write my subconscious the earth will be covered with paper.' Many women censor themselves in what must be the most powerful and pervasive form of silencing we know. What is it they fear? Loss of respectability? Loss of social acceptance? Ridicule? Rejection by family, friends, loved ones, a peer group?

The household or familial dimension impinges on women's writing in ways that are deeply gendered and internalised. Although, as Telugu writer Satyavathi says: 'We avenge the censorship we face in reality through our writing,' any number of women censor themselves for fear of how their families or communities will react. Censorship often takes place within the home, where manuscripts may be destroyed, suppressed or altered by husbands, parents or siblings because of what they reveal about 'family secrets'. Fathers or husbands may also appropriate the work of their

In 1997, some fundamentalist groups in Hyderabad prevented women clad in the burkha from entering cinema halls. It was my responsibility to raise my voice against such actions.

Wearing a burkha
I took a degree
Also took computers
And outshone others easily

Ammi was happy
Abba was very happy.
Hadn't I lifted Sinai single-handedly?

To crush the world underfoot
Was my heart's desire
Each breath said
Become a conqueror
An Alexander in burkha!

I went out to have fun.
Entering the cinema
I was stopped by the moral squad
Wagging their rods

Hey, young girl!
Burkhas not allowed entry;
Black smoke arose from my black mask
And off went the burkha!

When I sent the poem to Siyasat they declined to publish it. The same thing happened when I tried to read it on a radio broadcast. 'Why don't you read some other poem which doesn't hurt the sentiments of our Muslim brothers?' they said.

Jameela Nishat *Urdu writers' workshop, Hyderabad, 20–23 February 1999. From* The Guarded Tongue: Women's Writing & Censorship in India, *published by Women's WORLD/Asmita, 2001* daughters or wives because they do not wish them to have an independent identity, and feel that the work of women in their family properly belongs to them. The objection is often very violent. One Tamil writer told us that her ex-husband broke her right wrist for daring to write a poem about their divorce; and many others spoke about the physical abuse they suffered in the marital home because of their writing.

One wonders: would a meeting of 70 male writers have spoken about censorship in the home by mothers, wives, sisters or daughters in quite the same way? Would their poetry have been dismissed – as Volga says Telugu feminist poetry was – for being 'full of body-consciousness but lacking social consciousness'? Would their persons and personalities become an inextricable part of their texts? Would they be promised publication by powerful editors in return for sexual favours?

Nice girls shouldn't say such things.

But the market and literary establishments have their own subtle and unremarked forms of censorship, and equally subtle manipulations that sometimes barely conceal outright bias. More than one writer said she had been advised by literary 'well-wishers' to avoid certain subjects (feminist poetry, sex, politics, religion) if she wanted to be published – but if she was arrogant enough to persist the attacks could be vicious. But the opposite was also true! Writers in Kannada and Malayalam, for example, said it was fine for women to write about sex but when it came to exposing *sexual politics*, the battle-lines were clearly drawn!

Does subject matter determine form? Is poetry preferred because it allows concealment? The Urdu writers certainly thought so. But Malayalam poet Sugatha Kumari thinks it may be tolerated in women because 'society considers poetry a harmless activity, like buying a silk sari'. Are novels more difficult because they need extended periods of time, a luxury few of the writers present enjoyed? Could humour mask pain and so protect? If short stories are easier to write, they're harder to publish.

And so the thread that ran through most of the discussions was disconnection: the disconnection between what women said and what they wrote; between their spoken words and their silences; between their husbands' and fathers' apparent encouragement and support, and their explicit, disapproving silence when a norm was violated; between women as the subject matter of writing, and women as subjects and writers; between language, literature and social movements, and the emergence of women's voices; between language and gender, and gender and genre.

But it's not all gloom and doom – or, as some would say, whine and whinge. The fact that so many women persist with their writing in the face of so much resistance means something. It means, principally, that the dissenting voice will not be easily crushed. That women recognise that writing is a subversive activity in patriarchal cultures, especially when it is gender-conscious but refuses to be gender-bound. And that censorship emanates from many sources, and is chameleon-like: what was proscribed yesterday may be prescribed today but, equally, what is permitted today may be silenced tomorrow. In this time of Internet and electronic communication, the point of censorship – by state, street, family, community or society – is not to keep people from accessing a particular work, it is to keep them from *expressing* or *creating* it in the first place.

And this is why we need to redefine it: the better to be able to resist it. ❏

Ritu Menon is a writer and publisher based in India. She was a coordinator on the Women and Censorship project and co-editor of The Guarded Tongue, *an anthology of Indian women's writing based on the project workshops*

MORE BY TASTE THAN JUDGEMENT
EDWARD LUCIE-SMITH

MORE THAN ANY OTHER FORM OF CREATIVE
EXPRESSION, THE CONTEMPORARY VISUAL
ARTS HAVE A SYMBIOTIC RELATIONSHIP WITH
SCANDAL AND, THEREFORE, INEVITABLY,
WITH ATTEMPTS AT SUPPRESSION

In the 1970s, matters appeared to be relatively simple. Large tracts of the world were still dominated by the Soviet Union and by satellite regimes allied to it. In these regions, socialist realism remained the only officially sanctioned form of art. Things were, nevertheless, beginning to change. In fact, they had begun to change more than a decade earlier. This gradual thaw was abruptly checked when, in 1962, Nikita Khrushchev, then general secretary of the Communist Party and head of state, visited an exhibition held at the Manège in Moscow to mark the 30th anniversary of MOSKH (Moscow Section of the Artists' Union). This featured the work of a number of only marginally official Russian artists. Khrushchev was outraged with what he saw and had a noisy public exchange of views with the sculptor Ernst Neizvestny who, only three years previously, had won a national competition for a national memorial commemorating victory over the Nazis.

The thaw, however, cautiously resumed and, by 1974, matters had progressed so far that Neizvestny was actually asked to design the now fallen Khrushchev's tombstone at Novodevechiy Monastery. But 1974 witnessed another, less positive, event – the so-called 'Bulldozer Exhibition' held by a large group of 'dissident' artists in the Izmailovskii Park in Moscow, where the work on view in the open air was swept away and crushed by official clean-up crews. This piece of savagery, much publicised in the West, confirmed European and American perceptions that the censorship of art was primarily political, and was a feature of communist societies, not of democratic ones.

These perceptions have sometimes been challenged by later events. In the United States, the 1980s and 1990s saw a series of running battles between artists and the US art world in general, and conservative politicians often allied to the Christian right. Mostly these battles were to do with sex and representations of sexuality but religion also played a part.

One of the first of these controversies was aroused by Judy Chicago's ambitious feminist installation *The Dinner Party* (1979). The piece, a triple eucharist, with places provided for 39 celebrated women at a vast triangular table, was first shown at the San Francisco Museum of Contemporary Art where it was an immense success, attracting huge crowds. Later, other museums refused to exhibit it, apparently for fear of losing funding, and alternative non-museum spaces had to be found. When the artist tried to negotiate a permanent home for it at the University of the District of Columbia, the project foundered when the federal authorities threatened an audit and a reduction of federal funding.

The problem was not simply Chicago's feminist viewpoint but the sexual imagery. The vagina-like design of the plate provided for each guest aroused controversy. During a heated Congressional debate, Representative Dana Rohrabacher (R-Ca.) described *The Dinner Party* as 'weird sexual art', while Representative Stan Parris (R-Va.) condemned it as 'clearly pornographic'. Though *The Dinner Party* is now perhaps the most celebrated art work of its period, and is routinely illustrated in college textbooks about 20th-century art, it is still currently without a permanent home, and spends most of its time in storage.

Another major US controversy surrounded Robert Mapplethorpe's photography exhibit *The Perfect Moment*. This was organised by the Philadelphia Museum of Contemporary Art just prior to the artist's death in 1989 and was due to be shown at the Corcoran Museum in Washington, DC. News of its forthright sexual content reached members of Congress, among them the veteran conservative Senator Jesse Helms. In the face of their protests, the director of the Corcoran, Christina Orr-Cahill, lost her nerve and cancelled the event. When, in 1990, *The Perfect Moment* continued its tour, going to the Contemporary Arts Center in Cincinnati, the local authorities shut it down and arrested the CAC's director, Dennis Barrie, on charges of obscenity. The event became a rallying point for opponents of racism and homophobia. Barrie was eventually acquitted and the show re-opened. The exhibition itself was recently re-staged, more than ten years after the original tour, at the Santa Monica Museum of Art – something that demonstrated its now iconic status.

Many, if not quite all, of the major censorship controversies of recent years have involved photography. The reason is obvious. Though people are now at least intellectually aware of the ease with which photographs can be altered using digital means, a photograph carries with it an air of reality that is denied to most other contemporary art works. Examples are the work of

Andres Serrano, whose photograph *Piss Christ* shows a cheap plastic crucifix apparently immersed in a vat of urine – though the fact that the liquid *is* urine must, ironically enough, be taken on trust, since the camera itself cannot prove it – and pictures made by Sally Mann of her children.

Mann probably arouses more genuine unease than either Mapplethorpe or Serrano, because her work touches on the issue of paedophilia, and this is currently something that makes even the liberal audience afraid. Here, for instance, is an opinion from a lecture delivered by Christopher H Pyle, professor of politics at Mount Holyoke, a US women's college well known for its openness to radical ideas: 'It is not just the artfulness of Mann's images that shields her from condemnation; it is the artful way she excuses her transgressions. We look at the picture of the all-too-aware girl with the cigarette and fear she is headed for trouble. Then we read the caption and discover that the cigarette is made of candy. Similarly, those scabrous legs are not diseased; flour and water just made them look that way. The red liquid on the boy's abdomen is not really blood; it is raspberry juice. The children look wild, shameless, and out of control, but the captions tell us otherwise.'

And here is a more conservative opinion, from Dane L Peters, headmaster of a school in Connecticut: 'In this electronic era can we afford the subtleties and nuances projected in Sally Mann's art? Sally Mann

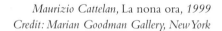

Maurizio Cattelan, La nona ora, *1999*
Credit: Marian Goodman Gallery, New York

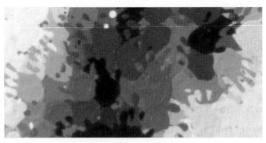

Marcus Harvey, Myra, *1995: and the children's*
handprints that made the picture . . .
Credit: The Saatchi Gallery, London / Stephen White

exploits youth's innocence, and while I am not in favor of censorship, I do take exception to art that uses children to pose in questionable situations, and the fact that Sally Mann used her own children should not legitimize her work. At what point does child art become pornographic?' Mr Peters' protestation that he is 'not in favor of censorship' clearly has to be taken with a pinch of salt.

It will, however, be noted that in nearly all these cases the impulse to censor has not been successful. Judy Chicago is the only one of the four US artists cited to have suffered long-term consequences. It is only in very special circumstances that avant-garde artists and their supporters now take a real battering, in the United States or out of it. A recent example was the row over the Italian artist Maurizio Cattelan's sculpture *La nona ora* (The Ninth Hour) when it was shown in Warsaw at the end of the year 2000. Previously seen in London, in the Royal Academy's 'Apocalypse' exhibition, this rather silly piece shows Pope John Paul II being crushed beneath a meteorite. The director of the Zache, the gallery where the piece was shown, was of Jewish origin, and anti-semitic right-wing elements in the Polish parliament seized on the excuse to get rid of her.

There is, however, another issue that even a very brief survey of this kind ought to mention, and that is an increasing tendency of today's avant-garde to exercise a fairly ruthless censorship of its own. David Lee, editor of a polemical London-based visual arts newsletter called *The Jackdaw*, recently carried out a painstaking survey of the way in which Britain's eight broadsheet newspapers reviewed art exhibitions during 2001. His research showed a remarkable uniformity, and his conclusions are disturbing. 'Even when simply computed,' he noted, '[my] survey demonstrated that coverage for the top galleries . . . far exceeded that for any others without taking into account the length and complexity of each notice . . . If you are an artist exhibiting anywhere but in these galleries, the chances of receiving serious coverage are non-existent.' He added: 'You may have noticed that there are no commercial galleries on the list which sell non-conceptual contemporary art. Indeed, in the 1,274 notices listed in the survey there were fewer than 20 such notices, all of them small reviews or mere mentions in passing.'

In Britain, exhibitions like 'Sensation!', drawn from the collection of Charles Saatchi and shown at the Royal Academy in 1997, often generate a great deal of heat. In that case, the tabloids worked up a furore over Marcus Harvey's portrait of the murderess Myra Hindley, and the work was duly vandalised. The exhibition itself was nevertheless an enormous success in terms of attendances – all the more so because of the fuss. The real current victims of censorship, it seems to me, are to be found elsewhere – among the artists whom the serious press simply refuses to mention, not because their work is bad per se, but because 'it isn't the right kind of art'. ❏

Edward Lucie-Smith *is a writer and art critic. His latest poetry collection is* Changing Shape: New and Collected Poetry *(Carcanet, 2002)*

JUST A SOLDIER'S TALE

ASAF ORON

*Opposition inside Israel to government policy in the Occupied Territories is not,
it seems, being given the attention it merits. With the presence of Labour veteran
politician Shimon Peres in Ariel Sharon's Likud government, 'official' parliamentary
opposition has more or less fallen silent. Protest has largely been left to civilian
movements such as Peace Now, which have recently been reinforced from a surprising
quarter. On 25 January this year, the first public statement by 52 veterans from
within the Israeli Defence Forces made clear the reasons why they could no longer
continue to serve within the army (see Asaf's story below). Since then, the numbers
signing the statement have continued to grow despite threats of retribution from the
Israeli chief of staff Shaul Mofaz.*

*While this is not the first time the IDF has had to deal with refuseniks – the
then IDF commander admitted that the rash of refusals was a key factor in inducing
the army command to call off the 1982–84 Lebanon war; further refusals during
the first intifada helped convince Israeli leaders they could not crush the Palestinian
uprising by military means, leading to recognition of the PLO and attempts at a
political solution – the public refusal of the present group directly affects policy-
makers, who have to take into account that the army is no tame 'military machine'
and its soldiers not mere robots, 'cogs in the wheel'.*

*Other events mid-March may help to swell the as yet small – according to
recent opinion polls only 31% of the Israeli population supports the soldiers' action –
opposition to the war against the Palestinians. On 15 March, as a result of a breach
in military censorship, Israeli television, followed by radio and the press, brought
the full horror of IDS search-and-kill tactics in the Occupied Territories into Israeli
homes. Efforts by IDS to contain the damage failed; the brutality of Sharon's strategy
is finally out there for every Israeli to contemplate.* **JVH**

On 5 February 1985, I got up, left my home, went to the Compulsory
Service Centre on Rashi Street in Jerusalem, said goodbye to my parents,
boarded the rickety old bus going to the Military Absorption Station and
turned into a soldier.

Exactly 17 years later, I find myself in a head-to-head confrontation
with the army, while the public at large is jeering and mocking me from the
sidelines. Right-wingers see me as a traitor who is dodging the holy war

that's just around the corner. The political centre shakes a finger at me self-righteously and lectures me about undermining democracy and politicising the army. And the left? The square, establishment, 'moderate' left that only yesterday was courting my vote now turns its back on me as well. Everyone blabbers about what is and what is not legitimate, exposing in the process the depth of their ignorance of political theory and their inability to distinguish a real democracy from a third world regime in the style of Juan Peron.

Almost no one asks the main question: why would a regular guy get up one morning in the middle of life, work, the kids and decide he's not playing the game any more? And how come he is not alone but there are 50 . . . sorry, 100 . . . sorry again, now almost 200 regular, run-of-the-mill guys like him who've done the same thing? [At the end of March, there were over 300 signatories – Ed]

Our parents' generation lets out a sigh: we've embarrassed them yet again. But isn't it all your fault? What did you raise us on? Universal ethics and universal justice, on the one hand: peace, liberty and equality to all. And on the other hand: 'The Arabs want to throw us into the sea.' 'They are all crafty and primitive.' 'You can't trust them.'

On the one hand, the songs of John Lennon, Pete Seeger, Bob Dylan, Bob Marley, Pink Floyd. Songs of peace and love and against militarism and war. On the other hand, songs about a sweetheart riding the tank after sunset in the field: 'The tank is yours and you are ours.' I was raised on two value systems: one was the ethical code and the other the tribal code, and I naively believed that the two could coexist.

This is the way I was when I was drafted. Not enthusiastic but as if embarking on a sacred mission of courage and sacrifice for the benefit of society. But when, instead of a sacred mission, a 19-year-old finds himself performing the sacrilege of violating human beings' dignity and freedom, he doesn't dare ask – even himself – if it's OK or not. He simply acts like everyone else and tries to blend in. As it is, he's got enough problems, and boy is the weekend far off.

You get used to it in a hurry, and many even learn to like it. Where else can you go out on patrol – that is, walk the streets like a king, harass and humiliate pedestrians to your heart's content, and get into mischief with your buddies – and at the same time feel like a big hero defending your country? The Gaza Exploits became heroic tales, a source of pride for Giv'ati, then a relatively new brigade suffering from low self-esteem.

For a long time, I could not relate to the whole 'heroism' thing. But when, as a sergeant, I found myself in charge, something cracked inside me. Without thinking, I turned into the perfect occupation enforcer. I settled accounts with 'upstarts' who didn't show enough respect. I tore up the personal documents of men my father's age. I hit, harassed, served as a bad example – all in the city of Kalkilia, barely three miles from grandma and grandpa's home-sweet-home. No. I was no 'aberration'. I was exactly the norm.

Having completed my compulsory service, I was discharged, and then the first intifada began (how many more await us?). Ofer, a comrade in arms who remained in the service has become a hero: the hero of the second Giv'ati trial. He commanded a company that dragged a detained Palestinian demonstrator into a dark orange grove and beat him to death. As the verdict stated, Ofer was found to have been the leader in charge of the whole business. He spent two months in jail and was demoted – I think that was the most severe sentence given to an Israeli soldier through the entire first intifada, in which about 1,000 Palestinians were killed. Ofer's battalion commander testified that there was an order from the higher echelons to use beatings as a legitimate method of punishment, thereby implicating himself. On the other hand, Efi Itam, the brigade commander, who had been seen beating Arabs on numerous occasions, denied that he ever gave such an order and consequently was never indicted. Today he lectures us on moral conduct on his way to a new life in politics. (In the current intifada, incidentally, the vast majority of incidents involving Palestinian deaths are not even investigated. No one even bothers.)

And in the meantime, I was becoming more of a civilian. A copy of *The Yellow Wind* [a book on life in the Occupied Territories by the Israeli writer David Grossman] which had just come out, crossed my path. I read it, and suddenly it hit me. I finally understood what I had done over there. What I had been over there.

I began to see that they had cheated me: they raised me to believe there was someone up there taking care of things. Someone who knows stuff that is beyond me, the little guy. And that even if sometimes politicians let us down, the 'military echelon' is always on guard, day and night, keeping us safe, each and every one of their decisions the result of sacred necessity. Yes, they cheated us, the soldiers of the intifadas, exactly as they had cheated the generation that was beaten to a pulp in the War of Attrition and in the Yom Kippur War, exactly as they had cheated the generation that sank deep into

the Lebanese mud during the Lebanon invasions. And our parents'
generation continues to be silent.

And I found myself volunteering in a small, smoke-filled office in East
Jerusalem, digging up files about deaths, brutality, bureaucratic viciousness
or simply daily harassments. I felt I was atoning, to some extent, for my
actions during my days with the Giv'ati brigade. But it also felt as if I was
trying to empty the ocean out with a teaspoon.

Out of the blue, I was called up for the very first time for reserve
duty in the Occupied Territories. Hysterically, I contacted my company
commander. He calmed me down: we will be staying at an outpost
overlooking the Jordan River. No contact with the local population is
expected. And that indeed was what I did, but some of my friends provided
security for the Damia Bridge terminal [where Palestinians cross from
Jordan to Israel and vice versa]. This was in the days preceding the Gulf War
and a large number of Palestinian refugees were flowing from Kuwait to the

*On the beach, Gaza, February 2002: Palestinian commuters bypass a road closed
by the IDF to protect Jewish settlers. Credit: AP Photo / Charles Dharapak*

Occupied Territories (from the frying pan into the fire). The reserve soldiers – mostly right-wingers – cringed when they saw the female conscripts stationed in the terminal happily ripping open down comforters and babies' coats to make sure they didn't contain explosives. I too cringed when I heard their stories but I was also hopeful: reserve soldiers are human after all, whatever their political views.

Such hopes were dashed three years later, when I spent three weeks with a celebrated reconnaissance company in the confiscated ruins of a villa at the outskirts of the Abasans (if you don't know where this is, it's your problem). This is where it became clear to me that the same humane reserve soldier could also be an ugly, wretched macho, undergoing a total regression back to his days as a young conscript. Going on patrol duty with these guys once was all that I could take. I went up to the placement officer and requested to be given guard duty only. Placement officers like people like me: most soldiers can't tolerate staying inside the base longer than a couple of hours.

And precisely because I knew so well, first-hand, from years of experience, what was going on over there, what reality was like over there,

I had no trouble seeing, through the fog of war and the curtain of lies, what has been taking place over there since the very first days of the second intifada. For years, the army had been feeding on lines like 'We were too nice in the first intifada,' and 'If we had only killed 100 in the very first days, everything would have been different.' Now the army was given licence to do things its way. I knew full well that [former prime minister] Ehud Barak was giving the army a free hand, and that [current chief of staff] Shaul Mofaz was taking full advantage of this to maximise the bloodshed.

By then, I had two little kids, boys, and I knew from experience that no one – not a single person in the entire world – will ever make sure that my sons won't have to serve in the Occupied Territories when they reach 18. No one, that is, except me. And no one but me will have to look them in the eye when they're all grown up and tell them where Dad was when all that happened. It was clear to me: this time I was not going.

Initially, this was a quiet decision, still a little shy, something like: 'I am just a bit weird, can't go and can't talk about it too much either.' But as time went by, as the level of insanity, hatred and incitement kept rising, as the generals were turning the IDF into a terror organisation, the decision was turning into an outcry: 'If you can't see that this is one big crime leading us to the brink of annihilation, then something is terribly wrong with you!'

And then I discovered that I was not alone. Like discovering life on another planet.

The truth is, I understand why everyone is mad at us. We spoiled the neat little order of things. The holy status quo states that the right holds the exclusive rights to celebrate the blood and ask for more. The role of the left, on the other hand, is to wail while sitting in their armchairs sipping wine and waiting for the Messiah to come and with a single wave of his magic wand make the right disappear along with the settlers, the Arabs, the weather and the entire Middle East. That's how the world is supposed to work. So why are you causing such a disturbance? What's your problem? Bad boys!

Don't you really see what we are doing, why it is that we stepped out of line? Don't you get the difference between a low-key, personal refusal and an organised, public one? (and make no mistake about it, the private refusal is the easier choice.) You really don't get it? So let me spell it out for you.

First, we declare our commitment to the first value system. The one that is elusive, abstract and not profitable. We believe in the moral code generally known as God (and my atheist friends who also signed this letter would have to forgive me – we all believe in God, the true one, not that of the rabbis and the ayatollahs). We believe that there is no room for the tribal code, that the tribal code simply camouflages idolatry, an idolatry of a type we should not cooperate with. Those who let such a form of idol worship take over will end up as burnt offerings themselves.

Second, we (as well as some other groups who are even more despised and harassed) are putting our bodies on the line in the attempt to prevent the next war. The most unnecessary, most idiotic, cruel and immoral war in the history of Israel.

We are the Chinese young man standing in front of the tank. And you? If you are nowhere to be seen, you are probably inside the tank, advising the driver. ❏

Asaf Oron *is a sergeant major in the Giv'ati Brigade and signatory 8 of the original 52 Israeli reserve officers and soldiers who signed the 'Fighters' Letter' declaring their refusal to serve any longer in the Occupied Territories. He was one of the first to include a statement explaining his action. Given the group's insistence on independent, individual responsibility, it is the closest thing to a 'manifesto' likely to be produced. Translated by Ami Kronfeld*

WINNERS OF THE 2002 FREEDOM OF EXPRESSION AWARDS

Courageous journalism

• **Anna Politkovskaia (Russia)**, a special correspondent for the biweekly *Novaia Gazeta*, has been reporting on the war in Chechnya and the human rights situation there. She has also written about human rights violations within the Russian army, and those carried out by it. Despite being arrested and abused by Russian soldiers, despite countless threats to her own safety and that of her children, and official pressure on her newspaper, she continues to return regularly to Chechnya.

Circumvention of censorship

• **Sanar Yurdatapan (Turkey)** continues to fight Turkey's harsh censorship laws. He initiated the 'Freedom for Thought' campaign which persuades Turkish writers and artists to sign themselves up as co-publishers of controversial books, making it much harder for the Turkish government to imprison the real publishers. The recent case against the publishers of the Turkish version of Noam Chomsky's *Rogue States* was dismissed, largely thanks to Yurdatapan's campaign.

Whistle-blower of the year

• **Jiang Weiping (China)** is a reporter for the state news agency Xinhua, and former Dalian bureau chief for the newspaper *Wen Hui Bao*. In December 2000, Jiang was detained for writing a series of articles exposing government corruption for the Hong Kong tabloid *Frontline*. On 5 September 2001, after a secret trial, Jiang was sentenced to nine years' imprisonment.

Services to censorship

• **Silvio Berlusconi (Italy)** With media, man and government all wrapped up in the single person of Italy's prime minister, Silvio Berlusconi, Italian critics are voicing growing alarm as he puts his unprecedented powers of censorship into practice. If, as alleged, Berlusconi replaces the present board of state-owned TV RAI with one sympathetic to his own ruling coalition, he will control about 90% of the country's television market.

Index would like to thank: Candace Allen, John Bird, Faber & Faber, Gary Fordham, John Fortune, FMCM – Annabel, Fiona and Hannah, Emily French, Michael Grade, Hamish Harper, Jane Havell, Geoffrey Hosking, Nadire Mater, Annalena McAfee, Sheena McDonald, John McFadden, Ross Miller, Ruairi Patterson, Andrew Puddephatt, Simon Rattle, The Royal College of Physicians, Ruth and Richard Rogers, Ros Sloboda, Jon Snow, Janet Suzman, Thanet Press, Sue Woodford, Kerim Yildiz, Yang Yo Yo

Corrections The editor wishes to apologise for the error on p185 of the last issue. Nigar's poetry should, of course, have been described as from Azerbaijan, not Uzbekistan. And on p54 the word 'terrorist' in the first line should not have appeared.

WWW.INDEXONCENSORSHIP.ORG
CONTACT@INDEXONCENSORSHIP.ORG
TEL: 020 7278 2313 • FAX: 020 7278 1878

SUBSCRIPTIONS (4 ISSUES PER ANNUM)
INDIVIDUALS: BRITAIN £32, US $48, REST OF WORLD £42
INSTITUTIONS: BRITAIN £48, US $80, REST OF WORLD £52
**SPEAK TO TONY CALLAGHAN ON 020 7278 2313
OR EMAIL TONY@INDEXONCENSORSHIP.ORG**

Index on Censorship (ISSN 0306-4220) is published four times a year by a non-profit-making company: Writers & Scholars International Ltd, Lancaster House, 33 Islington High Street, London N1 9LH. *Index on Censorship* is associated with Writers & Scholars Educational Trust, registered charity number 325003 **Periodicals postage:** (US subscribers only) paid at Newark, New Jersey. Postmaster: send US address changes to *Index on Censorship* c/o Mercury Airfreight International Ltd Inc., 365 Blair Road, Avenel, NJ 07001, USA